ALSO BY JESSA CRISPIN

The Dead Ladies Project
The Creative Tarot
Why I Am Not a Feminist: A Feminist Manifesto
My Three Dads

what is wrong with men

what is wrong with men

PATRIARCHY, THE CRISIS OF MASCULINITY,

AND HOW (OF COURSE)

MICHAEL DOUGLAS FILMS EXPLAIN EVERYTHING

Jessa Crispin

Pantheon Books / New York

FIRST HARDCOVER EDITION
PUBLISHED BY PANTHEON BOOKS 2025

Published by Pantheon Books, a division of Penguin Random House LLC, 1745 Broadway, New York, NY 10019.

Pantheon Books and the colophon are registered trademarks of Penguin Random House LLC.

Library of Congress Cataloging-in-Publication Data
Names: Crispin, Jessa, author.
Title: What is wrong with men : patriarchy, the crisis of masculinity, and how (of course) Michael Douglas films explain everything / Jessa Crispin.
Description: First edition. | New York : Pantheon Books, [2025] | Includes bibliographical references. Identifiers: LCCN 2024032096 (print) | LCCN 2024032097 (ebook) | ISBN 9780593317624 (hardcover) | ISBN 9780593469798 (trade paperback) | ISBN 9780593317631 (ebook)
Subjects: LCSH: Douglas, Michael, 1944—Performances. | Masculinity. | Masculinity in motion pictures. | Men—Identity.
Classification: LCC HQ1090 .C75 2025 (print) | LCC HQ1090 (ebook) | DDC 791.43/65211—dc23/eng/20240911
LC record available at https://lccn.loc.gov/2024032096
LC ebook record available at https://lccn.loc.gov/2024032097

penguinrandomhouse.com | pantheonbooks.com

Printed in the United States of America
2 4 6 8 9 7 5 3 1

The authorized representative in the EU for product safety and compliance is Penguin Random House Ireland, Morrison Chambers, 32 Nassau Street, Dublin D02 YH68, Ireland, https://eu-contact.penguin.ie.

For Michael Douglas

CONTENTS

INTRODUCTION   ix

PART ONE: MICHAEL DOUGLAS AND WOMEN

Fatal Attraction: Caught in the Crossfire of the Mommy Wars   14

War of the Roses: Court-Mandated Fatherhood   31

Basic Instinct: What If We Just Got Rid of All the Men?   49

PART TWO: THE ECONOMIC ACTOR

Wall Street: A New Economy, and a New Masculinity, Emerges   73

Falling Down: The Aspirational Mass Shooter   89

PART THREE: A WHITE MAN IN A BROWN WORLD

Black Rain: America Hits Its Midlife Crisis   113

The American President: Finding Meaning in the Drone Bomb   130

PART FOUR: THE PATRIARCH FALLS

Disclosure: Please Report to Human Resources   155

The Game: Bringing Patriarchs Back to Life   171

PART FIVE: WELCOME TO THE POSTPATRIARCHY

Teaching Michael Douglas to Love: Age Gaps,
Power Imbalances, and Other Heterosexual Indignities   196

Daddy Issues: Father Hunger and the Search for an Heir   211

Speculative Masculinity: The Rise of the Masculinity Influencer   225

Conclusion: Imagining a Post–Michael Douglas World   241

SELECTED BIBLIOGRAPHY   249

INTRODUCTION

"How can I possibly be a man?"

—Michael Douglas, as quoted in Marc Eliot's biography

The women of Pitié-Salpêtrière liked to put on a show. They were there in that French hospital at the end of the nineteenth century because something was wrong with them and no one could figure out what it was. Their symptoms were mysterious to the doctors. Their bodies would go as rigid as planks of wood, they would convulse and twist, they would retreat into childish delusion or sexual mania, welts would appear on the skin despite no injury or interference, and some of these welts seemed to spell out words.

In the hunt for answers, the doctors would display the women and their disorders to the public. There was a theater in the hospital for this very purpose. Doctors from outside the hospital would come from all over Europe to witness this new disorder and try to formulate a cause and treatment—Dr. Sigmund Freud was often in attendance. But it wasn't just doctors watching and gawking, a bored public would often attend. The painter Edgar Degas was frequently spotted. They loved to be entertained by the spectacle of it all.

The women would come to the stage and show the audience—

look, look at all that is wrong with me. The doctors would hypnotize them and have them perform tricks, like a little dog or a clown. Pictures of these performances are easy to confuse with circus acts. Here, a woman whose body is taut with a manic rigidity is balanced between two chairs, like a deranged magician's assistant. Another woman is touched lightly and she drops into a dead swoon, held up only by the strength of her doctor.

It was a wonderful entertainment, the audience at the hospital was always packed. And some of the women, who had previously been suffering in silence and neglect, started to like being the center of all this attention. How much of these little shows were real suffering or just the performance of suffering? Is there a difference?

The ultimate diagnosis these women would receive was simultaneously very old and very new: hysteria. It was an ailment that had been written about since the time of the Greeks: a feminine kind of madness, born not out of organic illness or physical trauma, but it would nonetheless come on suddenly, frightfully. The women would become violent or fall into fits of rage or weeping. They would hurt themselves or the people around them—most horrifyingly they would hurt their own children. They would spin out of control, dressing and speaking and behaving quite strangely. They would become unladylike.

In order to treat the hysterical woman, it was important to restore her to a ladylike state. Hysteria was born from the idea that in order to be well functioning, a woman needed to fulfill her biological destiny of caretaking and childbearing. Any other distraction, from work to romantic love to reverie, was a threat to her basic stability.

The Greeks took this literally, thinking that without a pregnancy to anchor the woman's womb into place, the uterus could wander around the body, causing trouble. Releasing vapor, snuggling in behind other organs and wedging between the heart and the lungs or tucking itself behind the liver, interfering with normal internal workings. The cure, for a long time, was to establish more strongly the woman in her traditional role in the family. Get her married, get her pregnant, destroy all escape routes.

Sometimes it worked. After all, this was a time before antibiotics, there was nothing riskier a woman could do in this era than give birth. And there is no more final cure for madness and suffering and being an embarrassment to your family than death.

Thousands of years later, in nineteenth-century France, the understanding of insanity and the female complaint was only slightly more sophisticated. And this diagnosis of hysteria still carried with it all the older ideas. Doctors knew by now that the uterus didn't literally wander around the body like a bored tourist, heading off to visit the spleen as if it were the Eiffel Tower. But the problems of the hysterical woman were seen through a similar lens: the issue was the woman's inability to fulfill her traditional role within the family. The solution was to make the woman ladylike again. To restore her to her feminine function. To force her back into caretaking and the roles of wife and mother.

In illness many women found a retreat from these feminine demands. As long as they were sick, they were the ones being taken care of, rather than the ones taking care of everyone else. The hospital was an asylum for them, in all meanings of the word. Because for some of these women, the family was not the solution to their problems but the source of the danger.

Louise Augustine Gleizes, who was immortalized in her medical case study as Augustine A., came to the hospital at the age of fourteen. Before she had fallen ill she had been working as a kitchen maid, forced into labor at a young age to help support her family.

Every place she went, she found violence. She was beaten at school, raped at home by her mother's lover, and abused at work. There was no sanctuary until her inability to deal with the trauma pushed her to the point of hysteria. As a daughter or as a worker she might have been exploited and violated, but as a patient, she was given kind attention by the esteemed Dr. Jean-Martin Charcot. And because she was so easy to hypnotize and so extravagantly performed her symptoms for audience and camera, she became a kind of star.

Augustine's story is the story not only of an individual, but of generations of women. In the aftermath of the Industrial Revolution, a huge sociological and demographic shift began. As economies changed from agricultural to industrial, people moved from the countryside to the city in huge numbers. Girls and women were removed from farms, where they had been embedded within their own families and small communities, and came to cities to work in factories or in the homes of the rich as domestic laborers.

If one looks at this era from the perspective of the wealthy, this time could be seen as one of liberation. After all, the new urban-centered existence gifted many women previously withheld freedoms. Sexual freedom, intellectual freedom, social freedom. Women of means at this time were holding salons, writing books, politically organizing. The traditional feminine role of being hidden away in the domestic space, taking care of the fathers and husbands and sons who were the truly important ones, was beginning to break down.

But one had to have money and power to enjoy that liberation. How wonderful that women didn't necessarily have to be wives now—but how was a woman supposed to live on the wages of an underpaid factory worker? How freeing to be able to enjoy the life of the mind as education opportunities expanded—but how to enroll when one must go into domestic work at the age of ten to survive? Life for girls and women in traditional villages had its own horrors, but structures of oppression can also sometimes be structures of protection. Whatever harm might happen within those structures, at least they are often predictable and therefore one can prepare a defensive strategy. Being out in the city, away from the protection of the family and the church and the social obligations one must perform, sometimes meant a chaotic kind of vulnerability. Some of these women became hysterical.

These hysterical women, born to be invisible and forgotten because of their poverty and gender, became a problem so large, so compelling, so unforgettable that they changed the world. The case studies, the art, the theories inspired by these women helped change the way we think about the human mind and mental illness, gender, poverty, and capitalism. Their performances were haunting, even for those who were skeptical about whether the women were faking or exaggerating. There is nothing wrong with these women. But there is clearly something wrong with these women. Just look at them!

As Mark Micale notes in his study of Salpêtrière neurologist Jean-Martin Charcot:

> The disorder has been viewed as a manifestation of everything from divine poetic inspiration and satanic possession to female unreason, racial degeneration, and unconscious psychosexual conflict. It has inspired gynecological, humoral, neurological, psychological, and sociological formulations, and it has been situated in the womb, the abdomen, the nerves, the ovaries, the mind, the brain, the psyche, and the soul. It has been construed as a physical disease, a mental disorder, a spiritual malady, a behavioral maladjustment, a sociological communication, and as no illness at all.

In other words, people have seen in these performances of the hysterical women whatever they want to see. Feminists saw oppressed women, made sick by their oppressed circumstances. Male doctors saw feminine frailty, proof that women were more vulnerable than men, therefore needing protection as if they were children. Artists saw them as muses, and the public saw them as entertainment.

Freud's work on the problem of hysteria would lead to the discovery of the unconscious and forever change our understanding of the human psyche. In *Studies on Hysteria,* in collaboration with Josef Breuer, they developed a theory on how experiencing violence and oppression could harm the subject mentally and physically. They wrote, "Psychical trauma or more precisely the memory of trauma—acts like a foreign body which long after its entry must continue to be regarded as an agent that is still at work." This confusion of the past and the present troubles the patient to such an extent that their well-being suffers, and they can struggle to adapt to and function in the world that surrounds them. This was an idea that would be developed into an understanding of everything from PTSD in soldiers and sexual assault survivors to the lasting effects of racism and discrimination.

The gendered quality of hysteria would be noted by many—although a masculine form of the disorder (more commonly referred to in men as neurasthenia) would be noted and treated—and lead some to wonder about the specific conditions and difficulties under which women labored in a society ruled by men. The hysterics would be written about by some of the greatest feminist thinkers of our time, not only theorizing what discrimination had led women to collect these traumas but also imagining what changes could be brought to society to prevent such harm from happening again.

Others looked at the problem from the perspective of poverty and the treatment of the mentally ill. Soon making a spectacle of the mentally ill, the way patients were asked to perform for the public and the way sightseers were allowed to tour the institutions and gawk at the unwell, would be replaced by a campaign for dignity. Muckrakers like Nellie Bly, author of *Ten Days in a Mad-House,* focused specifically on the unfair treatment of women in hospitals. Experimentation and quack treatments would be replaced with medical standards and scientific investigation into causes and treatments. Patients, of both genders, would start to be treated as humans capable of recovery and reintegration into society, rather than burdens to be housed and exploited until death.

By making a scene, by failing to thrive, by finding a physical way to articulate the way the ills of society were hindering their individual lives, these women had an enormous impact. And the artists and writers and scientists who found ways to translate their embodied distress into image, theory, and journalism, changed the way we see the world.

Which brings us to Michael Douglas.

Stay with me. After all, what did Michael Douglas present to the world in his string of blockbuster films through the eighties and early nineties but a performance of being extremely unwell? His was a performance of injury, oppression, and confusion, as he was traumatized by a world that was essentially working against him. In the same way that the hysterical women of Salpêtrière rolled their eyes and twisted their bodies to show the psychic harm being done to them, the typical Michael Douglas character will at some point dive into a state of frenzy and exasperation, shaking his head and waving his arms to say, Look at me! Look at what they are doing to me.

In *The Game,* a flummoxed Michael Douglas flings his briefcase about in a public airport, slamming it repeatedly against the wall and the floor and the bench, until he has reached a state of exhaustion. In *Disclosure,* he rants, wildly, about the unfairness of the state of the world, his mouth agape and twisted as his wife tries in vain to help him. In *Fatal Attraction,* he begs the police for help, he is the victim here, why can't they see that, why can't they help him, don't they know what he is up against?

There is another word for this behavior: hysterical. And there is a solution to this hysteria. We listen, we learn, we theorize. Maybe we can decode this sickness that seems to have overtaken him— maybe we can learn something not just about him as an individual but about the world. For if there's something wrong with Michael Douglas, the movie star and the symbol at the time of new masculinity, perhaps we can learn if there might not be something wrong with all of us?

In the age of Freud, there was one question that kept being asked: What do women want? We spent a couple hundred years figuring that out. We attended to their political situation, we built institutions and nonprofits and foundations to assist them, we probed into their psyches and their unconscious. We tended to them until they, at least some of them, could flourish in new and unexpected ways. Could the women of Salpêtrière have imagined the strides that the women who followed them would make? The laws they changed, the discoveries they made, the offices they led.

Now, it's a new question that dominates our age of inquiry. What is wrong with men? What is wrong with them?! Something surely has to be wrong with them, I mean, look at them! What on earth are they doing? Why in the world are they doing it? Is someone going to do something about this, for the love of god?

Men are failing to thrive. They are more likely than women to fall into addiction, suicide, and despair. They are going to university less than women. They are meeting educational goals less successfully than women. Their health is worse, they are dying younger, they are drinking more. And every day there they are, on the news, in our offices, in our faces, making a spectacle of themselves. The statistics about the problems of men are trotted out by politicians, anti-feminists, influencers, journalists, academics.

But we fail to answer our own question. Part of the problem is that we have become accustomed to seeing men in a certain way, much in the same way we became accustomed to seeing women in such a way for so long that we couldn't see their plight. Because we saw women as the role they were playing—wife, mother, daughter, caretaker—we failed to see who women might be outside of those roles. How confining and oppressive those roles might actually be. Only by seeing women as something else other than these roles—traumatized or brilliant or sexual—could we see what was really going on with women and begin to assist them.

And we, too, have mistaken the roles men play for the men themselves. And one of the most visible and important roles men have played in our society is the role of the powerful. In order to illuminate the specific position of women in an unjust society, we named the structure for that unjust society "the patriarchy." And then we got confused about just what the patriarchy is exactly. We confused the patriarchy with men.

Let's be clear and define our terms, because "patriarchy" has become one of those words that people use while having only a vague idea of what it means. It gets trotted out to take the blame for everything from body shaming to "late capitalism"—"capitalism" being another one of those words whose meaning seems to get blurrier upon every usage—to mass shootings. Having a precise, shared understanding of what the word "patriarchy" means can only help us moving forward. When I use the word "patriarchy," I am using it to mean the way society is structured through law, governance, social norms, and economics to keep money, property, and power exclusively in the hands of men.

This used to be overt. Throughout the Western world, money and property were distributed through inheritance from father to son. Women were prevented from inheriting estates, possessing property, and in many cases earning and controlling money. Women's only access to money, property, and power was through men. It wasn't until the mid-1940s that women could run for political office in France. In America, women weren't allowed to have their own lines of credit until the 1970s.

But now that's changed throughout the West. Yet, we insist, the patriarchy still exists. We still see its workings in everything from women's lack of full reproductive freedoms to the disparity between men and women in political office and the corporate world. Women still feel burdened by disproportionate expectations, and we are still trying to fit ourselves into a world that was built for and by men. Even if the laws have changed, we still feel the effects of patriarchy. This history lingers into the present. We are, in the Freudian sense, traumatized, as the past continually erupts into the present day.

As the legal, governmental, societal, and economic norms changed to accommodate women, no matter how unsatisfying or unfinished that project might be, a kind of liberation happened. For women, the barriers to creating a public life outside of the domestic sphere were removed. Women could find roles for themselves other than roles that were relational to men—and when they were in relation to men, they had the opportunity to redefine those roles to be less dependent, less submissive.

But there was a simultaneous, involuntary liberation happening. As women were liberated from their roles, men were liberated from theirs as well. Men no longer had to be patriarchs. They no longer had to hold the power of the household, the church, the society, the business, and the nation. They, too, could redefine their roles to be less dominant.

This is not how men commonly understand the changes of this era. There are a few reasons for that. For one, during this time, women put a lot of effort into creating networks to support women in their moment of liberation. There was an intellectual culture in universities, publishing, even in pop music to help women think through new ways to live a life. Women created nonprofits and organized themselves politically to advocate for themselves. Women wrote stories and made movies and sang songs about the changes, some of them celebrating this new era and others warning women of the downfalls of independence.

There was not a corresponding culture for men to explain the changes society was going through and how it would affect and influence men specifically. Men did not see this as a time of liberation; for many, it felt like a time of disempowerment. It felt like something was being taken from them, rather than an expansion of possibilities. Women were collectively creating new forms of meaning for themselves; men were isolated, failing to see their plight as a collective, political position.

The rules of the patriarchy had changed. The patriarchy sold men out, stopped honoring that old gentlemen's agreement. And no one told the men. You would think they would want to know. You would think they would be all over that. Ahem, alert, those old contracts are null and void. Please update your operating system and download the new user's manual.

That confusion led men to spin around wildly, trying to figure out what was going wrong. Hi, we pressed the lever, can we have our food pellet please? This goddamn thing, I swear to god it was working just a second ago, it's supposed to work, why won't it work. Cue red, sweaty face and an oncoming coronary event.

There were of course a lot of theories about the cause. It must be the fault of women. After all, things were fine before they got involved. It must be the immigrants, crowding in, taking what is rightfully ours. It must be capitalism! Or the gay agenda, or the work of Satan. Or any combination of the above. Power is accustomed to using distraction and misdirection to keep its workings hidden and protected, and many didn't want to face the reality that patriarchy was over. Patriarchy was over because it had been replaced with something worse.

Its successor retained its old structures of hierarchy, but the requirements for entry had changed. The top positions were no longer reserved exclusively for white men, now money is the only medium. Gone were the patriarchal values like stewardship, sacrifice, and charity—the only thing left was acquisition and avarice.

And the other reason men didn't understand this era as a time of liberation is because what they were liberated toward—the domestic and the private sector—was something they had been accustomed to denigrating. Care work is degrading. Sensuality is sinful. Emotions are irrational. Domestication is the same thing as castration. While the public sphere for women had looked like a prize, the private sphere for men looked like a trap. It was a definite downgrade, and there was little celebration of its pleasures in the culture. A stubborn refusal to participate in their own freedom overtook masculine culture. Suddenly everything looked suspiciously feminine, even the former rewards of successful past patriarchs. Is falling in love feminine? Is dressing well? Is eating vegetables gay? Rawr, I'm a real man, eating meat off a hunting knife, having sex without enjoyment, going into debt to buy the most manly of trucks. You'll never catch me holding a woman's hand—that's gay, bro.

Michael Douglas is a useful muse to tell this story. His father, Kirk Douglas, played gods. Kirk Douglas was Spartacus and Van Gogh and Odysseus, he played great lovers and great devils, he played war heroes and cowboys and villains. He portrayed the vast world of masculinity, and it was this that his son must have thought he would inherit.

Instead, Michael Douglas plays a man indignant and outraged at the reading of his father's will. The kingdom is not his alone, it is something to be shared and portioned out. Whether he's playing Gordon Gekko, who feels entitled to scheme and cheat to take as much back as he possibly can, or D-Fens, who slides into despair over a lost world, Michael Douglas throughout his oeuvre embod-

ied this new masculinity. He embodied the torments and the con-
fusions of the modern man, letting the invisible trouble become
discernible.

The peak of Michael Douglas's stardom corresponds with years
of tremendous social and economic shifts that would alter the lives
of many men. Whether it was the skyrocketing rates of divorce that
would change how and if men became husbands and fathers, or
the passage of financial laws that would fundamentally destroy the
masculine archetype of the breadwinner, throughout the 1980s and
'90s, men's roles were being upended.

Much like in the age of hysterical women, there were new possibilities for men opening up, but very few had or have the resources
to enjoy them. How wonderful not to have to be a provider for
an entire family, but as industrial jobs disappeared and wages for
blue-collar work stagnated, how to make yourself look desirable to
a prospective life partner without other assets? How freeing to lose
the stoic façade and get in touch with your emotions, but how to
explore your passions and find work-life balance and pursue a meaningful existence when working two jobs to get by? It's an incomplete
liberation, where the benefits are reserved for the wealthy and the
lucky and everyone else struggles to survive.

It's not Michael Douglas's personal suffering, whatever that
might be, that's important here. Too frequently we've dragged
celebrities and people on reality programming or just from videos
on the internet into the white-hot media spotlight, invading their
privacy and making them the subject of think pieces exploring the
burning question of the moment. What Taylor Swift's latest relationship says about the state of feminism. What this person having a mental health crisis in public and caught on video says about
the state of race relations. But that is mostly projection, and it feels
unfair at this point to turn the private lives of individuals into sen-
sationalized content.

It's Michael Douglas the performer who matters, the character he embodied in film during the era of the patriarchy's most dramatic changes. He is our little French hysteric, taking the stage to represent the state of an entire generation. And from his movements and his injuries we can theorize what is wrong with men.

It's common for us to say now that masculinity is in crisis. But masculinity is always in crisis. Because masculinity, as we traditionally have understood it, is something that men earn or develop through their engagement with the world. As R. W. Connell demonstrated in *Masculinities,* a century ago, a man fulfilled his public role by turning himself into the family man. He acquired a wife and a house, he sired some children, he provided for their needs with the work he did. Not having any of these markers of success—being unable to produce children or being abandoned by his wife—put his masculinity in doubt in a public way.

Today, in a much more atomized and disconnected society, masculinity is something more individualistic. It's about fulfilling certain metrics, like numbers in your bank account, your muscle to fat ratio, or your number of sexual partners. Pure masculinity is always glittering out there somewhere on the horizon, never fully achievable but something to be pursued at all costs. Just one more rep of squats, one more hour of hustle, one more breakfast of protein powder and a handful of supplements, one more match on a dating app and maybe one will finally feel like a real man.

Masculinity, then, is dependent on external, uncontrollable factors like the economy, the status of a nation on the geopolitical stage, or the housing market, yet it is rarely understood as such because to be a man is to be adaptable and competitive. It is to thrive no matter what environment you might be dropped into, like one of those reality survival programs where they film men scaling mountains with no equipment, eating snails pulled from the river, and building inadequate shelter out of sticks and rocks to silence some inner voice droning on and on about their inadequacies. Each of these external support systems of patriarchal masculinity went through radical changes and disruptions in the eighties and nineties. But this wasn't just your usual generational shift, where one father's priorities look old-fashioned and boring to the son raised on new technologies and ideas. This was the patriarchy abandoning men. This was about the disappearance of the actual structure of laws, cultural norms, financial regulations, and religions that withheld power from the many for the benefit of the few men who met their standards, to be replaced by a structure that instead benefited only the wealthy, no matter what their gender.

The shifts in the dynamics of heterosexual coupling are documented in three Michael Douglas films. In *Fatal Attraction, The War of the Roses,* and *Basic Instinct,* we see how women's change in status and values profoundly unsettles the men around them. Removing the obstacles, both legal and social, that prevented women from creating public lives for themselves and pursuing ambitions to the best of their ability destabilized the power imbalance between men and women and the traditional roles that had been created in order to maintain that imbalance. Both the role of the husband and the role of the wife underwent significant changes as a result of these new freedoms, as seen in the love triangle structure of *Fatal Attraction,* which involves the struggle between a successful man and traditional husband, his traditional stay-at-home wife, and the liberated, career-woman mistress.

One of the new freedoms made available to women between the mid-1970s and the mid-1980s was the no-fault divorce. Women were free to leave unhappy marriages—and they did, in unprecedented numbers. The modern woman's dissatisfaction, and the traditional man's refusal to adapt to new expectations in relationships, plays out in *The War of the Roses,* as family court becomes the newest, and most vicious, battleground in the war between the sexes.

The standoff that developed between men and women in the wake of changing gender roles created a state of heteropessimism and entrenched animosity between the sexes. Birth rates and marriage rates would fall steadily during the next few decades. Both men and women reported wild dissatisfaction with the state of dating, love, and marriage, yet endless negotiations did not result in any kind of peace treaty. This is the dynamic captured in *Basic Instinct,* where the female characters find it easier to murder—or, in polite society at least, abandon—men and forgo the fantasy of the happy lifelong marriage than compromise.

But strains on men's love lives are often just manifestations of economic anxiety. The economic changes of the 1980s put the middle class in peril and created a new demographic: the precariat. As seen in *Wall Street,* the financial deregulation, banking reforms, and corporate takeovers of that decade didn't only change the fortunes of men—it created a new form of competitive corporate masculinity. The respectable family man was turning into a ghost, and his sons were becoming increasingly reckless with the fortunes of the world. The switch from traditional finance to modern finance, also known as the onset of "casino capitalism," turned a stratified class system into a game of winners and losers.

In *Wall Street* Michael Douglas plays the decade's most notorious winner, Gordon Gekko. And in *Falling Down,* he plays the economy's archetypal loser, the middle-aged white mass shooter. The victims of the new corporate culture—the ones who couldn't or didn't want to compete in the new game—suffered layoffs, downward mobility, and chronic unemployment. Many turned to self-destructive, or just destructive, acts, lashing out as they failed to adjust.

It wasn't just masculinity in crisis during this time. America was suffering an existential crisis at the end of history as well. The country had for decades defined itself against its enemies, the Soviet Union and the specter of communism. But in the final days of this battle between the superpowers, America started to feel some anxiety about its position in an increasingly flat world. The country feared losing its status and its ability to order the world in a way that best suited itself, and that fear crept into its entertainment. In the films *Black Rain, Romancing the Stone,* and *The Jewel of the Nile,* released in the years leading up to the fall of the Berlin Wall, Michael Douglas plays the prototypical American abroad—arrogantly unworldly, impatient with different languages and customs—as American power overseas, spread more with the dollar than the bullet, entrenches itself.

And because the whole American Dream is tied up in the idea of clawing your way to the top, no matter how humble your circumstances, Michael Douglas also plays the American president in a 1995 movie. This is also part of the American Dream: the dream of power, of wielding the weapon of mass destruction that is the American military against enemies foreign or imaginary, of being able to shape the world through willpower and greatness.

With the changes in the family, the economy, the law, and the geopolitical hierarchy accomplished, the liberation of men from the patriarchy is almost complete. And yet no one is celebrating, no one even seems to be having a very good time. In the films *Disclosure* and *The Game,* Michael Douglas gives us two visions of men in this new ruling structure. In the first, the man refuses to adapt to the changing times, and he fails to relate to a world that is no longer meeting his expectations. He becomes bitter and paranoid, not to mention delusional about why his status is slipping.

In *The Game,* adapting to the new world without the collective project of making that liberation understandable as a political project turns out to be lonely work. Michael Douglas plays a man who struggles to liberate himself from the restrictive and ill-fitting costume of the patriarch, but it turns out not to be a personal project but instead one that requires the active participation of everyone around him. Without the money and leisure to rethink how to live a life, a man can find himself stuck in old patterns of behavior, handed down from the sad and angry men who came before him.

As the millennium comes to a close, we enter the aftermath of the patriarchal collapse and the era of stagnation and decline for men. Women are still benefiting from the parallel systems of support they created to help them transition out of oppression and into public life, but men—at least those lacking in wealth—are stuck with the outdated roles, insecure job market, and failing institutions of a bygone era. Michael Douglas looks upon the world he helped to create and he despairs. There is vast inequality, widespread suffering from addiction and suicide, and a catastrophic cynicism dominating the culture. In a time of uncertainty, con men and masculinity influencers make themselves rich by keeping the underclass hooked on their own resentment and sense of grievance. And yet Michael Douglas remains impotent and unable to intervene.

The benefits of patriarchy were always a trickle-down affair, men on the lower sections of the hierarchy always had to make do with scraps. But the benefits for even lower-class men in patriarchy, whether that was just having someone in a chronically lower status like women or racialized groups to feel superior to, were real. And the possibility of climbing up the hierarchy was dangled above them, to keep them compliant and well-behaved.

But now there are few automatic benefits bestowed upon members of the male gender. And while we are all still haunted by the ghosts of patriarchy, some of us fully driven mad by its specters and banging through the night, when daylight comes we can see that what we have instead is different. It might be structured like the patriarchy—with its hierarchies and systems of oppression still in place—but given the ways in which it functions and behaves, it reveals itself to be a different beast.

michael douglas and women

What did feminism have to do with Michael Douglas? This question lurks in the background of each of Michael Douglas's erotic thrillers, a big genre in the eighties and nineties and one that was especially successful for him as a film star. In each of his thrillers, his female partner goes from being an alluring mystery to an unknowable threat. Her motivations mystifying, her behaviors erratic, her presence menacing and monstrous. Did feminism change women from passive creatures into deranged beasts? Michael Douglas is stalked, harassed, threatened; women come at him with knives, poison, and ice picks. Is the real victim in all these changes in the lives of women . . . men?

Wherever you want to pinpoint the beginning of Western feminism—does it originate in the "first wave" during the fight for voting rights at the turn of the twentieth century? Or the 1869 publication of John Stuart Mill's *The Subjection of Women*? Or the first granting of individual legal status to women during the French Revolution?—the fight for equality between the genders has been a long one, with many stops and starts along the way.

But by the 1980s, the movement was at something of a standstill. The 1970s had been a busy decade when it came to legislating freedoms for women. The *Roe v. Wade* Supreme Court decision in 1973 standardized the legality of abortion in America, where previously each state had been free to determine whether it would be illegal or legal to access pregnancy termination services. Only in the previous year had the Supreme Court decision *Eisenstadt v. Baird* granted unmarried women access to birth control, giving women the right to control their fertility privately.

This was also the decade in which the federal civil rights law Title IX was passed, forbidding sex discrimination in education, and the Equal Credit Opportunity Act, which prohibited discrimination based on "race, color, religion, national origin, sex, marital status, or age," giving women the opportunity to open their own bank accounts and lines of credit. The previous decade had also seen great advances for the civil rights of women, as anti-discrimination legislation protected women and other previously marginalized groups in the workplace and enforced equal pay for equal work.

The result of all these changes was the ability for women to create for themselves a life and presence in the public realms of work and politics. To enter institutions of education and accreditation, to join the workforce while protected from discrimination, to own property and material resources in order to conduct business freely in the marketplace. But as many women quickly learned, the ability to exercise these rights was tied directly to their financial situation.

Most of these freedoms are considered "negative freedoms," or the freedom to participate in an activity without interference or obstacle. As in, the establishment of reproductive rights granted women freedom to pursue family planning services like abortion or birth control without the interference of the state. There were caveats and limitations on that, of course—term limits for abortion services, the need of a prescription from a doctor for the Pill—but this is how most of the feminist gains were granted.

Because for all the obstacles of the era that disappeared, one remained: money. But because the ability to pay didn't discriminate by gender, race, or religion, it was ultimately deemed to be a fair barrier. As the historian Robert O. Self has noted, "The more a right is rendered in negative terms, the more it becomes wealth sensitive—that is, the more it disproportionately benefits members of society who already possess resources." A positive freedom, for example, would have ensured that public institutions of learning were made available to all regardless of a person's ability to pay. This was a problem at the heart of Western feminism, which had focused its attention on freedoms (reproductive freedom, educational freedom, employment freedom) and neglected the pursuit of true equity, which would have required a more radical reimagining of society. Women were free to choose to attend college, but without the money for tuition, it was difficult for many to exercise that freedom.

After that, the goals of mainstream feminism became focused on individual achievement. Now that women were protected from discrimination in the institutions of education, they were encouraged to aim high and pursue degrees in the previously male-dominated fields of law, medicine, and technology. Now that women were shielded by law from sexual harassment, job loss for getting pregnant, or being paid less for equal work, they were encouraged to climb the corporate ladder and feed their ambitions.

But it wasn't just job satisfaction women were encouraged to aspire to. There was a whole masculine arena that had been refusing women access for years, and now they were encouraged by both feminist and mainstream women's culture and media to force their way in and revel in its delights. Sex! Money! Society! Politics! The world! Women were no longer confined to the dreary chores of the kitchen and the nursery, they were out to claim their stake in what had previously been denied to them.

While this was largely understood as an expansion of the world of women, something to grow into and explore with enthusiasm and delight, it was also seen as something wholly separate from men. The changes that were happening within the lives and psyches of women, individually or collectively, were not much discussed in the realm of men as an invitation for their own growth and exploration. At best, the work that women were doing to create a role in public life for themselves was seen as something that should be acknowledged and allowed. At worst, it was seen as a threat.

There were men who didn't just publicly take a stand against feminism, they professionalized their hatred. In one notorious example, Pat Robertson—a religious leader who founded Regent University, ran for president as a Republican in 1988, and had close connections to politicians like Bob Dole, George H. W. Bush, and Ronald Reagan—called the feminist campaign for the Equal Rights Amendment an "anti-family movement that encouraged women to leave their husbands, kill their children, practice witchcraft, destroy capitalism and become lesbians."

Robertson was one of the most visible representatives of a growing Christian backlash that (rightly) saw feminism as a threat to the traditional patriarchal order. If women were not forced, coerced, or made legally obligated to stay under patriarchal control, the whole structural hierarchy that placed a small segment of men on top would collapse. Politicians, talk radio hosts like Rush Limbaugh, and televangelists flooded mass media with hateful commentary. Feminism was incurring god's wrath and god was now punishing us with disasters like hurricanes and earthquakes, they insisted. Feminists were destabilizing society by working outside of the home. They were upending the natural order of things, and the progress of women must be stopped in its tracks. These men were on the radio, on the television, in the halls of Congress. They were often so extreme in their bigotry that they gave cover to the men with more moderate positions. After all, they weren't like that (gestures vaguely toward the man chomping on a cigar and stretching out the word "feminazi" on live radio). Feminism, they reasoned, could be something women had to figure out among themselves; what did any of this have to do with men?

The kind of man Michael Douglas represented in films was not a bigot. The Michael Douglas character was sophisticated, urbane. A walking embodiment of *Esquire* magazine, back when it was still good. He didn't demean women by calling them sluts or whores. He didn't explicitly say his wife should stay in the kitchen. He certainly wasn't on the side of the conservatives and the religious extremists who were outraged by the feminist movement, condemning the civil rights campaign as a tool of the devil. But he also didn't seem to think that the feminist movement and the changes happening in the political and cultural reality of women had anything to do with him. And in that way, he was a kind of cinematic stand-in for a lot of men of the time: liberal, tolerant, and clueless.

After a decade of cinema celebrating the rebel and the unconventional man, the vigilante, the hippie, the outsider, the junkie, the alienated, and the antisocial, the men of eighties film decided to settle down. Start a family. Go into business. Echoing the turn from counterculture to the suburbs that many of the baby boomer generation made, the film world of the eighties gave us a lot of family men and businessmen, men who traded in their dreams of cosmic harmony for dreams of financial abundance and white picket fences. Michael Douglas was a perfect representative for this man who worked in the city but lived in the wealthier suburbs; he was kind and gracious to his female employees and colleagues but didn't take them on as protégées or collaborators; he was thoughtful about his appearance but not so much that his heterosexuality would ever be in question. With the entry of a new kind of woman into his workplace, his home, his social circles, he didn't seem to think that his behaviors or expectations would have to change.

This new man was eager to benefit from the new roles for women that were being created. A new generation of women had been liberated sexually from religious shame and the weighty chains that had bonded sex with marriage and pregnancy. Maybe those women would like to have sex with him, if he showed up as sensitive and seductive. He could also experience the relief of no longer being expected to be the sole provider for his family, now that there were women with career paths. He could be lightly supportive, engaged with and encouraging of their ambitions.

But feminism as a political ideology didn't touch this man. It's not just that these ideas swirling around about femininity being a performance didn't penetrate his own thinking about whether masculinity could possibly be a performance, too. Or that if certain parts of the world had been kept from women, there might be a corresponding part of life that men had little to no access to as well. It's that a lot of men seemed surprised that they might have to behave differently now that women had new roles in life and new expectations for their existence.

If the changes feminism wrought were an issue for men at all, it was something that had to be negotiated one-on-one. If your wife has gained a political awareness about the injustices present in the heterosexual relationship as it pertains to an unfair burden of domestic labor or even the "orgasm gap," that is something to be met with not politically but through interpersonal negotiation.

In June 1990, *Esquire* released an issue devoted to "The Secret Life of the American Wife." And while throughout the features and articles there is an acknowledgment of things like how much more time even working women devote to childcare and housework, the wife is treated throughout mostly as a curiosity, a segment of the population that requires careful study. How curious these modern women, with their habits, their strange ways of dressing, their odd behaviors.

Esquire did seem to want to understand the modern wife. What was she doing for so long in the bathroom? The writers of "Your Wife: An Owner's Manual" (cheeky!) broke it down, giving a timeline for how long it takes women to wash their hair, polish their nails, curl their eyelashes. What secret treasures are women lugging around in their purses? The contents of the "typical" wife's bag are pulled out and explained one by one. This is a nail file, this is something they might stick in the eye of a man trying to attack them on the streets. What do they do all day? "The latest statistics indicate that lolling and bonbons are definitely not part of the current American wife's daily routine."

And what about all that feminism stuff? How were women reacting to that? In the feature "The Last Housewife in America," David Finkel profiles a woman who has decided to become a full-time homemaker. Her social circle is full of women who express anxiety and ambivalence about their decisions to stay at their jobs or to opt out to focus on family. One woman chose to stop working, only to be left by her husband after fifteen years. Another decided to go back to work after finding domestic labor too dull to handle. The husbands wander around in the background of the feature, not involving themselves in their wives' existential crises. "I was tired of hearing it," one husband reports to the journalist. It's not their problem, it's something for the women to sort out for themselves.

But if women were exploding their ideas about how to be a wife, doesn't it suggest maybe men should have been reconsidering how to be husbands? Many didn't, as was made evident by how the number of hours married men spent performing domestic or childcare labor barely moved upward through the eighties and nineties. (About eleven hours a week in 1987, up from seven in 1970, according to a University of Maryland study.) Nor did many want to think if there might be different ways to be bosses, fathers, sons, lovers, or friends. And the proof of that resistance to change can be found in the skyrocketing divorce rates, bloody custody battles in family court, and the increasingly toxic and frustrating dating scene. Or you could just watch some Michael Douglas movies.

Because the remarkable thing about watching these films now is seeing how exasperated and confused he is when talking to women. Why are you so unhappy? Why isn't this working for you when it's clearly working for me? What are you doing with that knife, honey?

That confusion stems from the fact that he is simply acting in the way he had been instructed by his parents, his teachers, his mentors, and the culture that surrounded him. And while that resulted in some funny fish-out-of-water stories—cue comedies like *Mr. Mom* that showed men flailing in the domestic role, realizing for the first time that raising a family and keeping a home is actual work—that confusion often twisted itself into something much darker and more damaging: into bitterness and resentment, into violence, into anguish. The confusion is a crisis point, one that could have been moved through with curiosity and adaptability.

But where were men going to get the information necessary to assist them through this process? What models did men have to learn how to adapt to the changing times? Men were still being asked to continue to fulfill those roles within the lives of women, of husbands and fathers and lovers and sons, but the rules for what those roles might look like or what behaviors were desirable versus problematic were in question. Their fathers' mode of masculinity was useless to them as a guide, but no new model was presenting itself, leaving men alone to try to navigate an uncertain time.

So imagine a game in which the balance and imbalance of power between two figures creates the fun and thrill of it. Maybe tug-of-war. While a perfect equality in strength and strategy creates a standstill—the death of fun—a mismatch creates tension and possibility. The weaker player has to be cunning to survive, they have to use surprise and strategy to turn their opponent's strength against them.

A tug-of-war is perhaps an overly simplistic way to describe heterosexual marriage during a time of patriarchy. And yet. For centuries, women's culture—their publications, the gossip, their entertainments, the information passed down from mother to daughter—taught women how to compensate for their disempowerment when it came to heterosexual marriage. How to use the imbalance not as a form of oppression and sadness—or at least not only as a form of oppression and sadness—but as a way to create fun and thrill. Women were taught how to be wily within the confines of relationships with men. They were taught how to scheme and manipulate, how to present oneself appropriately to attract men of higher status, how to charm and beguile, and how to avoid being just another body in Bluebeard's closet.

Men were given less instruction on how to win their tug-of-war, because they were the strong ones. Just pull hard. Sometimes they were told how to play fairly or how to pull their punches, literally—hence the laws that instructed on the size of a stick a man was allowed to hit his wife with. But ultimately, men didn't need a strategy to survive their game with women.

But now let's imagine the same tug-of-war. Only this time, the player who has always been the weaker one has bulked up. Maybe they got themselves a robotic arm. Whatever, I'm not going to belabor the metaphor. Now the opponent has strength and cunning. Not only that, they don't really even have to show up for the game if they don't want to anymore. Maybe they find a solo activity, like the swing set, just as interesting.

The game has changed. The traditionally stronger player is now at a disadvantage. He can't just pull really hard and expect to get the results he wants. And the men who have played the game before him are no help, because they were playing against a fundamentally different opponent. They're saying things like, "Just be yourself." Or if they can't believe it's going so poorly, "Are you even trying?" Or they start chiming in about how the game was better back in their day, and women should be forced to give up the progress they've made and come back into the game weaker and more vulnerable.

During this phase of skyrocketing divorce rates, when marriage was either delayed or never achieved, and there was greater dissatisfaction in heterosexual relationships, Michael Douglas appeared in three films that illustrate these changing dynamics between men and women. And in each film, he enters into a relationship with a woman while holding his old-fashioned ideas and is exasperated—shocked, even—to discover things do not go the way he expects. The game has changed. And not only is our male hero unprepared, he seems incapable of acknowledging the changes.

In three films, we get a sense of how the modern man responded to the mainstreaming of women into public life and the tumult this created in the domestic sphere. In *Fatal Attraction* (1987), we see a successful attorney who decides to have an affair, like many of the successful men before him. Only this time, the woman refuses to disappear or stay silent after he is done with her. His role as a husband, a lover, and a success are all put into jeopardy when one woman challenges him.

In *War of the Roses* (1989), the Michael Douglas character tries to build a home with his wife and his two children. Only his wife, a little bored with sitting around after raising two children and making a lovely home for their family, decides to start her own business. This act of independence destabilizes their marriage, and soon, thanks to the no-fault divorce laws, their marital problems become a legal battle.

And in *Basic Instinct* (1992), Michael Douglas falls in love with

one of the newly liberated women he's probably read about in magazines. She's financially independent, she's fulfilled with her job as
a writer, she's sexually adventurous, but still she finds herself drawn
back into the disappointing heterosexual dynamic. The women of
Basic Instinct start to contemplate the possibility that maybe a life,
or a whole world, might be better without any men in it.

FATAL ATTRACTION:

CAUGHT IN THE CROSSFIRE OF
THE MOMMY WARS

Gender is a performance. While this was a radical idea when Simone de Beauvoir mainstreamed it in her 1949 philosophical feminist masterpiece *The Second Sex,* it's become generally accepted thanks to the work of feminist thinkers who followed and the widespread introduction of gender studies classes in universities throughout the 1970s.

Gender is a role that we play in order to get along in society and achieve our goals and desires. It is shaped by our interactions with other people, through attempts—both successful and failing—to get what we want at our jobs or in our love lives, and the inspiration we see from other people performing the same gender.

But the roles we play, gendered and otherwise, are dependent on the roles other people are playing. If you're onstage in the middle of *A Streetcar Named Desire* and your scene partner launches into a soliloquy from *Macbeth,* the whole performance falls apart.

The roles of men in Western society were and are supported by the roles that women play. One woman's refusal to play along can disrupt the whole system. (Well, not literally—they'd just drag you off to give you a lobotomy and put you back onstage to dust the set pieces.) But in our understanding of a performance, someone refusing to do what is expected of them unsettles everyone else around them.

Which is why *Fatal Attraction* had such a tremendous impact on popular culture when it was released in 1987. The setup of the story was not radical—a married man cheats on his wife, so what. A tale as old as time. But the twist was so shocking that the film changed the lexicon (the phrase "bunny boiler" immediately entered slang to describe an unhinged woman), was quoted endlessly ("I'm not going to be *ignored, Dan*"), and spawned endless think pieces about the state of gendered relations. And that twist was simply that one woman refuses to play the role assigned to her, the role of mistress. Because rather than fading away after the man is done with their dalliance, she threatens and stalks him. She invades the private sanctity of his home, she shows up at his work and threatens his reputation. The man is supposed to be the one who is in control, but her refusal to play the role expected of her turns a romance into a horror movie.

To put it bluntly, the mistress's role is death. The mistress is supposed to die when the man is finished with her. The woman who is not fit for marriage, who does not exist within the protection of the family in a patriarchal society, is something to be used and discarded. This is the story of the murdered sex worker, the lesbians who die at the end of their films, the bohemian women who die of tuberculosis, and the rejected mistress who turns to suicide after her lover leaves her for another. It even shows up in *Fatal Attraction*, through repeated references to *Madama Butterfly*, Puccini's 1904 opera about a Japanese woman abandoned after her affair with an American soldier. When Butterfly is discarded by a man who marries a more appropriate match, she kills herself with a seppuku knife—the ritualistic death that restores honor to the subject after their disgrace.

Alex's refusal to die, her almost supernatural persistence and intrusive presence in Dan's life, marks a turn in the culture. Women could survive outside of men's protection. She has a job, a social life, love and sex, money, the kind of arty loft apartment in the Meatpacking District that your average Manhattanite would pay through the nose for these days. Alex refuses to play any role that someone like Dan could recognize.

But the fact that Alex does eventually die—not by Dan's hand but by his wife's—shows just how destabilizing the ability of a woman to live outside of men's structures really was. The patriarchal man isn't the only one threatened by Alex and the "career women" who crept around in the shadows of mass media's imagination like baby-eating Baba Yagas. Alex is also a threat to Beth, the traditional wife and mother.

When we meet Michael Douglas in *Fatal Attraction,* in a character named Dan, he is on his way up. We see the head of his law firm praising him and inviting him out for dinner, he's looking into buying a house in the suburbs, he is doing quite well for himself and his wife and daughter. He's doing so well, in fact, that he, like a lot of ambitious men, starts to feel cramped in his own home. He comes home from a successful business event to find his daughter has taken his position in his bed. His wife seems distracted and busy, her attention focused on real estate decisions and parenting obligations and her own parents, rather than on him.

And so, like any successful man in a man-ruled business, he decides to have an affair. He's entitled to one. Infidelity was supposed to be his reward for success. How many films, books, operas had taught our Michael Douglas figure and his upwardly mobile peers that this is what a successful man deserves? Isn't this why men ascend into the professional classes, why they fight their way into exclusive universities, why they work long hours to meet impossible expectations for billable hours, why they stifle anything interesting or unique about themselves way down deep to present a smooth, successful surface? Because once you accumulate enough wealth and power, the rules of morality and decency that govern other people, the common people, no longer apply to you. The king has courtesans; the big-name lawyer has mistresses.

There has always been a steady supply of extra women in the world, ready to service the great man's needs: secretaries, sex workers, mistresses, service workers, students, the unmarriable, scenesters. Women looking for a way into whatever industry he might be gatekeeping, women who can't find the loving attention of a husband and family themselves because they so poorly play the role of the wife, wild women who can't be domesticated, women with "daddy issues," naïve young women who are still confusing wanting to be like a certain person with wanting to fuck that person.

There have always been risks involved with straying outside the marriage for the successful man. There's the looming threat of divorce or scandal (or, depending on how you go about it, jail time). But these relationships with women usually have pretty clear trade-offs. Whether you are paying them off with money, romance, material goods, or access to your world, there are boundaries. Rules. Most of those boundaries, at least on the women's side, are maintained through fear. Fear of losing his affection, fear of getting dumped, fear of being publicly shamed or cast out of his society, fear of his displeasure turning into violence.

Because once they are no longer wanted, the extra women are easily discarded. Give her a cash settlement and an NDA, or maybe dump her body in the river if it's really not going very well. For the most part, the extra women of the world have known what part they are there to play, and there have not historically been many second acts for them. Mistresses, sex workers, and victims have often kept quiet, or at least waited until the man has passed to spill their secrets. Inhabiting the role of the successful man requires that women play their assigned parts with the same devotion and limita-tions. Men can get away with infidelity, rape, harassment, and other mistreatment without consequences only if women refuse to talk about it. Marilyn Monroe had an affair with a president and took the story to her early grave; Monica Lewinsky did the same and went on national television.

And it's not only Alex who is refusing to stay quiet after Dan tries to discard her after their passionate weekend. The only legal case we see Dan working on is related to a sex scandal. A woman who had an affair with a politician has decided not to stay loyal and keep his secrets for him—she wrote a book about it instead. Not even the threat of legal action will silence her. There is nothing the politician can do to prevent being smacked in the face with the con-sequences of his own behavior.

Ironically, Dan is working on the case on the side of the politi-cian's mistress and the publisher who wants to help sell her story. And yet still he naïvely has his own affair—with a work colleague—despite having this lawsuit right in front of him, the brief for which might as well have been written by Cassandra: Ruin is coming, Dan.

The reason Alex can pose a threat to Dan is because of the protec-tions afforded to her and other women like her by the feminist movement. Dan appeals to various forms of authority to protect him from Alex, but there is nothing to be done. Alex tells Dan she is pregnant; unable to coerce her into terminating the pregnancy, he asks for legal advice to see if there is anything to be done to pro-tect him from being declared legally responsible for this child. There is not. When Dan fears that Alex will reveal to his wife and child their affair, he goes to the police to see about a protection order. But since he can't prove she has done him any real harm, they can't intervene—not even to "scare" her, as he asks. These scenes are an interesting way of looking at how laws and regulations changed during this era. These institutions of law and order were designed to protect people exactly like Dan, property-owning white head-of-household men. Why won't they come to his aid?

As the Nobel Prize–winning economist Gary Becker noted, "The family is the foundation of all civil society." Which is why it was worrying to those in the American government when during this era the foundation started to show some cracks. Divorce rates were up, single parent households started to rise, and the middle-class nuclear family became endangered.

One major concern was that the welfare state was simply too robust. Families that split apart—leaving single women with low-paying jobs, or no jobs at all, responsible for the care of children—could turn to social programs like food aid and housing subsidies to replace the man's wages. The government would be expected to foot the bill for what some called man's dereliction of duty.

As Ronald Reagan ran for president in 1976, he frequently told the story of Linda Taylor, who he and other right-wing political figures deemed the "welfare queen." She had been receiving welfare checks under several different names and was accused of defrauding the government. The politicians who wanted to reform and gut the social welfare programs pointed to her as just one of many devious women who invented children who did not exist, created fake names to apply for benefits, and ran other scams to use welfare money to buy cars and fur coats. A backlash against welfare recipients started to grow, as people who relied on this supplementary income were tarnished as freeloaders and con artists. This created the pressure required to make sweeping changes to what was up until then a successful and efficient system for preventing childhood hunger and devastating poverty.

One thing both the political left and right agreed on in this era of increased political polarization was that welfare programs had to change. As Melinda Cooper writes in her 2017 book *Family Values,* both the neoliberals and the neoconservatives agreed that the restoration of the nuclear family to the center of the American economy was essential for growth. "Although they are much more prepared than are social conservatives to accommodate changes in the nature and form of relationships within the family," she writes, "neoliberal economists and legal theorists wish to reestablish the private family as the primary source of economic security and a comprehensive alternative to the welfare state." In order to decrease the burden carried by the government, the goal was to shift that burden over to the individual.

Many of these changes were designed to protect the state against irresponsible women: women who divorced their partners, women who had children outside of marriage, or women who birthed children without health insurance. Barriers were put in place to prevent these women from easily accessing welfare programs. But many of those barriers also punished men. And the more disadvantaged the men, the more vulnerable they were to these new policies that exposed them to increased surveillance and interference by government programs.

One major victory in this pursuit was the establishment of the requirement that before a woman could receive government support for her children she first had to attempt to collect child support from the father. The Child Support Enforcement program was established in 1984 to help ensure that men not present in the household, either because of divorce or children being born outside of wedlock, still contributed financially to the cost of raising children. These payments were a crucial part of creating financial stability for the rising number of single parent households, but they were also not directly tied into welfare programs. But in 1996, due to the "family first" welfare reforms, the establishment of paternity and the attempt to recoup funds from the absent spouse became a requirement for receiving welfare benefits. If the partner applying for benefits did not want to involve the other parent—and many people who had suffered domestic violence at the hands of their partner did not want to involve them in this legal process—then they were not eligible for benefits.

The parents who were involuntarily required now to make regular child support payments—and the vast majority of these parents were men—were subject to wage garnishment, loss of parental rights, and the threat of imprisonment if they fell behind, even if their failure to pay was due to job loss or other hardships. Failure to pay for more than two years became a felony, subject to fines and jail time. This burden fell disproportionately on economically disadvantaged men, men in prison, and men of color.

The politicians who wanted to slash these government programs helped to scapegoat these men as "deadbeat dads," who were failing to live up to the responsibility of their families. They were especially harsh in their rhetoric against Black men, who contributed, they said, to a scourge of "broken homes." This view of Black men had become mainstream with the release of the so-called Moynihan Report on poverty in the Black community, *The Negro Family: The Case for National Action* in 1965, which blamed not the higher rates of imprisonment or the lack of well-paid work for the economic position of Black men but instead "ghetto culture." These stereotypes would be amplified through this era of welfare reform, as Black men were demonized and blamed for irresponsibly leaving their children in single parent homes, and Black women were called lazy and entitled for expecting the government to pick up the slack.

The end result of all this was that men who could not or did not marry, men who fathered children outside of wedlock, and men who could not financially support their children were entered into this new system of surveillance and punishment. Dan's little "accident" of Alex's pregnancy, once something that could be easily denied and covered up, leaving the single mother solely responsible for the expenses of raising her child, now threatens his financial security and his social position.

And legally, if the child is his, there is nothing Dan can do. The establishment of paternity outside—and sometimes even within marriage—has long been fraught. During patriarchy, when inheritance and property rights and legal status were predicated on paternity, convoluted systems were sometimes necessary to establish the identity of fathers to "bastard" sons. Nara Milanich documents these systems in her book *Paternity: The Elusive Quest for the Father*, and the court cases that challenged them. Before the development of blood type science and DNA testing, legal paternity often came down to what was essentially gossip and guesswork: resemblance between father and child, eyewitness accounts of seeing mother and father together, the establishment of proximity and opportunity, testimony to the parents' characters, and so on.

But in 1988, DNA-based paternity tests became widely available. This was a vast improvement over blood type science, allowing for greater accuracy and near certainty. It was getting more and more difficult for biological fathers to deny their connection to their children, making enforcement of paternal responsibilities and the social shaming that came with denial and abandonment all the harder to escape. Cue a montage of men on *The Jerry Springer Show* leaping with ecstatic joy at the sound of the words "You are not the father."

So Dan is powerless. He finds himself trapped in this aura of the deadbeat dad, the disgraced man, no longer the powerful patriarch of his imagination. He can't even kill Alex, despite showing up to her apartment to do just that. She won't do away with herself, as expected. That leaves the responsibility of eliminating this threat to his wife, Beth, the stay-at-home mother of his child. Because if the working woman refusing to play the traditional female role destabilized the role of the man, she had an even more powerful effect on the role of the wife.

Many members of the contemporary "manosphere," the masculinity influencers who peddle casual misogyny and indoctrinate their lost and weary followers into far-right thinking, will ultimately lay the blame for men's contemporary problems at the feet of feminism. The reason you are not thriving, getting married, earning a decent living, having sex, finding public recognition for your efforts, is because of feminism. And they are partly right. Feminism greatly changed women's expectations for how their lives would play out, and it gave them roles other than the ones that supported men's traditional roles. It turns out men's power doesn't work without women.

But instead of seeing this as an artificial and dependent form of power, instead of seeing this as a moment to rethink and see the limitations of their own roles, these masculine influencers pathologize women who "step out of line." They're not really happy, they insist. They're deranged, they're selfish, they're sick. Women can only be truly happy when they are confined in the same dynamics that prop men up.

That vision of the derangement of the masculinized woman is alive in *Fatal Attraction* through the two competing female forces— the wife and the feminist. Dan, a traditional man with a traditional idea of how life should be lived, married a woman who is willing and able to meet the expectations that her role as wife and mother carries. She is soft, beautiful, and attentive. She doesn't work outside the home, and we don't get even the slightest glimpse into her inner life, because god knows she probably doesn't have time for one, what with the obligations of raising a daughter, finding them a new house in the suburbs, caring for the family pets, and balancing her various responsibilities as the other half of an ambitious and hardworking husband. And she's effortless at it, we don't see her going to Jazzercise to keep off the baby weight or taking a Valium to find the strength to be nice to people. There is not a thought in her head, just deep maternal and wifely feelings, and her name is Beth, not even a word, just kind of a sweet whisper.

And then there is her feminist counterpart, Alex. She's childless and single, but she's in a powerful position at her publishing company, so clearly she sacrificed the possibility of a family life to pursue her career. She's sexually voracious, sleeping with Dan just hours into their first date. She's going to fabulous parties not as a plus-one but as the primary invitee. She's living in an apartment that is basically a bachelor pad, devoid of any feminine touches, in the Meatpacking District. (Very subtle.)

This battle between two visions of womanhood became fodder for politics and mass media. The political left championed the freedom of the working woman, liberated financially and sexually, ambitious and fearless. The political right idealized the traditional wife and mother, imbuing her with a kind of sainthood for her endless patience and ceaseless love. Each side claimed the other was trying to oppress their imaginary woman. The right claimed the left was a bunch of baby haters who wanted to destroy the family and pervert the natural order of gendered differentiation. The left claimed the right was a bunch of misogynist religious fundamentalists who wanted to trap women in domestic spaces, silent and laboring unpaid forever. The media fed into this dichotomy, creating hysteria about working women dying unloved and unfulfilled (in 1986 *Newsweek* magazine falsely claimed that an unmarried forty-year-old working woman with a college degree was more likely to die in a terrorist attack than ever marry) and creating endless debates about whether or not women could "have it all."

The truth was that the vast majority of women lived somewhere in the murky middle. Stay-at-home mothers often had paid work of some kind, even if the work was only casual, off the books, or part-time. Many women who decided to forgo marriage or children did want them eventually but were unable to find suitable partners or simply wanted to wait until they established themselves in their careers. And just because a woman didn't carry a bachelor's degree didn't mean she didn't pursue education in one way or another, either through certification or vocational training, supplementary classes, or incomplete programs.

But in the *Fatal Attraction* battle between Alex and Beth, each woman is represented by the most extreme position. If men's roles with women were troubled by the changes brought about by feminism, women who wanted to retain a more traditional lifestyle, one with a clearly defined gender binary and prescribed role within the family and society, were finding it difficult to do so on numerous levels. Suddenly men had different expectations for their wives and might want to partner with women who chose to keep working after marriage, changing labor laws made it less likely to find a spouse who could earn a breadwinning wage, reforms to family law made it easier for men to leave their family without real financial support. Feminism had created new possibilities for how a woman could live her life, freeing her to make a stable existence for herself outside of marriage if she desired. But some women didn't want new possibilities. And they blamed feminism for gaining freedoms at their expense.

This viewpoint requires a misunderstanding of the timeline. When second-wave feminism emerged in the late sixties and early seventies, it didn't inspire a generation of women to abandon their homes to join the workplace—the political movement was the response to the changes that were already happening. Women had already started working in greater numbers—from 34 percent of women working outside the home in 1950 to around 43 percent by 1970, according to the Bureau of Labor Statistics—because of the decline in wages, the beginning of the stagflation that would persist through the 1970s American economy, and the first movements of what would become mass deindustrialization and globalization. Like most social movements, feminism was sparked by need, not by choice. It wasn't a luxury; it was a response to suffering and exploitation. Women who worked needed specific forms of support and protection, access to services like childcare and educational opportunities, comprehensive reproductive healthcare that included abortion rights, fair pay, and the ability to expand their career options outside of the so-called pink-collar paths like nursing, teaching, and secretarial work. Women had initially tried to fight for these rights within the larger pro-worker leftist movement, but they found the male leaders disinterested and hostile. The only way they were going to get what they wanted, they thought, was if they fought their own fights and insisted on the legitimacy and priority of their agenda.

Codifying the reforms to employment law did much to normalize the idea of the working woman, even after women had children. But the expectation that women could work and achieve financial independence meant that suddenly the financial security of married women who did not want to work outside the home was at risk. Part of the reforms to family law that feminists asked for was the creation of the "no-fault" divorce, allowing women to separate more easily from abusive, unfaithful, or otherwise dissatisfactory husbands without proving their unworthiness as a partner in the court of law. This, the conservative critics rightly believed, would make it even easier for men to abandon their families, leaving stay-at-home mothers alone to raise their children in diminished circumstances. Other parts of the feminist project (gay rights, desegregation, access to birth control and abortion, and so on) offended their sensibilities, which were often religious in nature.

We remember first the men who made such a fuss about feminism and impeded its progress, and how could you not, as loud as they were being. Besides the grandstanding politicians and preachers and talk radio hosts, there were the men of the media, who, just for example, made something like *Fatal Attraction,* where a woman who had prioritized career over family and marriage was turned into a covetous monster, absolutely deranged by her underused womb, a destructive whirl of crazy. It's humiliating listening to all this as a woman. It's degrading. But these sorts of stories weren't necessarily a threat.

At least not in the same way that other women posed to the feminist movement. Because it was mostly an organized lobbying effort of housewives led by attorney and anti-feminist spokesperson Phyllis Schlafly that blocked the passage of the Equal Rights Amendment. If women and men are made legally equal, she argued, women would lose more than they gained. Women would have to fight wars and get jobs, there would be gender neutral bathrooms and same-sex marriage. And it was often women spokespeople like Schlafly and Anita Bryant antagonizing the movement for the rights of gays and lesbians, using the language of family values and "for the sake of the children" to enforce heteronormativity. If traditional divides between the sexes are not enforced, these women warned, gender and sexual anarchy would follow.

But some of that animosity might also lie in the fact that feminists made traditional women look bad. The traditional mother was no longer the "Angel in the House." They were old-fashioned, dowdy, behind the times. (Schlafly's many public appearances admonishing feminists with her rock-hard hairdo didn't really help the aesthetics of the movement.) It wasn't just that they were losing ground culturally and legally, forced into a liberation they didn't ask for or want, they were seen and discussed as being oppressed. People felt sorry for them. They were talked about as if they were victims. I mean, no wonder Beth shoots Alex. It's not enough for you to fuck my husband, you want to destroy my way of life, too?

But the ambitious working woman of the eighties was neither the glamorous feminist fantasy of having-it-all success nor the hysterical shrew of men's fevered imaginations. She was left sort of flailing around. How to create a new kind of life, without any real models or guidelines for what that might look like? Your mother was no help, your office was unlikely to have a powerful woman for mentorship, and *Working Girl* wouldn't come out until 1988. The feminist movement had been successful in creating freedom for women, but it disappointed on the equality front. Feminism had liberated women into a world that already existed, but the liberation did little to change the world itself. A disappointment started to settle in. And the backlash from both men and women even to the idea of female liberation created an atmosphere of ambivalence and resignation.

Alex's ambitions aren't really being supported by the feminist movement of the time. She gets some encouraging slogans, maybe she would show up on a list of the "top 40 women under 40," but structural support? Such as a work culture that would guarantee her leisure time so that she could pursue a romantic and family life rather than devote all her hours to proving her worth in a male-dominated field? And then if she did have children, would she have people advocating for subsidized childcare or compensated maternity leave or flexible hours to manage her caretaking responsibilities? Sure, feminists like Gloria Steinem would go on television every once in a while and say it was really unfair we didn't have these things, but it wasn't like anyone was working to make it happen.

Women were being pushed to achieve, without the resources necessary to build truly independent lives, without a map for navigating hostile waters, and in an atmosphere of shame and terror. They were told, again and again, through the feminist discourse, that they were brave pioneers, breaking through barriers and ceilings and obstacles for the good of womankind, but the sacrifices that took were rarely rewarded with anything meaningful.

The big idea here was that if women managed to force their way into enough boardrooms, legislatures, and committees, they could make the changes that had stalled out in the late seventies. The political priorities of women were never going to be recognized by men, no matter how long women spent trying to persuade and cajole and insist. The only thing to do, then, was to change the makeup of the public world. And thus sparked the beginnings of corporate feminism, which became obsessed not with making working women's lives easier, but with simply pressuring women already under tremendous strain to do more and achieve more for the good of the sisterhood. Sadly, no matter how many CEOs or girlbosses or Olympians or representatives with hoop earrings we managed to put into positions of power, somehow the changes feminists had been dreaming of failed to materialize. (Somehow, they forgot success tends to erode sympathy, and people with hard-won victories are not so eager to ease the paths of the people coming up behind them. "If I can do it, no one else has any excuses" is the mantra of bootstrap capitalists of all genders.)

As much as Michael Douglas thinks this film is about him, it's the tension between the two women, Beth and Alex, the wife and the mistress, the stay-at-home mother versus the working woman, that makes *Fatal Attraction* work. But because Michael Douglas spends so much of his time exasperated and confused, he never gets around to wondering how any of this affects him.

The film ends with a close-up shot of the happy family photo. Husband, wife, daughter, all smiling brightly. But the reality is that his wife now knows that he cheated, the daughter is traumatized by everything that just happened, and his future as a family man is in peril. Will his wife take her cue from the culture of no-fault divorce that surrounds her, the feminist messaging that she deserves more, and liberate herself from this philanderer? And if the feminist movement breaks up his home, will he finally adapt to changing times? Love in a time of family court is coming up next.

When Betty Broderick shot her husband in 1989 and became an instant, if fleeting, household name with the help of tabloid media, was it simply a homicide or was it something more like the shot heard 'round the world? Was it an interpersonal issue or was it a decisive battle in the war between the sexes? The details of the crime were just a series of gendered clichés, and every new fact emerging from the case—gleefully broadcast for months through every stage of the trial—seemed to reinforce what everyone already believed about men, about women, about love and marriage in the 1980s. No wonder the entertainment industry played with the murder so frequently, turning it into a film, television movies, and trashy books (and much later a Netflix true crime series). When that abandoned middle-aged woman stalked off with a handgun to murder her ex-husband and his new young bride, she wasn't just killing two people. She was unleashing a cultural phenomenon.

Betty Broderick was the aggrieved first wife, a figure that would become almost archetypal in this era of no-fault divorces and tabloid television. Born in 1947, she was coming of age just as the second wave of feminism was telling American women, especially the

college-educated, white, upper-middle-class women like Betty—
women with the lingering sense of lost potential that Betty Friedan
so famously named "the problem with no name" in *The Feminine
Mystique*—that they could and should be more than just a wife.

But Betty Broderick chose a more traditional approach to plot-
ting out her life. Which is not to say she didn't work—she had a
degree in early childhood education and was the primary breadwinner, as a teacher and at a few other odd jobs, for their growing family
while her husband finished school. But once his career as a lawyer
started to take off, she and her husband divided up the roles of the
nuclear family along gendered lines. Betty would oversee the home
and their children's educations, and she would curate a useful social
life for the two of them that could help her husband fulfill his ambitions. And Daniel, her husband, would earn the money and develop
himself professionally and publicly.

Betty sacrificed the possibility of her own career and financial
autonomy to be a support system, sublimating her ambition into
her husband's. She was an educated and hardworking woman, but
she put all of that aside and boxed herself into the domestic space,
believing that her husband's riches were her riches, that his accomplishments were her accomplishments. That Daniel didn't see things
in quite the same way seemed to come as a shock to her.

Daniel, meanwhile, hit middle age. When men have their midlife crisis, or so the fantasy goes, their conventional little lives start
to feel too small. They feel the inevitability of death lurking just
over the horizon, and when they look at their wives, also middle-
aged, possibly wearing sweatpants to the grocery store because they
spent all night sitting up with a sick kid, they don't see the beautiful
young woman they married. They see a living, breathing reminder
of their impending doom sleeping in the bed right next to them.
They see their mortality and all the battles they have lost against it
staring at them from across the breakfast table. So they buy a tiny car

and drive around suburbia blasting "highway to the danger zone" on a cassette tape, they run off with the secretary, and maybe they join the Hair Club for Men. (Viagra wasn't around yet.) And Dan Broderick did almost exactly that. He got a sporty car, he left his wife for his young, blond secretary, and he dragged Betty into family court, fighting to pay as little spousal and child support as a successful attorney with his own practice could manage. When Betty broke into the new house he shared with his new, much younger wife and shot them to death while they were lying in bed, she became something of a folk hero. She received letters in jail from fans, written by similarly scorned and abandoned women, victims of the male ego and sense of entitlement, collateral damage of the crisis that is masculine middle age.

This was the kind of thing Phyllis Schlafly had warned American women about. That if the family structure was undermined by "progress," it was women who would suffer the most and be abandoned and impoverished. For women of the era the cliché wasn't really a midlife crisis, per se, but midlife anxiety. Women in middle age had outlived their usefulness, or so the gendered expectation of the time would have us believe. They had outlived their attractiveness and sexual potency. They would become invisible, easy to abandon. And then they would be left with no job, an empty nest, just a shell of a woman. This anxiety was very lucrative for some, fueling a surge in plastic surgery and physical fitness programs targeted at women (Jazzercise anyone?), and it played out daily on talk shows and soap operas. Daytime talk shows directed at women audiences exploited these fears by broadcasting cases like the Broderick murders or high-profile celebrity divorces to keep viewers hooked.

There was some truth to these fears. Divorced women with children were more likely to be downwardly mobile than their ex-husbands; single parent households that were financially unstable had poorer outcomes in wealth, education, and health than families with the presence of both parents. But the majority of divorces of the time were initiated by women, and those rates went up the more education the woman had.

It turns out the male midlife crisis, which became and remains such a potent cliché, was a self-serving fantasy. Like the man who bellows at his boss, "You can't fire me, I quit," it was a measure meant to protect the male ego in a time of rejection and difficulty. It took what was really happening—women divorcing their husbands in unprecedented numbers—and turned it into an ultimately destructive daydream about male autonomy. Because men didn't leave their homes in a triumphant huff. They were kicked out by dissatisfied wives.

Which is not to say that some men didn't dump their wives to marry their secretaries or buy fast cars. But the construction of that image of the balding man with the twenty-year-old girlfriend in the brand-new convertible—"a favorite gendered cliché... the images of male indulgence and irresponsibility," as Susanne Schmidt describes it in *Midlife Crisis: The Feminist Origins of a Chauvinist Cliché*—so prevalent throughout eighties and nineties entertainment, may have been invented to save men's dignity from the truth.

The construction of the midlife crisis marks the moment when the male imagination severed itself from reality. While women's entertainment was often a little silly—with wildly over-the-top titles like *Mother, May I Sleep with Danger* and *She Woke Up Pregnant*—it was at least engaged in the practice of trying to imagine for women new kinds of lives to lead and methods of navigating and thriving in a changing world. The men of film and television instead engaged in acts of disconnection and delusion—superheroes who can't be with the women they love because it's too dangerous, men riding a motorcycle right out of their wives' lives, the very cool antisocial antihero who is simply too brilliant to have a wife or follow the law or be nice to people.

It's worth considering how the myths and the anxieties of the era were in fact a reversed image of real social changes. Betty Broderick became a folk hero for middle-aged women who feared being traded in by their husbands for "a younger model," like they were run-down cars. Men were insisting they were choosing freedom over the old ball and chain. How did pop culture get it so wrong? And why did the fantasy deviate so extremely from men and women's lived experience?

If the cultural image of the male midlife crisis had been accurate, then its constant portrayal in media and entertainment could have been a way of assisting men through it, of helping them find meaning outside the traditional form of the family and the role as head of the household. But because it was a myth—or at least a very rare occurrence—it did the opposite. It told men that the family, a place where men found great happiness and meaning, was actually suffocating and emasculating. It replaced the joy of fatherhood with the crass consumerism of expensive cars and the intimacy of a lifelong partnership with the cheap thrills of promiscuity.

A more accurate representation of the actual state of 1980s heterosexual marriage (the only type allowed at the time, of course) was the series of films Michael Douglas and Kathleen Turner made together. Starting with *Romancing the Stone* and falling apart with *War of the Roses* the Douglas/Turner coupling (and decoupling) shows us how quickly the state of marriage was changing in the era.

In *Romancing the Stone,* Turner plays Joan Wilder, a single woman who has made her living as a romance writer, spinning fantasies of heroic love and adventure for all the disappointed women of the time. (The sales of romance novels were booming in the eighties, just as divorce rates were reaching 50 percent in all first marriages. I'm sure it's fine and says nothing about the state of love that the sales of romance novels have yet again been hitting record highs.) She's financially independent, so she doesn't need to find a spouse for material needs or for community respectability. Successful women of the era were finding they, too, could enjoy some of the benefits that successful men like Dan from *Fatal Attraction* enjoyed: the ability to evade the methods of conformity and moral righteousness that others had to follow.

Instead, Wilder wants all the romantic fantasy stuff constructed by the entertainment industry to cloak the reality of what a marriage is. It's too boring and disappointing to say that marriage is a contract that two people sign with a representative of the United States government; instead, it's a joining of two souls through a sacred vow blessed by god. It's not a series of rights (involving taxation and immigration benefits, among others) that are bestowed on an exclusive demographic, it's embarking on a lifelong emotional journey with another person that will deepen your capacities for love, meaning, and purpose in a frequently chaotic and scary world. That second version is what Wilder dreams of, a man on a horse sweeping her away, not a tax credit that saves her a couple thousand dollars a year and brings her access to his health insurance plan.

And she finds that romance and adventure with Jack T. Colton, an American smuggler (birds, not drugs) in the jungles of Colombia. He's not like other men. By which I just mean he doesn't shave. But he's bucked respectability and chosen a life of experiences and excitement over a life of asset accumulation and conformity. He's rootless, can't be tied down, he's a dreamer and a schemer. She can fall in love with someone unpredictable and financially unstable because she can provide for herself. And, like a lot of couples do in the glorious days before the wedding ceremony, they both believe this relationship will be different. There won't be monotony, there won't be resentment. The man won't hide from his wife in the most disgusting part of their house (garage or basement being the usual setting for a man cave), the woman won't start pouring vodka in her Diet Coke to get through the day. We're going to do things differently.

But how to do things differently with no working model for how to live a fulfilling and egalitarian married life? Particularly when women's culture might have been presenting visions of new possibilities for achievement and satisfaction, but the typical American marriage was slow to incorporate these new ideas about female empowerment and equality. Marriage had in fact retained its patriarchal nature, and therefore was structured in such a way as to benefit primarily the man, often at the expense of the woman. Married men statistically lived longer than single men; married women statistically died younger than single women. Married men reported more happiness and had better health than single men; married women reported less happiness and had worse health outcomes than single women. Married men earned more money; married women earned less.

In other words, marriage lengthened men's lives while shortening women's lives, essentially creating a parasitic relationship where a man sucked health and well-being directly out of his loved one's body. There was a conflict at the heart of a lot of marriages, and many women were giving up the fight (or at least changing the venue to family court) when it turned out that their new vision for what a life of love could be did not match the reality they encountered in heterosexual relationships.

When women filing for divorce were asked how things had come to this point, most of them very simply stated they were unhappy in their marriage. In survey after survey, conducted either by a governmental agency or a more informal media poll, things like unhappiness, incompatibility, and "lack of commitment" were the most consistently given reasons. Infidelity and abuse were mentioned in fewer filings. This has persisted since the no-fault divorce was slowly rolled out through the United States in the 1970s and '80s. As roles for the genders shifted, as women started contributing more money to their marriages, thereby fulfilling some of the more masculine elements of the household, they expected an equal investment from their male partners in the traditionally feminine realms of child-care, domestic labor, and emotional support.

These were not the "parallel lives" of Victorian era marriages, where husband and wife might occupy the same house and share children but found emotional and other assorted satisfactions through friends, family, and members of the outside world. As it became increasingly acceptable, even if not yet celebrated, to raise children in a single parent household or live partnerless or find sexual, creative, and emotional outlets in spaces other than the nuclear family, women wanted more from their husbands. Stephanie Coontz tracks these changes in expectations for marriage in *Marriage, a History*. When traditional, patriarchal gender roles were the norm in the heterosexual couple, each individual's expectations for their spouse were based on their ability to fulfill those roles. The success of a marriage wasn't measured by happiness and love for each other—it was based on a woman's ability to manage the domestic sphere and a man's ability to provide.

But as the twentieth century unfolded and women gained rights and started to contribute to their marriages in what had been typically masculine ways, they started to list love as a top priority in their partnerships. If they were equal in the eyes of the law, women wanted to be equals in their marriage as well. If they were going to marry, or stay married, they wanted things like companionship, emotional support, sexual satisfaction, and an equal partner in child-rearing and domestic labor. If women could work full-time at a job and still find time to make parent-teacher conferences and fold the laundry and vacuum the stairs and put dirty dishes actually in the dishwasher and not in the sink a mere six inches away from the dishwasher, then for the fucking love of god, so could men.

Divorce started to look like an exit ramp from an endless highway of tedium and dissatisfaction for a lot of women. If they had a decent financial foundation, why would they stay in an unhappy relationship? Family court could and did take on a substitute spousal role, like a third partner in the family, making sure the man was making child support payments and showing up for his days of visitation, doing his fair share of contributing to the raising of the child. No more yelling, begging, cajoling, crying, screaming. Why bother, when a judge could garnish a man's wages for child support, establish a custody agreement that split childcare responsibilities, and discipline partners who did not live up to their agreements?

These divorces tended to be timed around a woman's midlife—divorce rates in the 1980s dropped off considerably after a woman turned forty-five. And as Schmidt writes in *Midlife Crisis,* this troubling time in a person's life where they tend to wrestle with the life not lived and the roads not taken was first documented as a woman's problem. Women "reappraised their lives . . . They asked: 'What am I giving up for this marriage?' 'Why did I have all these children?' 'Why didn't I finish my education?' 'What good will my degree do me now after years out of circulation?' 'Shall I take a job?' or 'Why didn't anyone tell me I would *have* to go back to work?'" Schmidt writes. These questions often put them in conflict with their home lives, as Gail Sheehy, the journalist who originally popularized the term "midlife crisis," demonstrated in her 1976 book *Passages.* But as the media found Sheehy's work, they replanted these questions into the minds of men, constructing the fantasy of a man who can't be held back by the stifling domestic atmosphere.

Men found themselves dragged into family court against their will, by wives who previously did not have recourse to this institution to settle marital imbalances or unhappiness, and then they discovered women were often able to take advantage of the same stereotypes and prejudices that hurt them in their professional lives. Judges assumed women were better caretakers and parents, that they were powerless in relationships, and they needed the protection that the legal system afforded them.

As long, of course, as the women could adequately perform femininity. If you can't conform to your gender's standards you can be pathologized, so gay women, ambitious women, women who cheated or drank or had any other stereotypically "male" behaviors found themselves at odds with the system. But men were in a gendered double bind. If they behaved and presented themselves as gender-conforming men in family court, it was assumed they were bad, or at least deficient, caretakers. If they tried to present themselves as taking on a more feminine aspect, they made themselves look ridiculous to the authorities. If they were being abused by their wives, letting a woman humiliate or hurt them, they were pathetic. If they were the primary caregivers while the woman worked, or they were not adequately performing their breadwinning duties in some other way, they weren't man enough. Either way, men were not seen in family court as much more than providers, and by that, of course, the court meant providers of money. Up until 1988, women won sole physical custody of their children 80 percent of the time.

This is how family court became a proxy battle for the war between the sexes. Organizations that claimed to fight for "men's rights" highlighted the disparity between the genders when it came to custody cases, although they left out the fact that more than 90 percent of custody cases are decided with both parties consenting to the terms. The vast majority of mothers who leave a marriage with full custody do so because the father agreed not to have physical custody, not because a tyrannical judge forced him away from his children.

Much like the cliché of the midlife crisis, the myth of the man-hating family court judge was mostly a fantasy. Both of these fantasies allowed men to avoid taking the blame for how things turned out. The result was the same, but at least they could maintain the fantasy of control.

The bitter 1989 black comedy *War of the Roses,* about an affluent family breaking apart, was maybe too realistic to become a huge hit. This time Kathleen Turner is Barbara Rose, a homemaker who decided to sideline her own career to raise her family and make a beautiful home, and our Michael Douglas figure is Oliver Rose, a man who sacrificed his wild side to go to law school and then climb the ranks at his firm.

But Barbara's roles as wife and mother don't fit her well. In one excruciating scene, Barbara expects (and is expected by Oliver) to play the part of hostess to her husband's business partners at a dinner party. She's supposed to entertain effortlessly, tell witty anecdotes, and serve a perfect meal (that domestic workers probably prepared). But she can't. She stumbles over her words, she can't tell funny stories or overlook the bad behavior of her husband's colleagues at the table. And after everyone is gone, she mocks her husband's phoniness, his eagerness to please, and the way he changes himself to ingratiate himself with his bosses. She hates his inauthenticity as well as his expectation that she would be inauthentic on his behalf. This is the first bit of a crack in their happy marriage. From here it will only grow.

The conflict revolves around her desire to return to work. Her children have grown, her husband's place in the law firm is secure, and her house has been lovingly and perfectly restored and decorated. She is in fact facing a midlife crisis, asking herself the same kinds of questions women of her era were asking themselves. "What am I giving up for this marriage?" seems to haunt her. But she has also found a new passion for cooking, and her first attempts to turn her hobby into a catering business have been promising and lucrative.

Her husband is not actively discouraging. He agrees that she is a wonderful cook. But she is bothered by his reluctance to help her career the way she assisted him with his. He doesn't seem to take her idea seriously, and he occasionally speaks to her like he would a child. Again, the gentle misogyny displayed by our Michael Douglas figure throughout these films never comes in the form of outright hate. It's just a pointed refusal to update the ideas that have been deeply embedded in his brain about women, marriage, and family. He doesn't forbid her from pursuing her work. It's just a bit of a joke, a cute little lark that she'll probably drop once it gets hard. Maybe it's hormonal, maybe it's empty-nest syndrome, maybe it's her just being moody, you know how women are.

She's being asked to share a life, a bed, a dining room table, a home with a man who doesn't treat her like his equal. When she's fulfilling the role that he expects from her by raising the kids and buying decorative ceramics for the house and loading the dishwasher, they live in harmony. When she breaks away from his expectations, he teases and humiliates her. When she asks for more from their marriage, from him, he refuses her. And when she finally asks for a divorce, he doesn't even take that seriously. All his animosity toward her seems to be a self-constructed fantasy to avoid the knowledge that she is rejecting him because he has failed her as a husband. Even as he schemes for a way to win a better divorce settlement in court, he delays and fights because he assumes she'll change her mind. Until the very end, he is trying to restore their marriage to how it was in the beginning, when both of them were working for his success, back when he was happy and she was not.

. . .

One of the largest projects of second-wave feminism was to give women the narrative structures and the intellectual framework with which to understand their own unhappiness in contemporary society, especially as it involved domestic life. This was the meaning behind the slogan "the personal is political." Whether it was discrimination at the workplace or women doing three times as much domestic labor as their husbands, the problems of the modern woman could be understood—and remedied—collectively. These consciousness-raising sessions gave women the language to articulate to themselves and to the outside world what was happening to them in the private space. And these sessions helped women shape their stories into forms that institutions would recognize and take seriously.

Because the justice system is not an institution that rewards nuance or complexity. It likes clear dividing lines between victim and abuser, guilt and innocence. And in order to successfully seek assistance from such an institution, it is advantageous for people to use the language and stories that the institution already recognizes. Marital and family problems can rarely be so neatly narrated. In the muddle of a marriage that is coming apart, there can be violence, harm, emotional abuse, and infidelity by both parties. But creating blame—blame that can help you win a larger part of the shared assets, blame that can grant you or deny your partner custody rights, blame that can offer you legal protection from the person you pledged your life to—that is a matter of telling a story. Controlling the story means winning the divorce.

But the overarching truth is that the real advantage in family court went to whoever had the means. Whoever had access to the best legal representation, whoever had enough money to stretch out the proceedings, whoever could pay for private detectives to dig up dirt on their former partner, that's who won in family court. The

Broderick divorce lasted five years, with Betty alleging that this was part of Dan's strategy to drain her of her money and overwhelm her legal team. But he was hardly the only one who used this tactic. The eighties saw the rise of celebrity divorce attorneys, lawyers who got famous for representing high-profile or particularly contentious cases. (*The Hollywood Reporter* still does an annual list of the top divorce attorneys in the industry.) Divorce became something of a spectator sport, and the trashy television and gossip rags of the era flourished under the conditions of romantic despondency. Everyone needed an outlet for their own marital strife, everyone needed someone onto whom to project their own dissatisfaction, in order to keep their hostility toward their spouses at a manageable level.

The same year Betty shot Dan and Michael Douglas and Kathleen Turner were fighting on the big screen over the draperies, another high-profile divorce was taking over the tabloid headlines. In late 1989, Ivana Trump tired of Donald Trump's infidelity—his affair with Marla Maples had been chronicled in gossip columns for years by this point—and she filed for divorce. Every revelation during Ivana's attempt to overturn their prenuptial agreement was covered in the media. And why not? Divorce was entertainment by this point.

Here both fantasies of the midlife crisis and the poor disadvantaged man discriminated against in family court came in handy. Donald Trump was being spotted around town with a much younger woman, which made him look like the winner of the breakup, despite his abandonment by Ivana. The coverage of the divorce trial and other celebrity breakups of the time reinforced every ugly stereotype of women's behavior in romantic relationships: women are gold diggers, they're shallow socialites, they're vengeful harpies when crossed. That many of the women taking up headline space during the eighties were leaving their marriages due to abuse, infidelity, and mistreatment didn't matter. The tabloid press turned them into money-hungry monsters for asking for half of their more famous husbands' property. IVANA BETTER DEAL and GIMME THE PLAZA were the headlines chosen by New York tabloids to cover the negotiations.

This was a way of controlling the narrative. As Schmidt wrote in *Midlife Crisis,* the identity crisis that was described as hitting women at middle age was being relabeled exclusively "a male-centered concept . . . described midlife as the end of a man's family obligations and the moment when he would abandon his family to reinvent himself. This 'crisis of masculinity' upended visions of the nuclear family but bolstered gender hierarchies." While mental health crises have no gender, this notion of a typically male experience of being dissatisfied by and rejecting the domestic sphere was contrary to men's experience. The fantasy did little to help men come to terms with women's changing expectations of love and marriage, but it did assist Donald Trump in controlling the narrative about his experience of abandonment and rejection by his wife Ivana. After all, while Ivana got the greedy ex treatment, *The New York Post* went with a front-page headline of Donald as DON JUAN for accusations of infidelity.

What is striking now is how invisible this struggle for many men was to the culture at large. Maybe this is simply because those hit hardest were from lower classes, had prison records, and were often invisible to society in many other ways, but if anything, men's domestic incompetence was treated mostly as a joke. A man's inability to cook a meal, remember his children's appointments, put together a bunkbed from IKEA, meet the emotional needs of a partner or family member—these stereotypes all became sitcom fodder. Dad was no longer a hero, he was an oaf. The message was that the married man is an emasculated fool, the butt of all jokes, too pathetic to do what is necessary and flee the domestic prison. The wife and family went from being one of the rewards and pleasures of patriarchy to something a strong man should avoid.

So no wonder membership in men's rights organizations swelled in the eighties. The only surprising part about them is that they were so ineffective. Throughout time, men have been able to force institutions to cater to their needs, they have been able to find the resources to create organizations that prioritized their desires and protected them from infiltration. But the groups that claimed to care about male victims of domestic violence did not build shelters or hotlines for men. They simply complained. Groups that claimed that men were at a disadvantage when it came to custody disputes did not create centers to assist men with their needs as caregivers. It was almost as if the interruption, the distraction from the difficulty women were facing was the only real goal of the men's rights movement.

Women had built at tremendous cost and effort support systems to assist other women who had to flee marriages. There are still networks of shelters for women fleeing violent marriages, organizations to help rape victims, legal support, professionals and volunteers who can assist women in creating financial and existential stability after a family comes apart. For men? There are some angry forums one can visit, some angry books about the injustice of the justice system, there are any number of guns one can buy. Because as much as men insisted they, too, are abused and victimized and sexually assaulted by their female partners, they were unable or unwilling to create the same system of shelters, counselors, and aid that women did.

The patriarchy didn't have time or support for men who couldn't hold their families together, who couldn't fulfill the obligations of manhood. And instead of organizing around the idea of protecting men who were vulnerable or creating a sense of solidarity with women who suffered similar plights, the men's rights movement was almost entirely reactionary. A nascent attempt at forming a masculinist movement that paralleled feminism in the 1960s and '70s, one that understood the patriarchy and its hegemonic control over what a man was supposed to be was hurting men as much as it was hurting women, was crowded out by a larger (or at least louder) movement that blamed feminism for taking away what had been promised to men. As men lost control over their wives and children, as they struggled to get or stay married, they became aware they were failing to fulfill the expectations for masculinity. Where the first iteration of the masculinist movement sought to deconstruct their gender roles, much like feminism was doing for women, the men's rights movement that replaced it wanted to reinforce and solidify the status quo. This would continue to transform itself through the years until it found its new expression online as red pill culture.

Its slogans, aims, and rhetoric mimicked, usually in a mocking way, the slogans, aims, and rhetoric of feminist or woman-oriented organizations. In reaction to the creation of the National Organization for Women, in 1983 some leaders of the men's rights movement founded the National Organization for Men. In more recent years, the hashtag #MeToo, created to draw attention to sexual harassment and abuse faced by women, became #MenToo by men's rights activists (MRAs). When online activists and feminists coined the term "toxic masculinity" to discuss the problematic and mostly unexamined values and behaviors of men, figures like Jordan Peterson started to talk about "toxic femininity."

Not that Michael Douglas was in any way a supporter of men's rights organizations, but this reactionary mode is visible in the basic premises of most of his films of this time: What if men were the real victims of stalking (*Fatal Attraction*), what if men were the real victims of sexual harassment (*Disclosure*), what if men were the real victims of women's psychopathy (*Basic Instinct*). They didn't really have any other ideas than to take women's work and slap a man at the center of it.

The result was a Pied Piper movement away from adaptation and toward empty fantasies and narcissistic posturing. The effect was felt in dropping rates of marriage and childbearing to such a degree that heterosexuality itself seemed to be in peril.

Or, in the words of Joe Jackson, "If there's war between the sexes then there'll be no people left."

In the five years between *Fatal Attraction* and *Basic Instinct,* in the changeover from the eighties to the nineties, a third wave of feminism emerged. The cultural shift was as sudden and total as the shift on the radio from Whitney Houston to Nirvana. Born out of events like the televised Anita Hill testimony, a series of violent attacks on abortion clinics and doctors, and the emergence of a conversation about the sexual violence women and girls are subjected to, a new generation of young women strove to understand why the project of women's liberation still felt unfinished. The reforms of the seventies had cleared the way for women to rush into the world and transform it, and yet here women still were, trailing behind, blocked and thwarted.

Unlike the second wave, where actions were more targeted toward the political sphere, the third wave decided to take on the culture. With the DIY music scene of Riot Grrrl, a thriving print world with zines and independent publishing, and a grassroots movement that would soon move from Take Back the Night marches and campus organizations to the virtual communities of the internet, the new generation of feminists were focused not on external, structural change, but on change from within. Part of that shift was because of the political malaise the feminist movement had been mired in for the last decade or so. It was becoming clear that just because there were laws designed to protect women, that didn't mean women had access to justice. The Anita Hill allegations against Clarence Thomas might have found a national audience, and all the media attention and political speeches gave the appearance that we were a nation that was going to take sexual harassment and the mistreatment of women in the workplace seriously. But ultimately, the result was the same as it would have been in the fifties, and Clarence Thomas was going to be seated on the Supreme Court.

Same with abortion laws. Abortion might be technically legal, but if your local clinic was shut down by some nuisance legislation, if you had to fight through noisy protestors and abusive Christians to get to a clinic, and if you entered that clinic to receive healthcare from a doctor under threat of bombing or assassination, then maybe "rights" don't mean as much as you thought they would. And again, if you are raped but the police tell you it was your fault or laugh at you or refuse to investigate, does it really matter that rape is a crime?

The question then became, what is it that is keeping us from living lives free of violence and oppression? Well, men. It's men who are raping women, men bombing abortion clinics and assassinating our doctors, men harassing women on the street, men not giving us jobs or promotions, men telling sexist jokes at the party, men not taking our claims of domestic violence or sexual violation by other men seriously when we seek help and intervention, men leaving us with the childcare responsibilities, men in the White House, men following us too closely on the sidewalk at night, men refusing to reciprocate oral sex, men not doing the dishes. The political awakening of the third wave was one big muddle of the horrific and the mundane, the structural and the interpersonal, but there was one common factor: standing between the promise of liberation and the reality of oppression was men.

So maybe, just maybe, it would be better if some of these guys, the racists and the misogynists, the corrupt politicians and the hypocritical Jesus freaks, the cops and the boyfriends, gods and fathers, just weren't around anymore.

Enter Lilith. The folkloric figure of Lilith, the so-called first wife of Adam in Mesopotamian and Jewish stories who was too headstrong to submit to her husband, had long been associated with the feminist project, as activists through the generations tried to fend off the idea that women's subjugation was natural or necessary. The Christian story of Eve had been used for centuries, millennia, to explain why women needed to be kept in their place. The story of her betrayal of her husband and her god by eating from the tree of knowledge of good and evil in Eden was used to justify everything from denying women pain relief during childbirth to barring women from positions of power to supporting men as the head of the household. As documented in Per Faxneld's *Satanic Feminism: Lucifer as Liberator of Woman in Nineteenth-Century Culture,* the story of Eve was used for centuries for "legitimating the subjugation of women. Some have alleged that it also functions as a dangerous justification for violence against women, which is in effect even in our own time." Because Eve had been seduced by the serpent in the Garden of Eden, all women were made in her image and therefore are naturally sinful and devious. They would lead men astray. They need the guiding hand of man to keep the world safe.

Plus there was that whole "made from Adam's rib" thing that suggested women weren't even fully human. If women wanted to change their position in society, many believed they had to attack the stories that had been told about them. Stories had tremendous power over how people saw and understood the world, and there was no story in all of Christendom that had more influence over the way both men and women understood gender and power than the story of Eve. Overturning the subjugation would require overturning the story. Faxneld writes that "subordinated groups (such as women or people of colour) in a time of transition can transform motifs traditionally employed to vilify and denigrate them into something subversive and potentially empowering." If women were already going to be condemned for cavorting with the devil, they might as well have a good time.

Women needed a new story to tell about themselves. Not just for men, so they might see women as their equals, but for themselves, too. Something to counter this idea that women weren't as intelligent, as strong, as brave, as important as men; that they had not contributed significantly to history. And in this moment of publishing feminist fairy tales and biographies of great women of the past and correcting a written record that had managed to celebrate only a small minority of the population, women decided to rewrite the very first story, the creation myth, to help untangle everything that had followed. If Eve, this creature of temptation and humiliation, was the vision of womanhood under patriarchy, the symbol of a woman freed from those restraints would be Lilith.

Lilith was a perfect avatar for the modern woman. She was strong, determined, and certain that she deserved more. She was, in a contemporary simplification, the first wife of Adam, created not as an afterthought but as Adam's equal. It didn't work out, though, as Lilith was not interested in being submissive to her partner, sexually or in any other way. If, as the story goes, Lilith couldn't be on top during sex, then she was going to check out of the whole human project. From there she either becomes a consort of demons or a baby-eating monster, depending on who you talk to.

Lilith's act of rejection, though, was very compelling for young women who found their liberation stifled by the men in their lives.

Women had needed men for centuries for just bare survival. Prevented in various times and places from inheriting money, driving cars, voting, getting credit, owning property, and so on, the vast majority of women had decided to align themselves with men in order to get along in their lives. Some were happy, blissfully unaware or indifferent to all the forms their subjugation was taking, but some were acutely aware of the compromise. And how one of the conditions of that compromise was silence—about men's stupidity, their arrogance, how bad they were in bed. But these women kept quiet and accepted the conditions of their survival because this was easier than forging a life on their own. They were Eves, they were Beth in *Fatal Attraction,* they were, in the Protestant language of American religion, "helpmeets" to their husbands.

But then feminism and the advancement of women's rights gave them the possibility of saying no to men. And there was a lot to say no to! There has been a long conversation that started during the third wave about everything men do that we should reject. Some of this was structural forms of oppression that got filed under the heading of Patriarchy. Burn it down, they said! Build something better. (That "something" gets more and more vague the longer it goes undefined.) And some of it was personal, and those traits got labeled as toxic masculinity. Stop the toxic masculinity, they demanded.

As the project of voicing dissatisfaction and the celebration of rejection continued, Lilith showed up everywhere. Her name was given to a feminist magazine, an annual music festival, a much-celebrated astrological aspect, and a high-end perfume. She showed up on T-shirts and tattoos, she was the subject of artworks, she was even worshipped in a (very tiny) religion.

Rejection is not exactly a great model for how to live one's life, though. You wander out of the Garden of Eden and go where, exactly? Rejection is not enough to base a story on, let alone a whole political movement. Which sums up the political confusion of this moment in women's liberation. You burn down the patriarchy to build something new, but what exactly might that be? You reject toxic masculinity in theory and social media posts, but you quickly find it's extremely difficult to live a life entirely without men, especially if you are a heterosexual woman. Figuring out what you don't want has always been easier than figuring out what you do, and after some experimentation with new ways of living and loving, a lot of women made the decision to make the same kind of compromises the generations of women before them had as well. But frequently with a new sense of exasperation and frustration.

But if women had a new character to embody, men were still left only with Adam, the big dope. The man who just goes along with whatever he's told, either by his wife or his god, who seems incapable of thinking for himself or attempting anything new. Here, eat this, his wife says, so he does. Here, do this, his god says, so he does. Not a single thought in his head, just "yes, dear" and "I dunno, what do you want to do?"

The result is a pervasive sense of heteropessimism, or what theorist Asa Seresin defined as "performative disaffiliations with heterosexuality, usually expressed in the form of regret, embarrassment, or hopelessness about straight experience." It's a suspicious animosity between the sexes that has sparked both the #MeToo movement and the backlash to the #MeToo movement, an entire industry of masculinity influencers and gurus, a new generation coming of age without sexual or romantic experience, and a widening gap between the number of people who say they want to get married and have children and the number who are able to achieve this. The pessimism surpassed the usual dread of dating and romantic disappointments to encompass a belief that maybe heterosexuality was impossible. Maybe men could never see women as their equals. Maybe sex, love, marriage are all like Valentine's Day, a fantasy created by corporations to try to sell us things. Catherine Tramell is the Lilith of *Basic Instinct,* arriving, as she does, in the first scene astride her Adam. But, alas, despite her Adam's willingness to let her be on top, despite his devotion to her pleasure, she still finds herself dissatisfied and rather than walking off the edge of the known world she pulls out an ice pick and stabs him to death.

There were protestors outside the screenings of *Basic Instinct* when it was released in 1992, decrying what they saw as its reliance on an offensive stereotype about gay people being insane and violent. Catherine is bisexual, and there is a long history in film of trans and queer characters deranged by their sexual and gendered confusion and committing multiple murders as a result, from *Psycho* to *Dressed to Kill.* Catherine is portrayed in the film as a possible serial killer, a psychopath who has left a trail of dead bodies and boyfriends and parents behind her. It's up to our Michael Douglas figure to bring her to justice. The plot certainly looks like something a person tired of being told their oppression is all in their head would like to protest. But, as often happens with well-intentioned but mostly humorless and counterproductive protests against "bad art," they probably should have watched the film. Because the crazy queer and her other murdering lady friends are the only sane people in the whole movie.

It would be easy to read this opening scene, if one were a redpilled creep, as proof that women don't want equality, they want domination. Here we have our feminist beta male, willing to submit to his woman's desires, willing to let her have her way with him, and yet it's never enough. He gave Lilith what she wanted, and feminism has so warped her feeble brain with a lust for power that she ultimately wants to annihilate him, and by extension all men.

But as the film progresses, Catherine's murder of her boyfriend starts to seem reasonable. After the Garden of Eden, it was Adam's job to build the world as he saw fit. And in *Basic Instinct*, the world that Adam built is revealed to be pretty disappointing. It's a world of fluorescent lighting and linoleum floors, office coffee that tastes like cigarettes and is drunk from Styrofoam cups, polyester blends and suits bought off the rack without professional tailoring, sensible sedans, furniture that is neither comfortable nor aesthetically pleasing, venetian blinds and industrial carpets, long hours devoted to a job that is essentially useless and that they are not very good at. It is living a life that requires a person to ingest copious amounts of alcohol and drugs to sustain and survive, it is hedonism over pleasure and dominance over connection.

It is a world that is ugly, artificial, and enjoyed by no one. It is something to be endured. The film is set in San Francisco, but instead of reveling in that ecstatic natural landscape, the men stay confined in office buildings, police cars, and disappointing one-bedroom apartments. Compare that to the places Catherine inhabits, her house that overlooks the crashing shoreline, her chic and sporty car, the premium knits and well-tailored suits she discards from her luminous body as she ascends her staircase. When our Michael Douglas character Nick shows up in her house, he's smirking, he's rolling his eyes, he's refusing to acknowledge how ridiculous and out of place he looks here.

There is a very upsetting sweater in *Basic Instinct*. Nick is going to a nightclub, and he decides to wear a sweater. It has a V-neck. The neckline is just slightly too deep, showing off an unflattering amount of sagging chest and graying hair. It is one of those noncolors, not quite gray, not quite olive, not quite brown. It makes his flesh look slightly green, and it seems somehow to accentuate his jowls. It's almost certainly made of artificial fibers, something that itches a little and traps your sweat against your body. Whatever odors are in that club, smoke and booze and sex and the stink of moving bodies, is going to be absorbed into that fabric and will cling to it. And you just know he is wearing a cologne that he bought in a drugstore.

This is not about class. He's a police detective and she's an heiress, but the divide between their lifestyles and the way they present themselves is not only about money. He chose that sweater at least in part to signal his heterosexuality. Because with the mixing of gender roles and the increased visibility of the queer community, straight men were struck with a kind of anxiety, a fear that they might be mistaken for homosexuals. The purely masculine (which was defined in the era as heterosexual) territory was something that had to be demarcated and guarded. Certain activities—activities that straight men had for decades comfortably participated in, from dressing well to romantic gestures to physical affection shared between men—were now suspiciously feminine.

Ciara Cremin writes about this phenomenon and the rise of slobby heterosexual masculinity in *Man-Made Woman*. If a man could be emasculated simply by donning a dress or even something that used to be designated as masculine like high-waisted pants or a cashmere sweater, then that would reveal the fragility of male power. That it was simply an act, a façade. As she notes, "While evidence suggests that parents, and particularly fathers, dissuade their boys from dressing as girls for fear they will become homosexual, . . . the evidence is not an index of attitudes towards sexuality as such but rather what woman represents in patriarchal-capitalism. Clothes do not make the sexuality but they do denote gender and in turn a relation to power. . . . [In] 'women's' clothes, 'man' shows that male power is symbolic and contingent on appearance." But this jealous guarding of masculinity only served to make the men look ridiculous. As men punched each other and declared "no homo!" in the fear that any physical contact with one another made them look gay, everyone else simply got on with life. As women's lives got larger through this era of political liberation, it seemed like men deliberately made their own much smaller.

What Michael Douglas shows us in the nightclub, besides looking silly, is not self-consciousness or self-doubt but contempt. He's going into a space that is clearly ruled and created by people he is not familiar with, namely queers, Blacks, and Latinos, and women. It's the early nineties, the nightlife and the dance music scene, especially in San Francisco, is being created and celebrated not by Michael Douglas figures but by everyone else. House and dance music came out of marginalized cultures, not out of corporate focus groups. There's not even a flicker of feeling out of place or curiosity and excitement. He's fully confident that he can just swagger in, take what he wants (drugs and "his" woman), and leave.

So when a man shows up and tries to drag Catherine out of her bed (with, you have to imagine, exceptionally high thread count sheets) and her home and her car to trap her in this industrial man's world, that murder starts to look more like self-defense. At the end of the film, that's where she's been keeping her ice pick. Under the mattress, on her side of the bed. The same place just about every woman who lives alone and feels threatened keeps a baseball bat, a knife, or a gun.

Who (on the male side of the spectrum) is Catherine supposed to partner with? She's a successful writer, she owns her own home, she has no real financial need for a man, she doesn't exactly seem like the maternal type who might be looking for a father for her child. But how to argue with desire? Her potential suitors are a cop who shot unarmed tourists but swaggers around with unchecked arrogance, a has-been rock star still behaving like he's in his twenties, men speaking with absolute authority on subjects they know little to nothing about, compromised men who have sacrificed any integrity for the sake of ingratiating themselves to the powerful.

They want sexual contact with women they view with contempt. They don't want reciprocated pleasure, they want dominance and humiliation. This is around the time when the dumb dad and the lazy husband became tropes on sitcoms. The overweight and dull-witted guy with the inexplicably hot and intelligent wife. Men knew they were disappointing women, and they made jokes about it. In the generation to come, this trend would continue, as your average man started to trail behind women when it came to education and professional accreditation. Men used to attract and prove their worth to women by outperforming them in these areas, now they were struggling to keep up.

The heteropessimism that was developing was mostly one-sided. After all, Seresin concluded, "Heteropessimism generally has a heavy focus on men as the root of the problem" with heterosexuality. An increasing number of women decided to try to break free from heterosexuality, as best they could. They developed wedding ceremonies to declare a lifelong commitment to their own self. They developed platonic marriages with female friends. They proudly declared themselves spinsters. They chose themselves. But there were still men. And many women who sleep with men chose to stick it out with men and manage those relationships, whether because of need for the material resources one can find in marriage, or because of desire, or simply out of the exhaustion that can come from trying to live an independent life without massive wealth.

Dr. Beth Garner is not as capable as Catherine when it comes to exiting her relationship with the men of *Basic Instinct*. She thinks if she makes herself recognizable to these men in positions of authority, takes on their characteristics, and joins their team, she'll avoid the pain and suffering that is doled out to other women. She is the only woman we see on the police force, she uses their lingo and their manner of speaking, and she, too, has taken to wearing badly fitted suits that make her look far more dumpy than she is. (And under all of that is the most uncomfortable-looking lingerie, still needing to be a decorative object.)

The outcome of this negotiation is explicitly rendered through her encounters with Nick, with whom she has an on-again, off-again affair. He decides when they are on and off, and she seems powerless to establish any boundaries or persuade him into a more predictable or satisfying dynamic. Her only power with him would be to cut him off sexually and romantically, but she's already invested too much in him. Surely at some point, if she sticks around long enough, he'll be ready to settle down. They work together, making the relationship potentially coercive and inappropriate, and while he relies on her emotionally when in private, when he is with his colleagues he talks about her in a humiliating way, degrading her reputation. She doesn't get respect at work, she gets no real solace from her relationship, the only thing she has going for her is an alliance with the power structure that she hopes one day will somehow pay off.

This power struggle finds symbolic representation in her one sex scene with Nick. What starts from a place of mutual desire quickly becomes transgressive as Nick tries to find her boundaries. He pushes her into increasingly violent and upsetting acts, and all the while, because she loves him or because she doesn't want to seem high maintenance, she keeps trying to consent. But every time she adjusts and smooths away the look of alarm and pain that has overtaken her face, he pushes her further. He doesn't penetrate her until he hears her cry "no," because all along he didn't want sex, he wanted rape.

At the end of the scene, she's upset and accuses him of "not making love," which is the closest she will get in the film to calling out his terrible behavior. He smirks and leaves. This scene feels like it adequately represents how the culture of heterosexuality was about to go in the years that followed the film's release. Women tried to overthrow feelings of shame and a culture of purity by embracing sexual expression and pleasure, only to find that used against them in relationships (with the development of revenge porn, private nudes circulated around schools and workplaces, and the sudden normalization of everything from choking to anal sex in casual heterosexual encounters) and in the larger culture (Girls Gone Wild, Perez Hilton drawing cum on the photos of pop stars on his wildly popular blog, the businessmen who made billions from the newly mainstreamed sex industry, whether in the form of pornography, lingerie, sex toys, mass media, or strip clubs). Every time women thought they were about to get on equal footing with men the dynamic changed again.

And at each step, there was a desire to capitulate and consent, to try to bring these violations back under women's control. You can see this process on Beth Garner's pensive postcoital face: "I'm fine, right? That was what I wanted, yes? I consented but then I didn't but then I did so I didn't just get raped, right?" Michael Douglas remains blithely unconcerned, either unaware or uncaring.

Because there is a certain type of guy who can't even imagine being in a relationship where he is not dominant. He can't possibly function as an equal, he has to be the one on top. But there are also a lot of men who simply struggle with how to approach women, how to talk to women, how to get attention without domination, how to get pleasure from sex. They maybe don't want to dominate, but they're not sure how to connect.

When Catherine finds herself unfortunately in love with Nick at the end of *Basic Instinct,* she wonders what a life together might look like. Nick gives her the old patriarchal pitch: they should "fuck like minks, raise rugrats, and live happily ever after." In other words, the nuclear family. He suggests she insert herself back into the world of men, the world she worked so hard to escape. It's not even his original idea, he's just mimicking the language his partner in the police force used.

It shows how moribund the masculine imagination was in this moment. Men and women had been liberated from the traditional relationship structure. They can get divorced, they can have sex outside of marriage, they can love multiple partners. But our Michael Douglas character can't think of any other way to structure his relationship with the woman he loves than the form that drove his first wife to suicide and Catherine to murder.

This is all profoundly sad. It's pathetic that this man knowingly reproduces the systems that destroy the women he loves. Seresin writes, "For a long time, heterosexuality's normalization allowed it to endlessly repeat, immune from any substantial change."

With that being the case, the tendency of all the other women of *Basic Instinct* to murder the men closest to them starts to seem less like hysteria and more like logical responses to the stimuli. Every other woman character in the film has murdered a male member of their family—a husband, a father, a brother. One woman stabs her husband to death with a cake knife she received as a wedding present. Another kills her brothers with her father's razor. One day they just snap, pick up the closest symbolic phallus, and stab their way to liberation.

The fault with heteropessimism is that women will never find true liberation because of the persistent existence of men. Even if you refuse to sleep with or marry men, even if you find yourself a job while avoiding workplaces and corporations and institutions run by men, they are still there, hanging around. They are cops, neighbors, politicians, sons, pizza delivery guys, dudes on sidewalks, trolls on the internet, teachers. They insist on existing and being present, no matter how much a person tries to distance themselves.

The only reason Catherine is able to live her life of freedom is because she has enormous wealth (which she received as an inheritance after murdering her father, of course). Her money allows her to evade sexual respectability; her so-called deviance would put her at a disadvantage in male-run institutions like the workplace, family court, and church, had she any need for their assistance. She doesn't need the stabilizing force of a second income, her blithe admission that she hates children shows she won't want someone with whom to share caretaking responsibilities. And even if she did decide to have a child, a person of means can simply pay for someone to provide the services a partner would perform uncompensated. But even she is dragged back down into the world of men, even as she reaches for her ice pick to fight her way out again.

Ultimately what women are left with, speaking in broad generalities, is a choice between being a Catherine (a murderer) and being a Beth (who is in the end killed by her lover). Rejection or a twisted compromise. The real choice left in a relationship is a negative choice, much like the negative freedoms offered by feminism. And many women walk away. Women report a boost of happiness and a decrease in stress levels when they divorce their male partners. Women exist with a supportive culture that teaches them how to make and sustain close friendships outside of relationships; they are encouraged to explore what they truly want and enjoy.

That negative choice is pervasive. The American birth rate began its sharp decline in the early 1990s. There was also growth in the number of people delaying—or forgoing—marriage around the same time. Divorce rates seemed to stabilize after the peak in the 1970s and '80s, but this was possibly only because fewer people were getting married.

Without the guidance of traditional patriarchal forms of courtship, marriage, and family creation, the heterosexual couple proves itself to be a very fragile thing. All you had to do to destroy centuries of norms was give half of the participants a real opportunity to say no. And then it all fell apart. That should be a clue that maybe not everyone was enjoying themselves. And in the task of love, isn't a big part of the job making sure everyone is having a good time?

the economic actor

As utopian thinker Charles Fourier figured out over a century ago, men become obsessed with controlling women when they feel unable to control their financial and work situations. It's inevitable that a time of romantic turmoil would also be a time of economic turmoil. These two realms are intimately connected.

If one were to peek under the rhetoric of the men yelling about how women are wrecking the natural order of things with their feminism (a word Fourier coined, by the way), it's likely you'd find economic anxiety lying there. The difficulty men had in being husbands and fathers in the eighties and nineties during a time of peak divorce and the rise of the single parent household was rooted in the fundamental function of the husband and the father: the ability to provide.

The era in which Fourier lived and wrote was another that could be designated as a time of masculinity in crisis. His life span encompassed most of the Industrial Revolution, which shifted Western society from an agricultural economy to one dominated by manufacturing. This transition had a profound result on how families were structured, on where people lived and worked, and how money could be made. But it also created a lot of anxiety about how men should behave and dress and what defined manliness, as well as a general fear that men used to be better in some nostalgic and unspecified moment in the past.

New economies created new empires, and industries required strong male bodies to build their wealth. The birth of modern capitalism exploited men in previously unimaginable ways. But one thing Fourier noticed was that men who were incapable of acknowledging their own exploitation took out their anger and feelings of powerlessness on the women around them.

In a cheeky early-nineteenth-century essay translated into English as *The Hierarchies of Cuckoldry and Bankruptcy,* Fourier identifies the varied types of men who have been cheated, both by their wives and by their business. Overall, there are fewer types of bankrupted men than there are cuckolds—but the effect of this discrepancy is not to minimize the ruthlessness of the market but to underline a misdirected obsession. Even as men "let the merchants do as they will," Fourier writes, passively allowing them "full liberty in their sublime conceptions of treachery and pillage," they fixate, as if by way of compensation, on the tiniest fluctuations in their sexual prowess. Instead of admitting that they are getting screwed by business and the economy, men prefer to pretend they are getting screwed by women.

Same as it ever was. The problems of Michael Douglas the lover and the husband are actually the problems of Michael Douglas the working man.

Centuries after Fourier, men made a deal with patriarchal capitalism. If they sacrifice the idea of leisure, if they work so many hours they lack the time to participate meaningfully in family life, if they delay gratification and give up all their whimsical fantasies of pursuing what they truly love (art, music, literature, the life of the mind, adventure, and so forth) in order to shape themselves into a cog in someone else's machine, then when they hit the right age, they'll get to retire, finally take that cruise ship to Italy, enjoy some time with their grandchildren. If they don't drop dead of a heart attack ten years before their pensions kick in.

That was the deal. Work required men to cut out everything interesting about themselves in order to keep business and industry going, and in return they will be respected as productive and reliable members of society. Sometimes they will feel bad deep in their soul, but they will have social capital and a sense of authority and a recognizable role to play in the community. And in the meantime, they'll be able to buy a little house, put the kids through college, and pay for the benzo prescription that keeps their wives from running into traffic.

There are layers and layers of nostalgia, fantasy, and projection built into this idea of manhood, which vaguely resembles 1950s magazine advertisements and television sitcoms. This fantasy manages to excise the lifelong and often untreated trauma of the wars fought by (mostly) men through the generations, it neglects the hardship placed on men's bodies at work, and it disguises the way the labor of the many primarily benefited the few. The fantasy of respectable masculinity as defined by the breadwinner income also erases all of those who were prevented from participating in this version of manhood, the racialized citizens who could not find recognition as men, the underclasses who were prevented from rising into respectability by discriminatory educational and economic policies, and the domestic labor of women, both as wives and as houseworkers, who kept households running and new generations of workers coming.

But it also forgets that American masculinity has always included a dark pull toward more. That this kind of life is considered "settling," and what separates your average joe from a real man

is the courage to try to improve his status. True manliness is always
something out there glimmering on the horizon, something to be
fought for and striven toward but never fully achieved. There has
never been a model for American masculinity where a man is truly
happy with what he has. A real man takes risks. A real man makes
money in his sleep with passive income streams. A real man is ready
to pounce on an opportunity at any moment. A real man is a shark.
Call it manifest destiny, call it corporate imperialism, the American male has always been asked to prove himself by getting one
more dollar, one more promotion, one more car to show off to his
neighbors.

The economic changes of the 1980s, from the deregulation of
the financial sector to the privatization of public resources to the
financialization of every aspect of human existence, both material and speculative, essentially destroyed the possibility of a steady
middle-class life. Deindustrialization and globalization led to factory work disappearing or relocating to other countries. The disempowerment of unions through both legal and cultural interventions
decreased worker solidarity and led to growing dissatisfaction and
disharmony in workplaces. Wages for jobs that had once been pre-
dictably decent, from civil servants to office workers, continued to
stagnate as executive pay rose sharply. Tax reform and the restructuring of a once robust social welfare system put a new stress on
families. Masculine society was no longer stratified by class; there
was now a stark divide between the winners and the losers.

In *Wall Street* and *Falling Down*, Michael Douglas plays both
sides of this economic transformation. With Gordon Gekko in
Wall Street, Douglas offers up a vision of the new corporate masculinity, where it's not achievement but acquisition that is the true
marker of a man. It's not the man who builds who finds success,
it's the man who destroys, who breaks apart industries and jobs and
communities to suck out every dollar from their pummeled corpses.

And in *Falling Down,* he plays D-Fens, the aggrieved loser, laid off due to corporate restructuring. The loss of his marriage and employment has so destroyed his sense of self he doesn't even get his own name now, he's remembered by the vanity plate he drove to work. And his scattershot attempt at getting revenge, attacking women, queers, and immigrants instead of the executives and politicians who actually ruined his life, mimics the inability of the modern man loser to confront his true adversaries.

Loyalty was once a key masculine virtue. Loyalty to country, to community, to family, to business. But the political and economic workings of this era showed loyalty to be a fool's errand. If a man is loyal to his nation, the powers that be will send him to an endless war in Vietnam and keep him there past all hopes of winning just so they don't lose an election. If he is loyal to his company, the executives will pay him less than what he deserves and then they'll lay him off to hit some arbitrary number on a quarterly report no one reads. To be loyal is to be duped, dependent, and weak. It's only the man who honors nothing but his own self who succeeds, the man who values nothing other than the numbers in his accounts going up who wins.

The process of financialization, privatization, and the surrender of every aspect of life to market forces meant that only one thing was seen as being of value in public life, and that was the amount of profit. Whereas in the past one could expect a life of dignity and respect by doing a good job at something, how much one earned became the dominant marker of a life well lived. Oh, did someone spend five years making a work of towering artistic genius, a film that exposes the hypocrisies of modern life and the absurdity of life under capitalism? Well, if it didn't make as much as the latest superhero film it must not have been as good. Oh, are those men spending their time teaching the next generation not just how to read and write but to appreciate the elegant beauty of a perfectly crafted sentence? They should have learned to code, losers. Is this workplace oriented toward creating a product of outstanding and reliable quality, saving hundreds of lives each year caused by unnecessary accidents created by inferior products? Well, the shareholders are rioting and are about to remove the man who built the company so they can put in a CEO from a totally different industry who doesn't understand the work, so he can increase profit margins by slashing quality controls.

Again, this isn't necessarily new. American masculinity has always had its financial measuring stick. But the economic changes of the eighties and nineties brought this to prominence. And with the invention of the credit score in 1989, your exact value to society could be quantified and displayed for all to see. A bad number was inescapable and detrimental to your well-being, like a scarlet letter to be worn to every job interview and interaction with your bank, shown to every prospective landlord and colleague.

The scene of masculinity became a hierarchy of winners and losers, with a hollowed-out middle. And here is born hustle culture, a maniacal grind of side gigs, the hunt for elusive passive income, and the financialization of every moment of existence, in the desperate attempt to be a winner. Never a loser.

In a 2011 interview on Alec Baldwin's podcast, Michael Douglas expressed surprise that so many young men have approached him on the street over the years to tell him that his iconic *Wall Street* character Gordon Gekko inspired them to go into finance. "Hey, I was the villain."

And yes, how could anyone possibly make the mistake of wanting to be like Gordon Gekko, what with his sex workers on call and his stockpile of wealth and the stash of good drugs and the connections at the best restaurants and the best tailors and works by the hottest visual artists of the time hanging on all his walls? Everyone is either in awe of him or terrified of him, and everyone wants to know what he thinks. He's the villain, but he's also a tremendous success.

It was a problem of the eighties and nineties, with Scorsese's gangsters and Mamet's closers and Fincher's nihilists and Stone's bankers. Artists and writers and filmmakers may have thought they were depicting the thick filth that was running through the world of men, but a lot of men were taking it in and thinking, Yeah that looks pretty cool. A lot of men watched *Fight Club* and started their own fight clubs. A lot of men watched *Glengarry Glen Ross* and took Alec Baldwin's sociopathic monologue as an inspirational speech. A lot of men watched *Wall Street* and decided to go work on Wall Street.

(A lot of men also watched *Goodfellas* and then decided to endlessly quote *Goodfellas* rather than join the mafia, the inspirational mimicry could only go so far.)

What a lot of these films depicted was the severance of the actions of masculinity from the values of masculinity. The man's job is to provide through labor and the earning of wages. But severed from the values of selflessness and delayed gratification, not to mention that men were increasingly severed from their wives and children thanks to the climbing divorce rate, providing becomes simply mass accumulation. The man's job is to be strong. But severed from the values of protecting the weak and fighting for a cause, strength becomes mindless aggression. Guidance becomes control. Courage becomes destructiveness.

The process of that severance is often understood as happening on an individual level. When we talk about "toxic masculinity," we are usually solely blaming the man. His personal failings and corrupted character have allowed him to behave in these ways. Similarly, our solution to combating toxic masculinity is to shame, punish, and reform the offending man. At the end of *Wall Street*, Gordon Gekko is hauled off to prison for his financial crimes. The financial regulations that allowed—even encouraged—him to take the actions he did remain in place.

The truth is that this warping of the values of manhood was caused by very real material, political, and economic changes. And the solution to them is not a kind of progressive re-education program where we Clockwork Orange men's eyes open and force them to watch videos of wholesome fathers playing with their children and taking care of sick puppies. The problem can only be effectively addressed by creating new political and economic structures.

. . .

Wall Street presents two different forms of masculinity locked in conflict. On one hand, we have an example of the new corporate masculinity, the type of man American society and politics were, when the movie was released in 1987, setting up for success. On the other, we have the family man, a member of the working middle class, a waning demographic that is about to be pushed into precarity. And standing between them is their prospective heir, the young man trying to decide whose example he will follow. Who will be his real dad.

The new corporate masculinity is embodied in the character of Gordon Gekko. He's a corporate raider. He takes over a company, strips it of all its assets, and sells off its parts. He is also a popular example of the antihero who dominated entertainment in this era. The doctor who is too brilliant to play by the rules. The cop who is too brilliant to play by the rules. The chef who is too brilliant to play by the rules. Bad boys and renegades, the scourge of human resource departments everywhere.

Gekko is a banker who is too brilliant to play by the rules, and his business decisions are mostly based on insider information obtained and used illegally. The old way of doing things is illustrated in the character of Lou. He, too, is an investment banker, one who believes in the traditional values of respectability and stewardship. He believes the banks have an obligation to their customers and to the businesses with which they are involved. It is their job to invest in a company of value, to nurture its growth, and to profit through partnership. That way, the world is made better through a quality product, the bankers have the satisfaction of hard work done well, and the investors make money in a stable and predictable way. As Kevin Dowd and Martin Hutchinson define it in *Alchemists of Loss,* the values of traditional finance include "the importance of trust, integrity, and saving; the need to build long-term relationships and invest for the long term; modest remuneration for practitioners and a focus on the interests of their clients; and tight governance and a sense of harmonized interests and mutual benefit." A rising tide lifts all boats.

But Gekko and his proverbial sons instead want to crowd out every other boat in the water with their own superyacht. Lou is on his way out, he's getting old and doddering. His younger colleagues look at him like he's a ghost, a part of the past that is lingering unwelcomed in the present. Because it's not just that his ideas are no longer popular. They don't really work to make money anymore. Lou's character and his respectability and stewardship are a possible model for young men only if Lou's way of doing business can lead to a sustainable life. If by following his model they instead meet financial stagnation and frustration, it would be foolish for them to follow his lead.

What works instead is modern finance, defined by Dowd and Hutchinson thus: "a focus on marketing and sales, form over substance, and never mind the client; an obsession on the short-term and the next bonus; a preference for speculation and trading over long-term investment; stratospheric remuneration levels for practitioners, paid for through exploitation of clients and taxpayers, or 'rent seeking'; the erosion of the old governance mechanisms and out-of-control conflicts of interest." The Western financial system has also been described as "casino capitalism" by economist Susan Strange in her book of the same name. She warned that "from school-leavers to pensioners, what goes on in the casino in the office blocks of the big financial centres is apt to have sudden, unpredictable and unavoidable consequences for individual lives."

The eighties were an important pivot point between traditional and modern finance. Before the passage of the 1980 Monetary Control Act, the American finance system had not undergone any substantial reforms since those made in response to the onset of the Great Depression. But years of double-digit inflation put pressure on Congress to do something—and the choices they made in the 1980s affected not just American banks but also the fortunes of the whole world.

Playing by the old rules got you next to nothing, thanks to the recession and the government's confused economic policy. Banks like the old-fashioned savings and loans were failing in the early days of the decade precisely because they were operating in this more conservative mode. They were rooted in communities, restrained in their activities by law, and they were running out of money thanks to the various financial crises of the late seventies. And rather than fixing the banks by backing up their investments and allowing them to make adjustments to bring their policies in line with the rates of inflation, the advocates of deregulation chose instead to incentivize risk. To turn sturdy institutions into casinos. And these banks, which operated both as the casino and as the gambler, were not allowed to lose. But their clients and taxpayers were. People lost houses and a ton of money and their livelihoods and pensions, but the banks and the politicians and the executives who created the crisis were mostly allowed to walk away unscathed.

Savings and loans, also known as "thrifts," complained in the late 1970s that the high interest rates and the high levels of regulation and oversight were interfering with their ability to run their businesses. Before the eighties, the thrifts were run much like in the film *It's a Wonderful Life,* which immortalized them as mom-and-pop institutions where a warmhearted patriarch invested in the future of his community. Their primary function was in residential development, but that setup was straining their resources in this time of economic hardship.

Kathleen Day detailed what happened next in her book *S&L Hell: The People and the Politics Behind the $1 Trillion Savings and*

Loan Scandal. She writes, "By the early 1980s Maryland's thrift executives had used the high interest rates of the marketplace and deregulation-minded policies of the Reagan era to persuade Maryland's legislature to give them greater freedom to run their business." The Federal Savings and Loan Insurance Corporation–backed thrifts were given the green light to make risky investment decisions with the money deposited by their clients, confident that any losses they might incur would be covered by the taxpayer.

Day states the obvious: "Deregulation requires more cops." But the era of deregulation was also a time of gutting the government's oversight functions. Banks were frequently tasked with overseeing their dealings themselves, and they decided they were doing just fine, thank you. Unleashed from their original mission, incentivized to take wild bets, and left alone to determine the ethical line when it came to pursuing money, the thrifts began to invest in wild speculation. Savings and loans poured money into organizations that built housing based on subsidies and tax breaks rather than genuine need. When those properties failed to sell, the organizations filed for bankruptcy and left their debts to the S&Ls mostly unpaid. A few disasters in a row of the same kind left thrifts in Ohio and Maryland teetering on closure.

After the bailouts of the banks, some that failed due to bad investments and others due to outright embezzlement and fraud, the special investigator appointed by the state of Maryland pinpointed the culprit, as quoted in *S&L Hell:* "A total absence of regulation of savings and loan associations, individuals in the industry who took advantage of that absence of regulation to expropriate depositors' money for their own use, and a hopelessly flawed system which permitted the industry to make and enforce its own rules."

In other words, this is where a choice was made. A choice that would be continued by president after president, no matter which political party was in charge, no matter how many citizens began to protest. The choice was to keep the system in place that had led to disaster for the clients who lost their deposits and forced taxpayers to contribute to the bailouts.

The new banking regulations allowed the financial institutions to make riskier and riskier decisions, and they allowed the consequences of those decisions to fall solely on the individual bank customer. When the gamble did not pay off, the bank itself lost a couple of numbers on a computer screen, which were quickly replaced by the government in a series of bailouts and breaks. It was the individuals who lost their material goods, their pensions, their houses, their paychecks. It was the individuals who paid the taxes that should have been returned to them in the form of health insurance, safe bridges and roads, and Social Security and who instead saw that money diverted to the banking system. All they could do was watch as the infrastructure of their towns and their lives disappeared.

The power system took a side, and it revealed what side it was on in the decisions it made in the wake of disasters. Time and again, when corruption was revealed—the connections politicians had to the banks, or the misdeeds and crimes of speculators, developers, and businesspeople—charges were not filed. People were not arrested. Politicians were not sanctioned, they were not forced to resign in disgrace, nor did they lose their next election. And the taxpayers funded bailouts for the banks.

Instead, the choice was made to continue deregulation and privatization. Banks were given bigger piles of cash to make increasingly risky investments with. Protections that had been in place since after the Great Depression were quickly removed. Regulatory commissions whose job it was to safeguard the individual decided banks were capable of regulating themselves, despite all evidence to the contrary. And when things quickly fell apart again, this time on a global scale, once again, power chose a side, and the people who did wrong were not punished while the people who were harmed were not protected. This process was being duplicated in other ways with similar aims all across the world.

Gekko is merely a distillation of the whole system shaped into a man. The only unrealistic part of the film is when he is arrested and imprisoned for insider trading. Because in reality politics, business, and the global economy had reshaped themselves to protect and reward people like Gekko, at the great expense of everyone else. Gekko's form of masculinity, craven and rule breaking and selfish, became the new standard for corporate masculinity because it was consistently and profoundly rewarded.

Today's successful investors and hedge fund managers and bankers don't talk about responsibility or the importance of nurturing growth. They talk about numbers. About making the line go up.

The previous rhetoric defending a capitalistic system—healthy competition keeps businesses honest and accountable; it's the fairest system to make sure good work is rewarded and the lazy are incentivized to change their ways; every dollar is earned and reflects the value of the contribution—is not believed, let alone spoken of, much by Gekko's sons. This is a world of winners and losers, and cheating to win shows gumption and confidence. It's just another sign of a winner.

The other model of masculinity on display in *Wall Street* is Martin Sheen's Carl Fox. He's the patriarch, in the old-fashioned sense. He is concerned with his family, his union, and the company he works for. He is a steward, someone who prizes stability over risk and honesty over winning. He is a kind of stand-in for all the working middle classes, the laborers who in the postwar boom were able to get skilled work as plumbers, factory workers, carpenters, mechanics. They worked with their hands and made a good enough living to earn a breadwinning wage. They could buy a decent house, send their kids to a good school, and have a wife at home.

But the same financial pressures of the 1970s that pushed savings and loans into crisis were also affecting skilled laborers. The breadwinning wage—the ability of a family unit to survive on one income—had been the product of unionization and organization in support of workers' rights, but as the economy contracted laborers took the largest hit. While the bankers and executive class were being empowered politically, financially, and culturally, the power of unions was being undermined in all the same ways. Corporate management began to erode the collective bargaining power of unions. And when the boom of corporate mergers and consolidation peaked in the 1980s, the policy decisions were made to enable wealth and power to be transferred upward.

In Carl Fox's specific field, aeronautics, the 1980s were a chaotic time of change. There was a lot of money to be made in the world of air travel, but consistently it was the executives who profited, rather than the workers who powered the industry. Due to the deregulation policies of the Carter administration, which allowed airlines to set their own fare rates and routes, during the economic decline of the 1980s, much of the stress fell on the workers. Airlines had slashed the prices of their fares to attract a newly mobile population, and many of those savings came out of workers' pockets. Benefits were decimated and salaries became stagnant.

Smaller airlines were bought up by larger airlines, and the season of corporate consolidation began. Consolidation created a new corporate reality that is not often remarked upon, even though the consequences of it are huge: companies now have CEOs and executive rulers who have no experience in and know nothing about the businesses they operate. Companies get bought up by massive conglomerates, which often have their origin in entirely different sectors. Presidents of airlines don't come out of the airline industry, they come from other businesses. An executive might operate an entertainment company one year, a telecom company the next.

Executives don't know this specific business, they only know "business." They don't know about hospitality, travel, or engineering; they know numbers. The goal of executives who don't know their business is to make money, increase profit, and decrease costs. They don't care about the experience of passengers, the solidarity of their workers, the satisfaction of doing a good job, unless it affects the business's numbers.

Unhappy workers have two options: strike or quit. But striking, once a powerful weapon of the unions, has lost its power. Air traffic controllers went on strike in 1981 to advocate for better working conditions after years of intense pressure from their employers. Because they were federal employees, the strike was illegal, but the highly organized union had reason to believe their efforts would be successful. Politicians, looking to capture the working-class vote, generally offered half-hearted support of unions' efforts. Even if the union didn't get everything it demanded, it was reasonable to anticipate political support for a negotiation. But the political climate had changed. Media's coverage of the strike skewed toward the implication that the workers were selfish and entitled, disrupting the nation's economy and inconveniencing the average American. Democrats were no longer on the workers' side, and Republicans were active participants in the corporate takeover project.

President Ronald Reagan ended the strike by ordering the firing of all the participating union members—more than eleven thousand employees—and barred them from future government employment. According to Joseph McCartin, author of *Collision Course: Ronald Reagan, the Air Traffic Controllers, and the Strike That Changed America,* this one political act had a deleterious cascading effect for blue-collar workers. Unions declined in numbers, the once useful tool of the workers' strike was deployed less and less often, and corporations felt emboldened to bust up unionization efforts. Even when corporations engaged in illegal anti-unionizing efforts, the chance of prosecution was slim.

The dynamic between employee and employer was changed in that moment. What followed was increased employment instability and reduced collective bargaining. Due to the impotence of the unions to prevent layoffs and jobs going offshore, the average worker began to see unions as foolish investments that took more from the worker than they returned.

Those who lost their job in layoffs or quit in search of a better job found a smaller number of employers to choose from. Airlines were competing for customers, not for workers. And in the effort to make as much money as possible by lowering fares, operating with as few employees as possible, and cutting costs, many airlines were run into the ground. When they were dealing with unhappy unions, it was on occasion decided it made more financial sense to sell the business off than negotiate with their own workers. There were bankruptcies and liquidations and buyouts, all leading to massive job loss while the executives and owners took home millions.

What Gekko does to Fox's airline was happening all across the industry. Airlines were increasingly being run by finance guys and businesspeople who didn't know aviation, rather than specialists who ascended from within the industry. It was often decided that businesses were more valuable closed down and sold off than running, even when the business was turning a profit. It wasn't just airlines that were affected; once many sectors of American business were taken over by the financial sector, they found themselves liquidated. Local media, retailers, and healthcare providers—all sectors that traditionally have had powerful union representation—found themselves infiltrated and destroyed by investors and hedge funds.

Many sectors of working-class and middle-class American life were being squeezed for every possible penny of profit and then closed down. While politicians started to make grandstanding

speeches about main streets disappearing from small towns, they
made the legislative moves to ensure that the financial vulture class
was protected and massive corporations received incentives to take
over local economies. Small markets closed; Wal-Mart moved in.
Local media shut down; national conglomerates took their place.
Political representation was disappearing. The unions had once
been the bedrock of the Democratic Party, but a demographic shift
away from the working class toward a more affluent and educated
urban voter was already taking place. That left a large population
politically homeless. The Republicans maintained their focus on the
needs and interests of corporate culture, but they started to entice
the white working class to their side with rhetoric about strong
families and fearmongering about immigrants stealing their jobs.

As deindustrialization and globalization accelerated, communities and towns that had been centered on mining, manufacturing, and other forms of skilled labor were gutted. For generations,
skilled labor had netted its workers the ability to own property, raise
a family, earn a breadwinning wage. And for most of these jobs, a
college education was not required. Now, those lucky enough to
find warehouse or manufacturing work were being paid a third of
what their fathers had earned for similar hours and labor.

More and more forms of employment started to require a
college degree, even those that paid low wages. Other points of
entry, like apprenticeship, vocational school, and "starting in the
mailroom," disappeared. Traditionally working-class lines of work
like journalism and the arts became professionalized. Social mobility was always more of an American dream than a reality, but over
the past decades, it became more of a wild fantasy than a dream.
Avenues out of the lower classes were consistently blocked.

Carl Fox, then, is the representative of a dying way of life. The
lifestyle of quiet dignity and hard work is being actively hunted to
extinction. He has no inheritance to leave his son, other than a nos-

talgic fantasy of the nuclear family, the blue-collar job, and loyalty to others. If his son truly tried to follow in his footsteps, he'd end up laid off in the first wave of consolidation, then moving from job to job with no security and no benefits and no path to promotion. He'd find himself priced out of owning property in his old neighborhood, he'd find himself undesirable to women and unable to create an heir of his own.

Carl's life is the patriarchal dream of a good life, but it's conjured by a man asleep to social changes. He'll find himself not respected and emulated but hated as a baby boomer by the coming generation for not leaving behind a bountiful enough inheritance. He'll be scapegoated for not anticipating the changes that would give the next generation no room to expand but instead a poisoned future. He'll be blamed for not passing more sustainable environmental policies, for having it too good and too easy, and believing in the promise of technological ingenuity and American policy to keep all the lines going up.

Let's not get confused. Masculinity has always been about competition, war games, and who dies with the most toys. But the patriarchy, as we understand it, as a system of institutions, rituals, and roles, has for a long time encouraged, even if it didn't celebrate, hard work, delayed gratification, and public service. Now those material incentives like financial stability and property ownership and a sense of purpose have been destroyed and replaced with a mad scramble for acquisition and the hoarding of resources.

Wall Street portrays Bud's decision between these prospective fathers at the end as a personal choice. Which father will he be loyal to? Whose inheritance does he prefer? His choice is the choice between two dads, two models of masculinity. What kind of man does he really want to be?

When we meet Bud, he's already trying to distance himself from his father and his middle-class roots. He dresses the way he has seen successful men dress on television, in men's magazines, at his university and office. He didn't grow up in this world, and he doesn't have the money to buy anything that doesn't come straight off the rack, so it doesn't quite look right. Men who grew up rich spot the ill-fitting jacket and the artificial fabrics immediately. He's taken the mantra "dress for the job you want" very seriously, overdoing it with his hair gel even in his low-level position.

He is slightly embarrassed by his father, who wears mostly work clothes or maybe the one suit he has in his closet for "special occasions," which has the wrong kind of lapel and the wrong cut for the modern man. He wants to be better than his father, and not necessarily in the patriarchal way that each generation hopes that the one that follows will suffer less, have more, and build on what has already been established. He doesn't want to inherit the wisdom and resources his father has to offer, he wants to start fresh and prove himself in a totally different world.

This was part of the promise of the eighties and nineties, that education could bring social mobility and reinvention. The coming generations could break with past patterns of poverty and stagnation. It was different from the bootstrap rhetoric of the new conservatives because it was filled with promise and fantasy. The message was not that each individual is responsible for their own wins and losses; the prevailing idea was that with enough money and ambition, each individual can create the career and the life of their dreams.

But, of course, it was the same nonsense. Because the push for higher education—and the percentage of people who graduated high school and the percentage of people who continued into college both skyrocketed during this time—did not coincide with funding for higher education. It coincided with an increase in student loans. Many of the young people who were being sold a better future, one very different from what their parents had experienced, were the exact ones whose families did not have six figures to send their children to private universities. There were many banks and private companies that were all too eager to prey on those fantasies and hopes for an elevated existence and trap generations of students in decades of debt.

Same with Bud. Bud is so determined not to be his father that he, too, takes on student loan debt in the hopes of creating a better life for himself. How is he to know when he's signing those documents that the chances of that actually happening are incredibly slim? Because he's cursed with this idea of the value of hard work from his father, not knowing that the way you make it big in finance is to already be rich or to be a pure sociopath. He only starts to get ahead once he learns to lie and cheat and sell out his dad.

The reason he doesn't want to be like his father, by the way, is that he doesn't want to work as hard as he did. Which makes him sound a bit like a spoiled brat. Which he is. But this is the eighties, the era of the *Lifestyles of the Rich and Famous,* the Trumps, the gross displays of wealth and leisure. Bud has watched his father spend his life focused on the duties of manhood and the responsibilities he had to his family, his company, and his community, and, as his reward, enjoy absolutely nothing of the pleasures of the era. Not the women, not the money, not the cars, not the restaurants, not the drugs, not the nightlife, not even the cultural support. Instead his father's way of life was depicted in the entertainment industry and in mass media as outdated and sad.

So Bud goes with the flashier father, Gordon Gekko, and begs him to take him on as a protégé. He wants what he would have gotten had Gekko literally been his father: the connections, the lessons in how to navigate the social circles of power, how to order the right wines, the way to dress and present himself. Because that is what fathers do for their sons, they teach them how to live and succeed in the world. His own father can only teach him how to thrive in a world that Bud not only does not want but that is also quickly disappearing. The foundation of his paternal inheritance is made of quicksand, and neither Bud nor his father noticed how fast they are being swallowed up. Bud's one opportunity to survive in the new world, not having a father who can assist him, is to learn from someone else. He's lucky that he has Gekko, a person who exists in his (fictional) world. A lot of young men today instead find themselves with cyber daddies, parasocial fathers, trying to figure out how to be a man from dad influencers like Scott Galloway, Jordan Peterson, Stefan Molyneux, Andrew Tate, and Kevin Samuels.

It's no surprise then that when Bud gets a taste of success he immediately grasps for those pleasures. Fuck security, fuck saving something for a rainy day. Bring on the external markers of success! Bring on the sex workers and good suits and the fancy watch and the downtown loft. Bring on real estate and blue-chip artists whose work he doesn't in any way understand beyond its price tag. And by the end of the film, Bud sees that what was going to be his father's prize, his retirement and the time and space to for once in his life not work, will disappear when the company he works for is liquidated. For his father, the hard work would never end.

Bud thinks he is making a choice, but the choice has been made for him. The material conditions of the world have almost entirely washed out one path from his proverbial fork in the road. There is no future in respectable work anymore. There is no pension to see you through old age, no ladder to climb to financial solvency, no rewards for doing the right thing. We know the odds are against us, we know the system is rigged, but acknowledging that and walking away means accepting the loss and acknowledging that we are losers. Besides, someone has to win, right? Eventually? And who is to say that it can't be you?

FALLING DOWN:

THE ASPIRATIONAL MASS SHOOTER

In 1986, forty-four-year-old USPS employee Patrick Sherrill entered the post office of Edmond, Oklahoma, with a gun and murdered fourteen of his co-workers before killing himself. This was not the first post office massacre—there had been workplace shootings going back to the 1970s. But with the shockingly high body count and the overwrought media coverage of this particular shooting people recognized a pattern. Men were walking into their places of work, shooting everyone they could find, and turning the gun on themselves. And for some reason, this seemed to be happening most frequently at the post office.

Before the bullied teenage boy out for revenge at his school took over our imagination, the men who committed these workplace massacres were the prototypes of the mass shooter. They were often middle aged and white, strugglingly middle class, family men and active participants in their community. These were the mostly invisible men of our society, the men who worked in manual labor or bureaucracy or civil service, men who had maybe hoped for grander things but found themselves in disappointing circumstances. And one day, they just "snapped."

Late-night comedians made jokes about these men "going postal," and politicians sent "thoughts and prayers" to the survivors and families of the victims. Saying someone snapped is saying the fault lies with them. There was a psychological weakness to them, some fault in their wiring. Or maybe they were violent bullies all along, maybe it was inevitable that one day they would pick up a gun and go to work.

This was all a way of ignoring the conditions under which these men labored. People may have wondered why one institution was the repeated target of murderous rage, but it wasn't the investigations into the workplace culture of the postal system that made headlines. It was the number of dead, in massive print, and pictures of dead bodies in bags and under blankets that made the news.

The postal system had once been a symbol of efficiency and societal order. It was reliable and friendly. Mailmen were the subjects of Norman Rockwell paintings and greeting cards. You put a stamp on a letter to your mother and then a kindhearted man hand-delivers it to her. It was part of the thread that holds us all together.

But that system started to break down in the eighties due to privatization, reforms, and union busting. Up until 1970, the mail had been handled by the Post Office Department. But after an eight-day strike for better pay and working conditions by employees that year, the decision was made to reconfigure the organization as the United States Postal Service. Once it became an independent agency, there was a new pressure for the USPS to function as a corporate entity. The subsidies on which its functioning had been dependent were slowly reduced until they were ended in 1982, and after that the USPS was trusted to operate not as a service but as a business. Expected to be self-sufficient, the agency was under pressure to cut costs, automate its processes, and operate with the fewest number of employees possible. Investigations by government agencies found that across the United States, management was rewarded for running bare-bones operations, even if it took harassment, labor law violations, and cruelty to get the job done. Individual workers, however, instead of being rewarded for hard work found their paths to promotion blocked, productivity expectations increased, and wages stagnated.

The post office had long been a reliable employer that offered respectable income and benefits, a decent place of work for those without college educations or grand ambitions of becoming a self-made man. Do your job, be a vital part of the community, and go home to your family. But for your average worker, it was becoming a dead end, both financially and emotionally.

This is where an economy that prioritized the financier over the worker ended up. Unionization was low and privatization was high. Globalization was sending well-paid factory work overseas, hollowing out communities in the Rust Belt. Workers were being squeezed for every minute of productivity they had in them, and every dollar created seemed to be sucked out of the community to be put in some distant stockholder's pocket. And while a lot of people in the country couldn't afford mental health care services, this being America they could afford guns.

The Italian philosopher Franco "Bifo" Berardi contemplated the rise of the mass shooter in American society in his book *Heroes*, where he argued that it was impossible to remove these figures from their economic context. The changes related to the transition from traditional to modern finance had a profound effect on the individual economic actor. Money is no longer "an indicator of value," Berardi writes. Modern finance had turned work into primarily a function of building wealth for a small handful of people who are uninvolved in the workplace. Likewise, the sense of stability that came with the postwar American middle class was replaced with scarcity.

Berardi continues, "Work, production, and exchange are all

transformed into a battlefield whose only rule is competition. Our entire precarious life is submitted to this one imperative: competition. All of our collective energies are enlisted to one goal: to fight against all others in order to survive." A new American archetype was being created, the mass shooter. And he looked an awful lot like Michael Douglas in *Falling Down*. The story of a man who abandons his car after getting stuck in a traffic jam and decides to "walk home," despite the restraining order his wife has filed against him and the bad neighborhoods he has to traverse, *Falling Down* is ultimately the story of white male grievance. The city used to be his domain, the family used to be his kingdom, and the institutions like the police used to be there to serve him. In his final moments he seems confused about when he became the bad guy and it's a question worth considering.

How, a college-educated liberal will say, shaking their head, can a working-class man blame immigrants for his inability to find a job, rather than the real culprit, globalization/corporate tax rates/the billionaire class/and so forth?

Well, one could answer thus: How can a college-educated liberal blame personal failings for so-called toxic masculine behaviors, rather than the real culprit, globalization/corporate tax rates/the billionaire class/and so forth?

When the postal shootings were still happening, it was easier for everyone to think these men were just crazy. If the shooter is insane, then the problem is solved, because that man is now dead. Many of the original mass shooters killed themselves or were killed by the police at the end of their sprees. Manifestos written before the mass shootings were not yet part of the process, so often people were left to speculate about the reasons, whether they were racially motivated or the result of personal hatreds.

Falling Down is essentially the story of misdirected rage, all the way around. The character's real problems have been caused by his employer, who recently laid him off, the implied abuse doled out by his father (itself probably exacerbated by a military industrial complex that traumatizes young men in war and refuses to take responsibility for the lingering effects while finding ways to deny mental health services to the men and women who served this country), which has created his inability to manage his temper, resulting in his ex obtaining a restraining order against him. And yet he lashes out instead at the minor inconveniences and indignities of urban life, the more visible signs of society's decay and a world gone mad.

From *The Bonfire of the Vanities* to *Judgment Night,* there were multiple stories at the time whose entire plot hinged on the idea that if they take one wrong turn in an urban environment, if they dare to get off the freeway that safely glides them past urban blight and gang warfare, an innocent white person will find themselves in scenes of unspeakable deprivation and vulnerable to violence at the hands of Black and brown people. In the white middle-class imagination, inner cities are filled with trash cans on fire, young boys armed like African child soldiers (another thing they don't actually know anything about but saw on the news once), and women in a permanent state of peril.

Times in the cities were tough during this era. Violence, poverty, and homelessness were all on the rise in the eighties. As Donovan X. Ramsey shows in his social history *When Crack Was King,* the closure of factories in South Central Los Angeles left unemployment and economic hardship in their wake, and the streets were flooded with cheap and highly addictive drugs. The crime and violence that resulted, as well as the media hysteria over myths like crack babies and the young Black male "superpredators," were used to justify long-term prison sentences for even nonviolent drug offenders, who were disproportionately Black and Latino.

It was good business to keep the middle-class whites afraid. Politicians used their fear to scrounge up votes and donations, media escalated their coverage to keep viewers too anxious to look away. The so-called War on Drugs boosted incarceration rates in America to some of the highest in the world, created the private, for-profit prison system still in use, and substantially increased police budgets in cities across the country.

Professor of sociology Robert P. Weiss describes this process in "Privatizing the Leviathan State: A 'Reaganomic' Legacy": "The 1980s was a watershed decade in the racial and class history of US criminal justice, repudiating 20 years of political and social activism that expanded civil liberties and due process and fostered liberal and 'critical' criminology movements stressing prisoner rights, decarceration, decriminalization, and socioeconomic 'root causes' of criminal behavior." Criminals were dehumanized in the media and politics, which gave cover to the rise of the for-profit prison system, where prisoners were more likely to suffer harsh and violent conditions and less likely to receive services that might offer the possibility of rehabilitation.

The crime statistics were real, cities had big problems keeping their residents safe. But often the "white flight" of the postwar era preceded these problems, rather than being caused by them. When the middle class abandoned urban areas for the suburbs, the cities' tax base shrank, leaving many cities in a state of budgetary crisis. A nationwide policy shift toward privatization and deregulation meant public assets from utilities to street parking to prisons were sold off and their new owners attempted to provide as little service as possible for the highest price. Services like healthcare, public transportation, and education took a big financial hit as municipal governments sought to slash city expenditures.

These problems almost inevitably lead to an increase in crime, drug use, and violence. But that violence was felt not by white tourists or suburbanites or the affluent residents who stayed. Their crime statistics barely moved. (Although multiple people, from the supposedly grieving mother Susan Smith in South Carolina to the fraudulently heartbroken widower Charles Stuart in Boston, during this time invented Black male perpetrators of the murders they themselves committed, blaming phantom carjackers for the deaths of their loved ones.) The victims of the violence were mostly the poorer residents of the city.

But when the middle class left, it wasn't just buildings and former revenue streams that were left empty. The imaginative space was left wide open. Without the steadying guidance of the stable white middle-class patriarch, many seemed to believe, surely everything would steadily descend into chaos. A gap widened between how violent cities were and how violent people thought they were, and flourishing within that gap was the entertainment industry, eager to taunt their target audience of white suburbanites with fantasies of race riots and gang violence and drug wars, way beyond the reality of these problems.

It is easier to hate a stranger's face than a corporate entity. It is easier to take a baseball bat to a human body than to a municipal policy. And it is easier to force repentance or redress from an individual than from an international banking system. Which is just one reason why, when the anger becomes too much to be contained in an interior space, it spills out and is directed at people who have nothing to do with the source.

In *Falling Down*, D-Fens's life became harder because of corporate reorganization in an entire economic sector, the defense industry. After the fall of the Soviet Union and the liberation of its communist empire in Central and Eastern Europe, America had an identity crisis. Without its most powerful enemy, who was it anymore? The Cold War had helped to define America in both the international imagination and its own since the end of World War II. America was what the Soviet Union and its communist sat-

ellites were not. Where communism was repressive, America was
liberating. Where communism was about sacrifice, America was
about abundance. In the years between 1989 and 2001, the military,
the intelligence community, the defense industry, and other communities with connections to America's global presence struggled.
D-Fens is a symbol of this identity crisis, standing as he does
between these various overlapping pressures. The retreating white
presence in the urban center, the fear of the non-white other, the
financialization of everyday life, the failed and useless patriarch in
the broken nuclear family, and the loss of meaning and identity at
the end of history. And then he gets a gun.

One by one our Michael Douglas character airs his grievances with
the world and the way it has ceased to operate in a way that makes
sense to him. The movie was an instant sensation. Its strength is the
same as a lot of the conservative and radicalizing materials that we
have examined so far: it is very good at describing the symptom, terrible at diagnosing the cause, and delusional about its cure.

There's a video game element to the plot of the film. At each
stop, D-Fens escalates the encounter (going from threatening someone to assaulting them, from shooting to injure to shooting to kill)
and he levels up his weapon from bat to gun to rocket launcher.
Everything that inconveniences or creates an obstacle for him is
treated as an existential threat. It must be eliminated so he can continue on toward his goal.

His first stop is a convenience store, where he is initially angered
by being asked to pay more than he expected for a can of soda. He
attacks the owner with a baseball bat and trashes his store. The real
culprit here is the monopolization of food businesses. Large conglomerates are able to negotiate lower prices from suppliers. Small
independent businesses must pay more for the same products, forcing them either to manage slim profit margins or increase the cost

past what a chain grocery or drug store can offer. Corporations raise prices independent of the real costs of manufacturing to push the limits of consumer loyalty and to spike profits.

But who is it easier to get angry with? The guy working behind the counter, who irritates him with his less than immaculate English and his refusal to genuflect to the superior white, U.S.-born, middle-class, red-blooded American man standing before him? Or the corporate executives who made a series of decisions that cascaded downward until they influenced a store owner's decision to raise the price of aspirin and batteries beyond the customer's expectations?

To whom is D-Fens to address his grievances with the Latino gang culture of Los Angeles? When he wanders into gang territory he is accused of trespassing, even though he, as a white citizen of the United States, believes he should be able to go anywhere and do anything he wants without consequences. Who is going to take responsibility for the violence he faces? The generals of the Mexican-American War? The city councils who generations ago redlined neighborhoods and sequestered racialized groups in substandard housing? The CIA for destabilizing South American countries in the name of preventing the spread of socialism and communism, causing mass northward migration?

Next he must wander through a public space that is filled with the mentally unwell, the unhoused, and those asking passersby for funds. According to him, their complaints are exaggerated and their circumstances overstated. He seems offended that he is being approached and asked to share what he has. During that time, the late eighties and early nineties, the issue of taxation dragged middle-class voters over to the right. But, of course, it was the fantasy of freeloaders and "welfare queens" that haunted the tax nightmares of your average citizen, not bloated military budgets and corporate bailouts.

And how different are our grievances now from the grievances of D-Fens? How to trace the origins of the precariat of American society? There's the refusal of cities to build affordable housing in keeping with the pace at which the population is increasing, meaning almost every urban area in the United States now has a housing deficit. Throw in an economic crisis that resulted in massive foreclosures and evictions, and you've got a growing population with insecure housing. Cities continue to cut public services like public healthcare, homeless shelters, mental health and addiction recovery facilities, and public transportation, deciding to prioritize instead police departments and enticement packages for corporate entities. More people are not in a mental or physically stable enough state to work to afford rising rents and vehicles. More people have no place to go, with no home and no office, and cities increasingly have more private than public spaces. People with no private space collect, then, in the limited public spaces like sidewalks, under bridges, and in parks.

The decisions that caused these various crises go back decades and involve shifting and overlapping systems of political, corporate, and public power. There is no one person or decision to blame if one is accosted by someone loud, violent, unwell, or obnoxious in a public space. There are so many people whose financial and social well-being were prioritized over this other person's that it is much easier and more satisfying to blame the individual than the system around them.

D-Fens continues through the city, complaining about fast-food employees instead of the corporation that made the decisions these workers are forced to follow lest they be released into a terrible job market. Or threatening the lives of construction workers because of some municipal corruption they have nothing to do with. Everyone in this city is being forced to be the stand-in for the government or corporation that is controlling their lives, and they must withstand the threats, complaints, and violence of D-Fens because he's having a bad day.

D-Fens himself would argue that everyone has to take responsibility for their position in life. This was the prevailing political idea of the time, that a person's economic and social position was tied to their performance and work ethic. Call it the Protestant work ethic, call it bootstrap capitalism, but pointing out structural obstacles like racism and misogyny to explain poverty or criminal involvement was widely thought to be making excuses to hide an individual's personal failings. If a child failed to get good grades, they had failed to apply themselves; if a worker was struggling financially, they weren't making themselves indispensable to their employer; if a whole sector was laid off, they weren't adding enough value to the marketplace. And it is true, every failure is a frothy mélange of the societal, the cultural, and the personal. But then D-Fens is also not eager to take responsibility for his wife leaving him (women are so irrational) or for his job loss. Which is part of the mass shooter psyche. Everyone is benefiting from the way things are except him.

D-Fens twice makes reference to himself as a consumer. He pays his money, so he should get what he wants in return. "I'm just standing up for my rights as a consumer," he tells the owner of the convenience store, right before he trashes the place. "Rick, have you ever heard the expression 'the customer is always right'?" he asks the manager of the fast-food restaurant. "Yeah, well, here I am, the customer."

The world is a buffet. For the consumer, the most important act is making a purchase. Under this consumerist mindset, taste becomes synonymous with character. Consumers define themselves by their preferences and broadcast their preferences to the world to tell everyone who they are. A consumer who buys tickets to the opera and expensive wines tells the world they are refined and cul-

tured. (Just kidding, no one goes to the opera anymore.) The consumer who eats vegan, watches all the documentaries about social
injustice, and carries a tote bag with the logo of a local bookstore
or NPR to the farmers market tells the world they have progressive
politics and empathy for the downtrodden. The consumer who eats
factory farmed red meat, drives a massive truck with a National Rifle
Association sticker on the back window, wears a Fuck Your Feelings
T-shirt, and spends their leisure hours watching every action movie
that the coastal elite critics gave bad reviews is doing the same thing
as the consumer who puts their Harry Potter house in their social
media bio and their favorite films in their dating profile. They are
using their purchases to communicate something essential about
themselves to the people around them.

This is part of the process by which the values of masculinity
have become severed from the actions of masculinity. The role of
the patriarch—providing for their family, participating in their
community—has been replaced by the role of the consumer. This is
the mindset that drives the acquisitive man who has found the traditional pathways of community recognition, whether it is membership in a religious organization or providing a service through the
work one does, replaced only with this monetary exchange. What
was once an object with meaning has become only a financial asset.
The family home is an investment; the car meant to take a worker to
the office is a status symbol, modified to make even more noise to
draw the attention of everyone around. Every existential problem
can be solved not with self-development but instead with shopping.
Can't sleep? Any major retailer has available an array of products to
sell you, whether it's a white noise machine, over-the-counter medi-
cation, high thread count bed sheets, a memory foam mattress with
cooling technology, nose strips to reduce snoring, or black-out cur-
tains. Sexually unfulfilled? Here are pole dancing classes, sex workers, entire shops devoted to every specific kink, intimacy experts,

interior designers to help build a "sex playroom," whips, feathers, gels, handcuffs, butt plugs, vibrating butt plugs, books, dungeons, harnesses, and strap-ons.

These options are made available to the potential customer using the language of play and exploration, but they are all existential dead ends that are incapable of addressing, let alone fixing, a person's real problems under a system that has been designed to exploit and manipulate them.

The financialization of human existence does two things. As Berardi explains, it turns every peer into a competitor. "The post-Fordist worker no longer shares the same interest as his/her colleagues, but, on the contrary, is forced to compete every day against other workers for a job and a salary in the deregulated labor arena," he says. There are finite resources, and each individual must fight to gain access to those resources. Solidarity between competitors is not only unlikely, but also foolish. Men who once banded together to accomplish collective goals are now told to get what they can for their own selves out of every situation.

The second thing this does is discourage the tasks of creation and participation. If everything in the world already exists, made for cheap overseas out of plastic, then the consumer only has to find and acquire from what is already available. Any inadequacies can be compensated for with enough money. For people who are struggling to find affordable healthcare providers in their area, it can be easier, rather than fighting politically for a nationalized healthcare system, to buy a plane ticket to India and have the necessary procedure done there. For those who disagree with the local government, it is easier to move to another district or state that better aligns with their political beliefs than to work for change.

Politics and community become just new things to shop for. They are nouns to a consumer, not verbs. They are not something to be done, they are something to be bought. There is no collective project for the consumer. There is simply an interaction between consumer and product, with a service worker as the intermediary. And if the service worker (and in this category falls everything from the Starbucks barista to the president of the United States) fails to be a satisfying intermediary, boycott becomes the only possible solution.

"I pay your salary" is a frequent cry of protest against politicians, the police, school boards, and service workers. (It's also a frequent complaint against people living in countries receiving American financial aid that are coincidentally frequently places where America has waged war.) It is a demand not for rights but for satisfactory customer service.

D-Fens should have solidarity with each of the people he meets on his journey across the city: the convenience store owner, the beggar in the park, the gang members, the fast-food workers, the construction workers, the Nazi . . . okay, maybe not the Nazi. In fact, the reason that the Nazi is the only person he does kill while on his rampage is to prevent a kind of identification with him. He says he is not like the Nazi, the man who is trying to sell him Holocaust souvenirs and German military memorabilia. But he is. Like D-Fens, the Nazi is nostalgic for a world he could control, one where he had all the power. D-Fens wants to destroy anything that reminds him of his similarity to the Nazi.

Everyone in the film is suffering from the same affliction, and that affliction is global finance. But because everyone is also being told that resources are scarce and that the rights and social improvement of one group comes at the expense of all others, there is a profound irritation with the others. The long afterlife of *Falling Down* supports this, whether it is the re-creation of D-Fens's walk across Los Angeles in a beloved Foo Fighters video or the many fan edits of the film on YouTube. The focus is on the inconvenience of other people's existence. Everyone is in someone else's way, and without a sense of shared purpose or belonging, the mere physical reality of other people becomes a source of stress, pain, and outburst. Daily life is a series of indignities and obstacles. The only vision of liberation is one where we are freed from obligations and ties to other people: the retreat into private property and wealth and leisure through mass accumulation of capital. This is certainly the mindset that plagues D-Fens. But when he loses the possibility for retreat, suicide by cop liberates him in another way.

The only man D-Fens feels solidarity with throughout the film is a man protesting the bank for denying him a loan, because he has been deemed "economically unviable." Much like D-Fens, who was just deemed inessential to his corporate overlords. The protestor is Black, but he is dressed exactly like D-Fens, from the short-sleeved button-up right down to the shoes. Some might see this as making some broader statement about the plight of the middle class in this era, but the only person D-Fens feels sorry for is himself.

At the heart of *Falling Down* is an identity crisis. Masculinity defines itself through its accomplishments: you are what you do. Stripped of his family, his job, his money, he loses sight of his self. It's what is often said about mass shooters today, whether adult or adolescent; they are losers. Unable to achieve most of the standard trophies of masculinity—family, career, money—they are left with only one marker. Violence.

But that accomplishment of violence, too, has become warped and twisted, divorced from its traditional setting—the theater of war—and thereby let loose on the home front. With Korea, Vietnam, Iraq, Afghanistan, Iraq again, we are very far from the heroic and glorious deeds of the wars that came before. America won World War II and saved the world from a Nazi threat. But with every conflict that followed, that fantasy of America as the savior or the liberator became more and more polluted, more corrupted by corporate interests, war crimes, and imperial intentions. D-Fens asks a Korean man why he's not more grateful to his American liberators. After all the money they spent, all the blood spilled, how dare he not spend every day on bended knee in appreciation of America. Never mind the fact that perhaps not everyone in Korea was so pleased to have their homeland be the site of a proxy war between two global powers, maybe not everyone was thrilled to have their world destroyed so the Americans and the Soviets could move some pieces around on their game board. Not everyone thinks there is glory in dying so the Americans could feel a little bit better about themselves.

D-Fens's identity crisis is tied up with America's identity crisis. The country had defined itself through its enemies for a century now. Through the First World War, the Second World War, and then the Cold War, America could know it was good because its enemies were bad. And now that they had "liberated" the whole world and communism had finally fallen, the country wasn't sure who it was anymore.

a white man
in a brown world

The performance of masculinity is as much about what is left unsaid, undone, and unexplored as it is about what a man accomplishes. The dividing line between masculinity and femininity has always been anxiously guarded. There's the line between the work world (competitive) and the domestic world (nurturing). The line between masculine gestures (playful re-creations of violence) versus feminine gestures (elegant and fluid). Or the difference between masculine hygiene products (scented with bourbon, pine trees, or "sport") and feminine hygiene products (scented with flowers).

For a man to cross the line between masculine and feminine means to risk contamination. This is why young boys' playground taunts are based on this potential for transgression. Women's boundary crossing into traditionally masculine territory carries none of this risk or taboo, because for them it's climbing the social hierarchy, crawling out of their degraded state. For men, the taboo is in falling downward.

So Michael Douglas, as our prototypical modern man, does not lose himself in a work of art. He does not go to Paris to pursue his passions. He does not experience a moment of intimacy, emotional or physical, with another man. He does not humble himself before God, nor does he seek counsel from a philosopher or poet. He does not work the land. He does not paint something beautiful. He doesn't cry at a sunset, and he doesn't try to solve one of life's intractable existential questions.

Each of these activities at one point or another has been part of the masculine domain. But as women expanded their reach, men retreated into a smaller and smaller territory, sacrificing activities and forms of self-expression in order to maintain this masculine signifier.

One way of seeing this shrinkage is to notice the gap between father and son, between what Michael Douglas's real-life father, the megastar Kirk Douglas, was able to portray on-screen and still be seen as a "real man," and what Michael Douglas himself was able to portray. Kirk Douglas played the painter Vincent van Gogh, the mad genius. But by the 1980s, the art world was deemed the province of homosexuals. Paintings could be bought or sold as assets, and their acquisition could be bragged about because of how much they fetched at auction, but heterosexual men no longer made the works of art themselves.

There are several tender moments of affection that Kirk Douglas shares with his male costars throughout his films. Meaningful glances, embraces, even kisses. None of these moments appear to emasculate Kirk Douglas's characters. But these are strikingly absent from Michael Douglas films. Other than an arm slung over a shoulder or a playful punch, there is no real touching between male characters in his films. Women easily show affection with each other, but the idea that a man would embrace another in the way that just a few decades ago showed camaraderie is now taboo.

But perhaps the most remarkable thing that Michael Douglas does not do is go to war. Some of Kirk Douglas's most iconic roles are in war films. From *Spartacus* to *Paths of Glory* to *In Harm's Way*, he portrayed the masculine virtues of sacrifice, courage, and loyalty. But by the time his son came of age, the idea that a real man is one who proves himself in battle had dropped out of the working definition of masculinity.

The difference is that the wars that followed World War II are not shown as places where men prove themselves. They are places where men are broken down. War becomes something that happens to the American male, rather than being an essential part of their identity. Robert O. Self wrote about this change in *All in the Family: The Realignment of American Democracy Since the 1960s*. "To serve one's country was a duty and an honor but also believed necessary for the survival of the 'free world,'" he writes. "Beginning in the early 1960s, however, the citizen soldier came under intense national scrutiny, as the nation was asked to answer for what the soldier did in Vietnam. Under that pressure, on a peninsula a world away, and equally in the living rooms, courthouses, and college campuses of the United States, Cold War American manhood frayed, split, and ultimately came undone."

Part of that process is visible in American films. The eighties were a huge decade for Vietnam films. But the messages of the World War II films and the Vietnam films were distinctly different. Michael Douglas's absence from these films is notable. Every hot actor of the decade was making one of these movies. There was Matthew Modine in *Full Metal Jacket,* Sean Penn in *The Casualties of War,* Charlie Sheen in *Platoon,* Tom Cruise in *Born on the Fourth of July,* Tim Robbins in *Jacob's Ladder,* Robin Williams in *Good Morning, Vietnam,* and Sylvester Stallone in *First Blood.*

The first thing you might notice about this list of actors is that they are all white. White, and, with the exception of Stallone, playing characters who are middle class or above. This wasn't who really fought in Vietnam. Vietnam was the first American war in the twentieth century where class and race divides were dramatically

different for soldier populations. Where the "we are all in this fight
together" proved to be not only a lie, but an obvious, flagrant lie.

It's true that the contributions of working-class and racialized
soldiers have long been written out of the histories of previous wars.
Even today, many World War II films have all-white casts, or sideline the stories of everyone else so the white guy can have his big
heroic moment. But Vietnam was the first time that the stories of
middle-class white men were written into the record.

The type of men most of these white actors were used to portraying on-screen—college educated, professional, well bred—were
the exact demographic of men who found it easiest to evade war.
From deferments for university education to pulling nepotistic
strings with politicians to paying a doctor friend of your father's to
write you a medical exemption, a great number of these men found
ways around the draft.

Vietnam was the moment in which one major requirement for
American masculinity, soldiering, essentially disappeared. For centuries, the military and the theater of war had given men the discipline and the sense of brotherhood that was a central part of male
identity. So many of the noble masculine virtues, like self-sacrifice,
and vices, like cowardice, were taught on the battlefield. A good
man died so others could live. A bad man surrendered to fear or
self-interest and avoided the conflict.

But now, the sacrifice of the self for a noble cause, whether that
was to kill Nazis or to spread democracy, was a task for those who
weren't smart enough or privileged enough to find a way to avoid
it. It wasn't only that the causes were becoming less noble, although
there is a steep slide from the reasons for fighting World War II
(complex and now oversimplified to present America in the best
possible light) all the way down to the protection of corporate interests in the Gulf Wars. The fantasy of the Greatest Generation and

the brave, heroic young men who liberated Europe and the Pacific was mostly manufactured by Hollywood. Decades of movies where complications were reduced down to good versus evil conveniently hid American war crimes and the rapes of the women "saved" by American troops and their allies, as well as the American origins of the German eugenics programs. But it's true that the wars that followed, from Korea to Vietnam to the Gulf to Afghanistan, didn't make quite as satisfying stories.

If Hollywood producers couldn't depict the American soldier as the conquering hero, they would make Vietnam films about his inner torment. The war became a metaphor for a white man's loss of place in the world. His confusion, his sorrow, his suffering. A world that doesn't make sense anymore, a world where the rationality and enlightenment of white civilization is subsumed by an irrational brown violence. These films were not so much about Vietnam— except in the way that they kept the story of that war centered on what Americans suffered and lost, rather than on the people who were invaded, murdered, and poisoned—as they were about the anxiety of America's place in a flattening world. The Vietnam War had proved that America couldn't shape the world into what it wanted it to be through violence and force. Not that this would convince America to stop trying.

But the country need not have worried too much, as it still would find its culture contagious and its capital desirable. America would continue to dominate the world in the softer fields of entertainment and business. It would find in a post–Cold War world that its money was a greater weapon than its bombs. Since Michael Douglas was a representative of this new American power and masculinity, he didn't need to conquer the world on a literal battlefield. He did it from an executive suite.

Michael Douglas never went to war because men like Michael

Douglas did not go to war. For them, the world was not a source of trauma and alienation, it was a source of pleasure, wealth, and adventure. It was a place to dominate, not to get lost in. Michael Douglas did not take a journey into the heart of darkness. He had an adventure through a world that was waiting, open for him to take what he wanted.

BLACK RAIN:

AMERICA HITS ITS MIDLIFE CRISIS

Americans were very worried about Japan in the Michael Douglas days. Our once bitter enemies at war had confronted us on a new battlefield: the global economy. And they seemed to be winning. They were making more money, they were selling more cars, they were buying up American real estate. Even worse, they had the audacity to be doing this while looking better, being better educated, and being more efficient and loyal workers than Americans.

Much of this anxiety was filtered through the American cultural imagination, which depicted the Japanese in film as both mindless hordes and as evil genius masterminds. Watched today, *Blade Runner* seems chaotically Japanese-phobic, imagining a Los Angeles both run by brilliant Japanese elites and overwhelmed with Asian refugees and poor immigrants. Novels like Michael Crichton's *Rising Sun* imagine Japanese culture as mysterious, perverted, and ritualistic; the Japanese are powerful because they are corrupt and violent. There were even comedies like *Gung Ho,* where Japan's industrial and intellectual superiority is somehow a character flaw, and Americans' slovenly laziness and provincialism is nothing but the secret to their inevitable success.

It wasn't just Japan that Americans perceived as a threat. But the buying spree Japanese companies and moguls went on through New York City real estate, including a 51 percent stake in the iconic Rockefeller Center in 1989, made it feel like a full takeover was imminent. First Pearl Harbor, now this? It didn't last. Japan's economy started to crash in the early 1990s, and it has never recovered to the grand heights of the eighties. But America's anxiety about having to compete with other nations, rather than just dominate them militarily, brought up certain fears. Maybe America isn't number one.

The Cold War was ending. And while America rushed to declare itself the winner over communism, that warm glow of victory didn't last like it had after World War II. The termination of the war troubled American identity rather than crystalizing it. In a newly open world that privileged free markets over military alliances, Americans found themselves a little flat-footed.

Americans had always prided themselves on being exceptional and different from the people in the rest of the world. And by different they, of course, meant better. But those claims to superiority were built on ground that was getting shakier and shakier. It wasn't just the embarrassing loss in Vietnam, being outfoxed and outfought by a significantly poorer and less well-equipped army. In comparison to other nations, in surveys backed up by real statistics, America was slipping.

American children were slipping in the ranks of math and reading comprehension. Americans started to have worse health outcomes than people of other nations. Our citizens were dying from things that were almost entirely preventable, such as car crashes and complications from childbirth, more than in other industrialized nations. Hell, Americans were less happy than people of other nations. When other citizens of the world envisioned your typical American, it was no longer as the bright shining face of a strapping young soldier, giving a poor kid of the country we just liberated a Hershey's bar. It was as a fat, dumb, insolent, ignorant rube.

And did America respond to this slippage with a moment of reflection, perhaps with a humble pause and a recommitment to the values it held most dear? Hell no. America responded with a renewed patriotic vigor, with deafening chants of We're Number One. It responded with geopolitical chaos, making monsters out of molehills, invading other countries and bombing the hospitals and embassies of nations it said it was trying to protect. It renewed calls to protect its borders, making immigration one of the most contentious issues of the era. And when that wasn't enough to make us feel good, we decided to cheat at the Olympics.

During the Cold War, the athletic competition between America and the Soviet Union acted as a kind of political propaganda for a way of life. Which form of government, communism or capitalism, would lead to a better society? Which would conquer the world? Who ruled the future? The Soviet Union understood this implicitly, devoting itself to crafting perfect athletes with medical and social interventions. Their doping technology was both an open secret and a cause of international envy. And each Olympic match, whether it was in hockey, swimming, ice skating, or basketball, was infected by this clash of the civilizations proxy war. Every medal the Soviets won seemed to be wrested from the grasp of not just the American competitor but democracy itself.

For as long as the sport had existed, basketball at the Olympics was reserved for amateur players. This was true for every sport. Paid athletes from professional leagues were not allowed to represent their nations at the international competition. But then, in 1988, the American men's team lost to the Soviet Union. This was never supposed to happen. America invented basketball. America dominated basketball. American basketball players were international superstars, people came from all over the world to watch Americans play basketball. Losing to the Soviet Union was humiliating. Devastating. Unacceptable.

This loss revealed something pretty mortifying about America: it wasn't that great at sports. At least not in international competition. America was good at playing sports that it invented, when played only against other Americans. Americans were good at playing American football against other Americans, a sport that is violent, boring, and slow. Americans were good at playing the American sport of baseball against other Americans. But soccer? Rugby? Until recently, the American presence at the World Cup was a reliable spectacle of incompetence. When Americans set the rules, the scoring system, and the standards, they are really good. But truly competing against others on a level playing field? America has failed even to qualify for about half of the World Cup competitions for soccer. The last American to win the Tour de France was stripped of his title for cheating.

Now that the Cold War was over, the Soviet Union had fallen, and America had declared victory, an American loss to a team from a postcommunist nation would be even more humiliating. So America went about changing the rules so professionals could play at the Olympics for the first time ever in the 1992 summer Olympics. They got their way, whatever their methods with the other members of the international federation might have been. And suddenly here's the Dream Team, some of the highest-paid athletes in the entire world, coming to crush the competition.

And they did. The rule for allowing only amateurs in competition at the Olympics was meant to keep something of a level playing field. Bringing in professionals meant richer countries with richer athletes could essentially buy their medals. They had advantages that smaller nations could only dream of, from cutting-edge medical technology to the ability of their athletes to devote themselves full-time to their advancement. The players of Croatia, the team that went up against America in the final game in 1992, were playing for a country that hadn't even existed in the previous Olympics. But America won their proxy war. They would maintain their position at the top, even if they had to stomp on everyone below them to stay there.

As the Cold War was ending, America had big divorced-man energy: walking around with an unearned arrogance, refusing to acknowledge past mistakes or screw-ups, taking credit for other people's accomplishments, showing defiance in the face of other people's boundaries or rules, attempting to woo partners that were way out of their league, and basically running from the confusion that was lying just beneath the surface and bothering other people with it instead. It was the midlife crisis fantasy on steroids. It was Michael Douglas driving a motorcycle in a leather jacket through the streets of Tokyo.

Black Rain, released the year the Berlin Wall fell, is essentially a midlife crisis movie. For the Michael Douglas character, but also for America. Michael Douglas can't pick up his daughter from school because he traded in his car for a motorcycle. Recently divorced from the partner that had defined their existence for most of their adult life—for Michael Douglas, his wife; for America, the Soviet Union—our hero decides to let his hair grow out, get a leather jacket, and generally be an embarrassing cliché in front of everyone. He's got a chip on his shoulder, something to prove, and a total absence of shame.

Michael Douglas plays Nick, a detective who sets off for Japan to chase the suspect in a mafia hit in New York City. And despite not knowing the language, the laws, the culture, the legal procedures, or any of the people, he is able to solve the big mystery at the heart of the murder before any of the actual Japanese people he is forced to work with.

Black Rain asks an important question: Does the NYPD have jurisdiction to run investigations and arrest criminal suspects in Japan? If not, who has the courage to try to stop them? The rest of the world's "rules" don't apply to the American man, or America in general. Americans have no problem violating treaties, the sovereignty of another nation, international law, and peace agreements in order to avenge minor slights and grievances. It doesn't matter how many people our American cop gets killed or hurt, as long as he gets his man.

However you want to understand this character—the white man, the American man, the colonizer man—he believes himself to be naturally dominant. He is lit in a certain way, he has a certain kind of swagger, he is being played by Michael Douglas. This is the man who is going to set things right. So if he is struggling in some way, it's because something has gone wrong—not with him, but with the system. If our Michael Douglas is not on top, it's because the world has turned itself over.

That's why it was so important in these films about Americans encountering Japanese culture for the Japanese culture to seem insane, violent, racist, irrational, and so on. The only way these people could be doing better than Americans, than the country that defeated them in war, is if they are in touch with dark forces or they are cheating or they are a dishonorable people.

This is part of the same process that Elizabeth D. Samet documents in *Looking for the Good War: American Amnesia and the Violent Pursuit of Happiness*. The stories Americans told about World War II, primarily through Hollywood films, helped to create a narrative in which America was the unsullied victor in the battle against Nazi evil. "The depravity against which Americans had fought, most clearly evidenced by the Nazi death camps, ultimately came to gild the unprecedentedly intense and indiscriminate violence that achieved victory," Samet writes. She continues, "Miraculously, the deadliest conflict in human history became something inherently virtuous." Hollywood films retold the story of World War II to an eager American, but also an international, audience. The civilian deaths in Dresden and Tokyo, the horrors that followed the bombings of Hiroshima and Nagasaki, the crimes committed against the women liberated in Allied countries, this all was either covered up or justified in the blinding light of heroic propaganda.

But that propaganda can fail retroactively if the enemy can show itself to be different from how they've been depicted. It wasn't only Japanese business that was thriving in this era—its culture was also proving to be a robust export. The video games of Nintendo and Sega had stomped all over Atari's market. Manga in the 1980s was seen as a sophisticated alternative to childish American superhero comics, which had not yet seen their artistic and economic revival. And anime from *Akira* to *My Neighbor Totoro* were becoming cult hits in the States. America had never really been forced to reckon with what it had done to defeat Japan in World War II. Japan's emergence as a competitor posed a peculiar existential risk to the country, not because the risk of a financial takeover was real, but because it threatened America's conception of itself.

Much in the same way the midlife crisis fantasy could give cover to men's sense of losing control over their families and their women, America's depiction of other countries in its films gave American men power over that country's narrative. American films were not only watched by Americans—they were popular all over the world. In *Black Rain,* the Japanese have two modes. The first mode is hopelessly corrupt. It is a society that is run by yakuza, who without repercussions are allowed to just chop people's heads off with swords while riding motorcycles. In director Ridley Scott's version of Japan, the society is managed via a series of backroom deals in mafia-run nightclubs, and everyone knows this but is either too powerless or too stupid or too corrupt or too cowardly to do anything about it.

The other mode of the Japanese is the beta male: weak, emotional, and lower in rank compared to the American alpha. This is the yes-man who can only do things by the book, is terrified of authority and his superiors, who is incapable of thinking outside a very narrow set of instructions and regulations. He lacks the American ingenuity and swagger to bend the rules, so ultimately he will always be powerless and ineffective.

When Michael Douglas steals money from a crime scene, his Japanese partner turns him in. The film makes it clear that this means his partner is inferior. Michael Douglas did not steal money from the crime scene to enrich himself—although if he did, that would somehow be okay, too—but because he knew if he turned it in, he couldn't trust the Japanese police to do the right thing with it. He had to break the rules in order to protect Japan from itself.

This is in line with how the police were portrayed throughout the eighties and nineties in entertainment. Their violent attacks on unarmed men and women were often played for laughs. Their flouting of laws and regulations made them smarter, better police officers than those who studiously went by the book. In a world gone mad, the people tasked with putting it back in order must do everything within their power to make things right again. Even if they must use violence, even if innocent people get hurt along the way. It's all just collateral damage, part of the price of doing "the job."

There's something that happens in a lot of American action films set in other countries. During a chase scene, our American hero will run or drive through a crowded urban marketplace, chasing or chased by bad men. Fruit carts are overturned, goods for sale are thrown into the air, poorly built structures are smashed to bits, and the injury or death of unseen natives is heavily implied. It happens in *Mission: Impossible* films, *Fast & Furious* films, *Bourne* films, pretty much any action sequence set in a Central American, North African, Middle

Eastern, Central Asian, hell, any non-American or non–Western European country.

The meaning of this scene is not that subtle. This is the marketplace, a place of commerce, industry, and gathering. The arrival of the American disrupts these processes. But what the American is doing is so exciting/important/interesting/sexy that the cost, borne by the people who live and work in these countries, is worth it. There's no follow-up with the witnesses of the mayhem. We may see a body spinning through space as they are hit by a motorized vehicle, but no one checks in to see if the person made it or not.

This scene happens in both the films about Jack T. Colton, the Michael Douglas character who gets into wacky scrapes in Colombia in *Romancing the Stone* and a fictional "Middle Eastern kingdom" in *The Jewel of the Nile*. In *Romancing the Stone*, the destruction serves the pursuit of a mythical gemstone, an enormous emerald that has lain hidden for centuries but is now sought after by various treasure hunters and looters who are looking to take it for themselves. We're asked to root for the Americans to find it first, because, well, they are American, and they want it, and the Colombians also pursuing it are corrupt gang leaders who probably will use it to buy more guns and drugs, unlike the Americans who want to buy a yacht.

The writers and producers chose Colombia as the film's setting because it held a special place in the American imagination during the 1980s. It was dangerous. Sexy. Mysterious. Cocaine was the key drug of the 1980s. It fueled both the financial and cultural industries, as both Wall Street bros and Hollywood players glamorized the stuff. It was an aspirational drug, just one of the accoutrements of wealth and social success. Its sister drug crack destroyed whole neighborhoods in urban areas, but more than that it was the bogeyman of the time. Crack, or the nightmare version of it, was used by politicians and mass media to scare the middle classes and the suburbanites. One hit, they said, was all that was needed to turn a respectable person into an addicted monster, willing to commit any crime, kill any person, rob any house or store, for just one more score. It was mostly Black users who showed up in these mass-produced fantasies—the Black man as the violent addict, the Black woman as the uncaring mother addicting and then abandoning her baby.

Colombia was the mother of these angels and demons. It, too, was a daydream and a nightmare. It was an exciting place of rebellion and lawlessness. A man could make his fortune in Colombia and live by his own rules, killing anyone who crossed him and taking any number of lovers. Stories of kingpins like Pablo Escobar had a powerful effect on the American imagination. But Colombia was also an evil place, the source of the despair of addicts and the horrors of the drug trade. It was condemned in the institutions of Washington, D.C., and, it was said, bore the responsibility for the lack of progress in the War on Drugs. Many people made a lot of money maintaining these fantasies about Colombia, and most of them were Americans.

Much of the reason for Colombia's political instability, suffered through both civil war and the battle with the narcos during this time, had to do with international interference. Leftist movements and socialist revolutions throughout Central and South America had been squashed with the help of American forces and an uncontrolled (and uncontrollable) CIA. Colombia's production of cocaine and other illicit substances made it a desirable asset to other nations, as it became both a scapegoat in the global War on Drugs and a precious resource. And its civil war made it a proxy for larger struggles between Far Right and socialist movements. Money and weapons washed in and out of Colombia, drugs fueled multiple international conflicts, and all this meddling from outside forces prolonged the country's civil war.

And yet in *Romancing the Stone,* the danger of Colombia is

merely the thrilling setting for two bored Americans in need of some adventure to shake up their dull lives. Their existences have become too comfortable, too predictable. Other nations suffering through chaos are places where Americans can go to prove themselves. The lived experience of Colombians who had to endure the violence and corruption had been ignored in favor of an Americanized version of Pablo Escobar, a man who was in the American imagination a dangerous madman, a Robin Hood–like folk hero who built houses for the poor in Medellín, the town where he grew up, and an embodiment of the American dream of wealth and limitless power, all at once. That makes Colombia a perfect setting for adventure in the American imagination.

This time Michael Douglas is Jack, a man who says he "could've been a cosmetic surgeon, five hundred thou a year, up to my neck in tits and ass" but instead moved to Colombia to become an exotic bird smuggler. Instead of a life of affluence and comfort, he chose to go to the jungle to have a more adventurous, authentic life. Americans who find it impossible to have an authentic existence within America—because of its romantic disappointments caused by feminism's gendered confusion, because of the staid conformity of its suburbs—is, of course, a running theme in cinema, and the adventure story, whether it be *Indiana Jones* or a *Fast & Furious* film, is just one part of that.

America is too civilized. What authentic people need in order to find their true selves is to be uncivilized. So they go to countries experiencing war, poverty, or violence. It's a modern version of the Western, that most American of genres. But instead of ugly stereotypes about Native Americans that are used to define, by contrast, the white American character, it's ugly stereotypes of South Americans or Middle Easterners or Africans. The setting is always vague. Your typical American wouldn't be able to find Colombia on a map, let alone tell you what distinguishes it from, say, Argentina.

The dawn chorus of accents throughout this film, none of them Colombian and yet all of them "Colombian" is just one part of that. The filmmakers know Americans can't tell the difference, let alone care, so any brown actor, South American or not, can be used as a stand-in.

Somehow the qualities that emerge in American men who are able to survive in these conditions for a week or so are never transferred to the citizens of the country who live there all the time. The Americans may show themselves to be gallant, courageous, and strong for trekking through the jungle or making their way through battlefields or evading certain death, but the people who have to live their lives around war or unrest or poverty are generally depicted as craven or stupid or unsophisticated.

Romancing the Stone also has the gender-flipped version of this masculine adventure story—a woman goes to a foreign nation to prove herself strong and adventurous and has a love affair along the way—that is so popular it keeps being retold, from *The African Queen* to *Out of Africa* (a lot of Africa in both gendered stories, it is always an easy stand-in for the undeveloped and uncivilized) to *Under the Tuscan Sun* to *Eat Pray Love*. The implication here is that there is something wrong with American men, either they are too dull or they want their women to be meek and small or they aren't macho enough. Women need to go overseas to find men to love them in the right way and so that they can come into their authentic selves.

In the end, the Americans get what they want. The woman finds love, the man gets a yacht, and each of them proves something to themselves and to others through their ability to survive a week or so in the Most Dangerous Place in the World. They go to the Underworld, the Heart of Darkness, the Edge of the World and come back with the riches they so justly deserve. And a lot of the Colombians die.

But at least all they were ultimately looking for was a little adventure. Have a little fun, take some photos you can post on Instagram, do some property damage, and get people wounded so you can feel alive again. Worse is the arrogance of the American who goes to a foreign nation, runs into some difficulty or maybe the place just doesn't look like the travel brochure that inspired his trip, and he starts thinking, "If I was in charge . . ."

When Jack and Joan's relationship grows stale, they decide to raise the stakes in *The Jewel of the Nile*. Joan Wilder decides she is exhausted from all the excitement, and she wants to accomplish something meaningful. "How much romance can one woman take?" she asks Jack, complaining that their lives are too full of sunsets and glamorous locales and true love. She wants to do "something serious," which for Americans often means meddling with other people's lives. She feels limited by her successful career as a romance novelist, and she wants to try some real journalism or writing something more substantial instead.

Luckily for her, a dictator with an eye for imperial expansion "on the Nile"—the word "Egypt" never comes up—hires Joan to write his biography. This is a chance to get out of romantic nonsense and into really important work and make a difference, despite having no previous encounter with this man or his country. It's the same impulse that leads young Americans to volunteer to teach English or build schools or dig wells for the "disadvantaged," rarely taking a moment to wonder if they should possibly learn the language or something about the country where they are going. It's the same impulse that drives some young men to join the military.

In the end she sees through the dictator and notices he is actually bad (thanks to the screams of a tortured prisoner who is for some reason being held in the presidential palace). So now it's up to her and her boyfriend to bring his reign to an end. A group of Middle Eastern men implore Jack to topple their tyrant and restore their one true leader. Jack doesn't speak the language, doesn't know anything about the region, has no local contacts, has no historical or cultural knowledge, has a fundamental misunderstanding about the project, and has not met any of the figures whose fates he is deciding. He has American gumption, and that's what matters. And he mistakenly believes he is going to be richly rewarded for his efforts, so the rest of it doesn't really bother him.

In the geopolitical time line, *The Jewel of the Nile*'s 1985 release date lies between the American involvement in the coup in Iran and the repeated conflicts with Iraq. The scenes where women are shown as oppressed by tradition and religion predate the feminist justifications for the invasion of Afghanistan and Iraq following 9/11 but come after the concern trolling international feminists did in Muslim nations like Algeria, imploring women to take off their traditional scarves—and the influence of patriarchal religion the scarves represent—and display their beautiful hair and bodies in the Western fashion.

The people in *The Jewel of the Nile*'s Tribes of the Nile live in a permanent ancient present, with no history to speak of. Meaning they have no universities, no politics, no intellectual tradition, no art. They have superstition instead of religion. Their prophesied leader is a clown, literally. The "Jewel," the leader our Americans help bring into power, is played by an American performer in the clown arts, made up in brown face and with a funny, indistinct accent. He does silly dances and tricks and delights the childlike Middle Easterners and solves all their problems (which are just "tribal" and not material, because, again, they are a people without history who can be manipulated and controlled easily) by making them laugh.

It's not so much that these films are propaganda, although it would be easy to read too much into them and start making parallels between them and the twentieth-century American habit of handpicking "clowns" to be the leaders of other nations, whether that be South Vietnam, Iran, or Afghanistan, and then being surprised when those leaders are rejected by the people they were meant to lead. That part of the American masculine experience is one of dominance and arrogance. There is no encounter with the Other here, the other is there to entertain or enrich or please the American man.

These acts of intervention and disruption are often done in the name of care. Joan gets involved with the plight of the tribes out of tremendous concern; Jack is just looking to get paid. But her sympathy eventually rubs off on him, and his desire to plunder and profit is overwhelmed by his desire to do good. It's much like the charities that were set up in Afghanistan after the American invasion, that built schools no one used, that were used to funnel money to international leaders rather than to locals, and that offered pretty photo opportunities to American volunteers and did no real material good.

Joan's and Jack's hearts are clearly in the "right place," but as Americans they can only engage with the world with sympathy and not empathy. Part of American exceptionalism is the belief that only Americans have gotten this nationhood thing right, and that the most important act in liberating the world or at the very least improving it is to make it as American as possible. Every other way of organizing a life, city, or society is at best misguided and at worst evil. Intervention, then, whether it is done by the military or the international market, is for the country's own good.

There is, of course, a small question here about why these films tended to do so well overseas. Everyone loves to be pandered to. Everyone screams when the rock star calls out their city's name, even though, if they thought about it for more than a second, they'd realize someone probably had to remind that rock star which city they're playing in tonight. Everyone loves the thrill of seeing themselves on-screen, even if it's under terrible circumstances. Everyone just likes being paid attention to.

In January 2017, Meryl Streep used the occasion of being awarded the Cecil B. DeMille Award for lifetime achievement at the Golden Globes to congratulate Hollywood on its inclusivity, its moral center, and its opposition to the Trumpian ideology of the newly elected president. By portraying the lives and truths of people different from themselves, actors are engaged in a heroic work. "We have to remind each other of the privilege and the responsibility of the act of empathy," she said. "We should all be very proud of the work Hollywood honors here tonight."

She was not, apparently, talking about movies like *The Jewel of the Nile,* where the producers used extras with a wide variety of ethnicities and nationalities to portray its Middle Eastern characters because they only saw them as brown. She didn't mention how many film studios take money from the Department of Defense to portray the American military as brave and forthright, creating propaganda for war and imperialism. She also left out the way Hollywood has in the past coerced and still in the present coerces its racialized actors to portray the worst stereotypes of their people. The Black men who played violent and menacing predators and criminals, the Black women who played hypersexualized addicts and losers, the Latinos who played drug kingpins and gang members, the Middle Easterners who played terrorists, the Asians who played martial art masters or sexless nerds.

For many Americans, entertainment is how we get our news about the rest of the world. An American who watches one Hollywood film about the Middle East, if not given contradictory imagery from other sources or personal experience in the region, can unconsciously refer to these images when picturing a place. If all one knows of the Middle East is one movie where the people are shown to be lazy, violent, or corrupt, then maybe when the news tells them America has invaded a nation in the Middle East, they think not about imperialism or corporate interests, they think about Matt Damon rescuing a child from a Middle Eastern terrorist. If they see a brief snippet of Colombian police officers shooting unarmed men and women protesting government corruption, they think about those Colombians probably being drug traffickers and guerrilla fighters.

The American man, juxtaposed against these brown and Black men, starts to look like the beacon of sanity and safety. The carrier of democracy and freedom. The liberator. So often when a person is down on their luck, their sense of self shaken by unemployment or divorce or illness, the last certainty they hold on to is their national pride. It's the chant of U-S-A, U-S-A at every ball game and every political rally, it's the active hostility to anyone who dares besmirch the name of our great nation, it's cheering for the explosion of bombs over nations we aren't even pronouncing correctly in conversation.

THE AMERICAN PRESIDENT:
FINDING MEANING IN THE DRONE BOMB

P eople don't like to admit it when they start to slip. They don't like to admit it to themselves, and they certainly don't like to admit it to others. That things just aren't going as well as they used to. Their star is not burning as bright, their luck has turned, that soft spot on the apple turned out to be rot that goes all the way to the center.

And most everyone has some experience with being around a person still intent on keeping up appearances, despite the obvious problems just beneath the surface. We call it a midlife crisis, or Divorced Man Energy. They've still got it, they insist. While everyone around them knows, is absolutely certain, that even if yes, one time it could be argued that possibly this man was in possession of it, at some point it slipped out of his grip. It fucked off, it ran off into the night, it fell through the hole in his pants pocket he kept forgetting to have mended. It's gone, it's not coming back, and the longer this guy insists it's still in his possession the sadder this spectacle is going to get.

America is in a period of decline. But instead of dealing with that fact, it remains in denial, lost in nostalgia. As Jed Esty writes in *The Future of Decline: Anglo-American Culture at Its Limits*, "The narcissistic goad of 'lost greatness' still resonates for many Americans, and not just right-wing patriots. . . . It resonates because Americans do not have access to a galvanizing alternative language for a common national purpose." Americans who were raised to believe their country is the best nation that has ever existed do not have the capacity to think about the potential of a world that operates outside of American control. Much like men have struggled to think about relationships with women where the women aren't subject to the men's will.

Instead, America is trying to suck in its gut, trying to disguise its alarming hairline, trying to walk with the same swagger it once had. It will do everything it can to keep reminding the rest of the world, hey, remember what I'm capable of, remember what I can do. But that fantasy originates in a brief sliver of time, from the New Deal to the edge of the Vietnam War. During that time, America dreamed big and it built big. It cared for its poor and vulnerable, it rebuilt Europe, it put men on the moon. Its leaders were men of towering greatness. Other nations looked to us for aid, for leadership, for guidance, for entertainment, and for inspiration. They did what we said, either out of fear or out of respect. To Americans, the difference between those two motivations didn't matter much.

And much like the former football quarterback still telling the story of his big save at the big game every time he reaches his fifth beer, we use that peak to avoid looking at the reality as it currently exists. Our golden boy tells that story so he won't have to notice his wife hates him, his queer son thinks he's embarrassing, he's not the big shot at the office, and no one else laughed when he mimicked the waiter's accent. The world has moved on. It doesn't need him anymore, at least not in the same way. But somehow that information is too excruciating to acknowledge, let alone adapt to.

Why is it so difficult for this guy to just admit his diminished capacity? Why can't he enter his age of decline with grace and elegance, why does he feel the need to impose his will, prove his prow-ess, take up as much space as possible?

But people don't tend to respond well to such dressing-downs. President Jimmy Carter gave his "Malaise Speech" about the "crisis of the American spirit" after a long run of economic, diplomatic, and military failures. America had gone years without a functional energy policy, as the nation continued to use more than it produced with no thought to the by then obvious imminent environmental collapse. It had failed in Vietnam, the extent of its crimes in Cam-bodia and Laos were just coming to light, and it had created a diplo-matic quagmire in Iran. America was in crisis, and its leader got up in front of the nation and said exactly that. That America's people had turned toward cynicism and consumerism over optimism and citizenship. The country no longer believed it was capable of great things, or perhaps it no longer had any interest in doing truly great things, so it refused to sacrifice or put in the difficult work necessary to accomplish things like a shift to renewable energy. The media went crazy over that speech and politicians made wild statements along the lines of: How dare he insult the honor and integrity of this great nation? How dare he call his own people lazy and greedy, how dare he impugn the military, how dare he suggest that America is doing anything other than what it was put here on the planet by God himself to do?

Carter didn't win his re-election bid.

"Americans can no longer afford to pretend they live in a great soci-ety." This is a line from the speech of the fictional American presi-dent Andrew Shepherd in the hit film *The American President*. It's the true American dream—our Michael Douglas character can ascend from the depths of the unemployment and mass shooter potential of *Falling Down* to *The American President*'s Oval Office. The film was released in 1995, more than fifteen years after Carter's speech, but the two addresses share a similar meaning. America has gone off-track, it has a "lost greatness" it must return to. Wisdom and strength are required to get things moving in the right direction again.

Between Carter and Shepherd (a fictional stand-in for the recently elected, not yet scandal-ridden Bill Clinton) had been twelve long years of conservative leadership. The Reagan and Bush presidencies had created an administration of nostalgia, as they romanticized the postwar boom times. The calls to "make American great again," which originally came from a 1980 campaign speech by Ronald Reagan, refer to this sliver of time when all the engines of American power—cultural, economic, social—were working together. If we can simply re-create the conditions of that era by jacking up the (white) birth rate, re-creating the racial, gendered, and sexual roles of the time, strengthening the powerful institutions of Christianity and the military, then America can recapture its glory.

Andrew Shepherd's administration is also nostalgic, but for a different era. The character is very much of the Michael Douglas mold—he is professional, cosmopolitan, educated, with liberal politics (vaguely defined). He has a Kennedyesque air to him, an East Coast and handsome version of Clinton. His administration longs for the ambitious days of the FDR administration, when the government did the right thing whether the American people wanted it to or not. Back when Americans didn't fight sweeping structural changes and a powerful leader was able to mold the world into the shape he knew was right. All that is needed to get us back to this place, the movie suggests, is another bold and intelligent father figure put into a position of power.

Two competing nostalgias, both powered by romanticized fantasies of what was accomplished and how the machinery of that era worked. The Reaganesque fantasy of the postwar era excises all racial strife and oppression, the burgeoning feminist movement, the monotonous and atomized hellscape of the suburbs, and the unacknowledged and untreated PTSD of soldiers who saw, experienced, and committed horrors during the wars of the era. The conservatives see only what they want to see, which is a strong, white nuclear family in a cute little house with a white picket fence.

Likewise, the nostalgia of Shepherd and his creator Aaron Sorkin (who would later adapt this film into his wildly successful television series *The West Wing*) clings to a rosy vision of FDR and the New Deal. This was the time of rising sympathy for Hitler's Germany in politics and society, the internment of Japanese citizens and the exploitation of their labor, and the development of horrific weapons of war. But all the liberals see is an erudite and sophisticated father figure guiding the unruly masses toward a better version of their selves with subsidized art programs, social welfare programs, and an overwhelming war machine.

Nostalgia is an active form of delusion, a story you tell yourself purposely to avoid seeing reality. This is why nostalgia takes over in times of great strife—it's a coping mechanism that tells us there were better days in the past, so surely there are better days to come. This is also why it's a useful political tool. It distracts citizens from the disappointment of reality and disguises political violence.

And the Reagan/Bush years were certainly a time of great strife, in more ways than one. Much the way the behavior of men and their mistreatment of women was becoming a mainstream topic of conversation with the rise of feminism's second wave, the post-Vietnam era had a lot of Americans asking a relatively new question: Are we the baddies? The origin story of the United States was being retold through different perspectives and in a different tone. Books like Howard Zinn's *A People's History of the United States* and Edward S. Herman and Noam Chomsky's *Manufacturing Consent* sent a younger generation buzzing with questions about the story of American exceptionalism and natural dominance they had been force-fed in school.

Has America misused its power? Has it committed war crimes? What about its history of slavery and genocide, are we really past that? Have our leaders done evil things to other countries that we don't even know about, like toppling foreign governments or stealing resources? Are the stories the government tells us about why we are running a military intervention right now a total fabrication? Is our enemy—the Soviet Union or "socialism" or Iraq—really as bad as they say they are? Is mass media complicit in the political propaganda that has created these false narratives? Is the educational system?

But questions like these are tough to bear after a while. "Have I participated in or celebrated atrocities committed in my name?" is not really something most people want buzzing around in their heads while they're standing in line at the grocery store checkout. After all, what is your average individual, carrying credit card debt and with high blood pressure and a sixty-hour-a-week work schedule, really supposed to do with this information? Easier to find a way to manage it, either by falling into cynicism, doubling down on patriotism (or antipatriotism and the belief that America is the greatest evil in the world and to blame for every bad thing that happens on the world stage), or deciding where you live is merely a minor detail that doesn't have any real influence over your life or any great meaning for you.

Another way to avoid these questions is to believe America (or masculinity) just needs to be fine-tuned. Get it a new outfit, refresh the wallpaper, maybe take it into the shop for an upgrade. It's not that the foundations are rotten. It just needs a facelift. Maybe some filler. Cue the makeover montage. This requires what Esty calls "restorative nostalgia," the fantasy that these things used to be better and uncomplicated, in some ever-shifting moment in the past.

Esty writes, "The melancholy and defensive belief that supremacy is an American birthright . . . is gaining ground in the US as hegemony ebbs. It encourages Americans to invest in past glory rather than work through a complex history."

One of the fantasies of the era of decline was that if we just got a different guy in charge of stuff, that would fix the problem. This was mostly a fantasy for the political center and left because this was the demographic most afflicted with the questions and doubts about America's history and future. When Reagan was in office, the fantasy was: What if someone else had overseen the AIDS crisis? Would fewer people have died? What if someone less warmongering had overseen the military and intelligence services during various conflicts in Central America and the Middle East? Would there be peace and stability?

Screenwriter Aaron Sorkin made a lot of money during this era providing entertainment to satisfy these fantasies, first with *The American President,* then *The West Wing,* and finally *Newsroom.* Sorkinland was a parallel universe where good leadership and intelligence and good intentions circumvented the great troubles of this time. His work was as nostalgic as the Reagan vision for a lost American greatness, it's only the content of that nostalgia that was different. And in the end, Sorkin invented a kind of nostalgia for a lost present, with misty-eyed eulogies for our lost potential. As liberal leaders watched their potential for greatness squandered by their political opponents, they fantasized about how the world of today could be different and created entertainment out of that nostalgia.

The two problems that are preventing Americans from having a "great society" in Sorkinland's *The American President* are gun control and environmental policy. Here, the right president can establish a mandatory reduction in greenhouse gases and our future is saved. It's not important to the film, or to many Americans, it seems, how this reduction is going to happen. There's no word on the specific policies or changes that will achieve this goal.

It is a world that is changed by a spell, through a magical edict. "Cap greenhouse gases" and they are capped. No one has to build a high-speed passenger rail system, no one has to give up their air-conditioning or deal with energy shortages in the winter, no one needs to fundamentally change the way Americans travel, eat, live, or communicate, it just happens because the president says so.

It's the same with his declaration that he's "coming for the guns." This was filmed a couple of years after Waco, during a rise of white nationalism and militia culture, but the president says people are going to have to get rid of guns and everyone cheers. And this is going to solve the problem of "crime," but how criminalizing individual gun ownership is going to lower crime rates across the board is not explained.

It's not so much about whether or not a Hollywood movie and a television show on a major network should function much like C-SPAN, giving a full (and tedious) look at how government works. The question is more about why the Sorkin properties were so overwhelmingly popular with both audiences and the media, and how they functioned within the American imagination. It's relevant not only because masculinity in the West is strongly tied to nationalism, but also because American nostalgia functions very similarly to masculine nostalgia. In both circumstances, the nostalgic are willing to overlook who was suffering in order to allow their demographic to thrive, and they carry with them a nostalgia for the lost present that would be possible had (insert women/immigrants/other demonized group here) not been allowed to take over.

One of the Sorkin fantasies is that there are good Americans and bad Americans. Much like there are good men and bad men, this idea suggests that in order to solve our problems with American power or masculinity, the solution is to elevate the good actors and diminish or punish the bad actors. These are the fantasies that propelled politicians like Bill Clinton and Barack Obama into the highest office in the land, as well as the justification for turning a blind eye to the way they wielded its power in destructive ways. This keeps the focus on the individual, rather than on the system that created them.

In *The American President,* an international incident interrupts date night between the president and his paramour, Sydney. Libya, he's told, has just bombed C-STAD, killing almost two dozen American soldiers. C-STAD is a fictional stand-in for the Iron Dome, a mostly American funded defense system for Israel that was operational a few years after the release of *The American President.*

President Shepherd must decide if and how to retaliate. American soldiers are dead. The refusal to retaliate would show weakness to and embolden an enemy. (At least our Middle Eastern nation has a name in this film.) It would reveal Israel to be vulnerable, and it's just sort of assumed that the audience will innately understand Israel's importance as an American ally in a hostile region without the need for a grandstanding speech.

It's a pivotal scene. "What you did tonight was very presidential," a staffer tells him solemnly. It's a scene meant to show the burden of power. To show our leader's great heart and concern. His empathy and strength demonstrate that he is a different kind of leader than the Republicans who were dragged into scandals like the Iran-contra affair. It's funny, though, that even if this good leader has a different haircut, different romantic proclivities, has different opinions about homosexuality (it's okay) and the French (they're great), a bunch of people who were just minding their own business in Libya still end up dead.

Nothing makes approval ratings jump like military action. Americans love it when people overseas are killed on their behalf.

Whether it's Bill Clinton bombing Iraq and Serbia to distract from his sex scandal or George W. Bush's approval ratings skyrocketing when he announced America would invade Afghanistan or liberal commentators declaring on social media that "this is the night Donald Trump truly became the president" when he bombed Syria, it makes us feel good and patriotic and righteous to exercise power. What is strength for, if not to make others bend to our will?

But whether a military action is right or wrong is often judged by who is ordering it. When a liberal administration assisted in the assassination of Libya's president Muammar Gaddafi, this was good, according to people who supported the president of the time. Because our leader is intelligent, sophisticated, reasonable, then this act must be all these things, too. But if our leader is the wrong leader, then committing the same act is obviously the wrong thing to do. The 1980s through the 1990s was a time of intense political polarization, which only accelerated in the new millennium. Both parties demonized each other, and whichever one you chose membership in was meant to broadcast something about your character.

In *The American President*, the wrong side is personified by Senator Bob Rumson, a mash-up of various conservative Christian ideologues of the era. In the first full scene we see with him, he's literally doing backroom deals with cigars and brown liquor. He's a stand-in for the old white men who defended segregation, withheld care from the gay community during the AIDS crisis, stood in the way of feminist progress, and preached righteousness while exercising hypocrisy. The type of man who said vile and hateful things about Hillary Clinton during her husband's 1992 presidential campaign. He is a moral vacuum, a barely breathing body with poll results in place of a heart, a pork barrel in his back pocket, and dollar bills for brains.

He is running his campaign against President Shepherd on the platform of "traditional family values" and speeches about how

"the pride is back" (not very catchy, admittedly). It's not even that
he has sincerely held values or beliefs that might make his desired
aims different from Shepherd's; it is that he is duplicitous, power
hungry, manipulative, and craven. If he bombed Libya, the viewer is
asked to consider, he'd do it in the wrong way. Or he wouldn't feel
bad enough about it. Or he'd take it too far. The idea that America
shouldn't be bombing Libya at all, that we have destabilized the
Middle East through decades of misguided policy and thought-
less intervention, that Americans perhaps shouldn't get to decide
whether Libyans live or die, doesn't really come up in the film or in
much of the media discourse of the era. The political polarization,
then, hasn't created different political agendas or different ideas
about how the world should be. But each side has created fantasies
about its enemies across the divide, and each side blames the other
for why things have not improved.

Near the end of *The American President,* speechwriter Lewis Roths-
child, played by Michael J. Fox, confronts President Shepherd about
his reluctance to take a stand on a particular issue.

"People want leadership, Mr. President," he tells him, "and in the
absence of genuine leadership, they'll listen to anyone who steps up
to the microphone. They want leadership. They're so thirsty for it
they'll crawl through the desert toward a mirage, and when they
discover there's no water, they'll drink the sand."

The president responds, "People don't drink the sand because
they're thirsty. They drink the sand because they don't know the
difference."

This is a bizarre and insulting way to think and talk about the
electorate. It's also another sophisticated dodge. It's a point of view
that suggests the average person doesn't know what they really want.
That they must be guided, in a paternal manner, into believing the
right things, wanting the right things, behaving in the correct way.

That they are children in need of a strong controlling hand, to encourage them in the right directions and steer them away from the wayward path.

This was an essential part of Sorkin's entertainment properties, and while it's not surprising that this might be the thinking of powerful people of the era, it's strange that it became so popular among viewers. But then, of course, the people who loved these movies and shows were often people who agreed with the center-left politics of the characters written by Sorkin; part of the pleasure was probably believing the characters expressing disdain for the childlike citizens were talking about their political enemies, not them.

It might be insulting to think of grown adults as children in need of instruction and correction, but this mindset also offers easy solutions. Those questions you might have, about America's role in the world, about the legacy of evil acts, about why there is war and poverty and racism, they don't need answering. Nothing is truly broken. We just need to choose the right leaders, assign the right reading material, cast movies in the right way, and we'll be back on the side of good again. This is top-down politics, which treats structural issues as personal problems. This is why the Clintonian era of dismantling social welfare programs coincided with a hard push into university education. If people failed to thrive under the administration's policies, it would be because they didn't go to college, didn't apply themselves in high school, weren't ambitious enough to get a business degree instead of trying to make do with work in the factories or the mines.

This is very similar to the commentary about how boys just need better role models to become good men. It's not that the problems of masculinity have their origin in the political, economic, and social changes we've detailed throughout this work; it is simply that men are "toxic." And if they consume pornography or radicalizing alt-right YouTube videos, that's a personal problem that can be corrected on a personal level (i.e., they need to be redirected to the right viewing material and that will solve their problems). If larger solutions are needed, it's simply that certain people need to be deplatformed, algorithms need to be redesigned, and content needs to be restricted to keep our impressionable youth from falling under the sway of masculinity influencers and right-wing content creators.

The American President was released about halfway through Bill Clinton's first term as president. There was still optimism for what the return of the liberal imagination could accomplish in a powerful position. This was before his disastrous military interventions in the Balkans and Iraq. It was before his disappointing backsliding on things like gay rights, healthcare reform, and environmental protections. And it would be years before the consequences of his tough-on-crime policies or his dismantling of food aid programs for single mothers would be widely felt and understood. So the nostalgia for the present of *The American President* is gentle in comparison to what would come in *The West Wing* or *Newsroom*.

In the Sorkin properties that followed, the tone became more hectoring, the monologues more arrogant, the grandstanding more dramatic. This is what a leader is, this is the policy that is needed, these other ideas are all wrong. And much in the same way that young viewers of *Wall Street* were inspired by Michael Douglas's character to go into finance, people who would eventually become staffers for the Obama and Biden administrations credited these Sorkin shows with inspiring their career path. That they were confusing drama for real life and a warped vision of politics for the legislative process didn't seem to matter.

In an interview with Errol Morris for the 2003 documentary *The Fog of War,* former secretary of defense Robert McNamara discussed his military career during World War II. He had been part of the team whose job it was to decide strategy against Japan. When regular bombing campaigns over military targets failed to have the desired results, McNamara said, the decision was made to use incendiary bombs in urban areas. A hundred thousand people died in Tokyo in one night. In other cities, the equivalent in population and development to American cities like Cleveland, Chicago, Memphis, and others, the majority of the infrastructure was destroyed. The civilian casualty toll was enormous and unprecedented in a war between two nations. McNamara says very clearly, "I was behaving as a war criminal." And yet in the history of World War II, in the big splashy Hollywood films, in the stories told by veterans, survivors, and politicians, there was little to no mention of the firebombing of Japan, or the similar destruction waged against Germany. McNamara remembered his superior General Curtis LeMay telling him, "If we'd lost the war, we all would have been prosecuted as war criminals."

Japan was widely seen as both the aggressor and the loser in the war. Japan had attacked America first, and at the end it surrendered and admitted defeat. That makes America both victim and victor. And when you're assigned these roles, it just so happens that whatever you had to do to survive and win doesn't really get questioned. But, McNamara asks, directly into the camera, "What makes [something] immoral if you lose and not if you win?"

One wonders, then, if the inability of American masculinity to admit its failings and its state of decline is, in some part, a fear of being held accountable. If there is an admission that America is not number one, that the American self-image is in some crucial ways a lie, then will America be hauled in front of a tribunal and asked to explain? Even if the nation admits that it is no longer part of a "great society," it was, *The American President* insists, and can be again. The scramble to get back to the top of the hill originates in a fear of what is waiting at the bottom.

This might also be why the solution to injustice and inequality is so frequently about empowering those who were previously marginalized. If people are pulled up, no one has to fall downward. What if America puts a woman in charge? Or a Black man? Someone gay? A Muslim? Would that make it okay then? Anything to delay the realization that it is the unquestioned and unchallenged power that is the problem, not the person sitting behind the desk.

Which is a bit like the frantic posturing of today's modern men. What if men cry now? What if they go back to wearing really good suits? What if they're sensitive to multicultural issues? What if they return to the light of God? What if they have elaborate facial hair? What if they're socialists now? Or communists? Or anarcho-capitalists? What if they're into crypto? What if they're geeks instead of tough boys? Tough boys instead of geeks? Geeks who lift? Tough boys who do jiujitsu? Soft boys who cry while doing jiujitsu? What if they refuse to watch football because organized sports are "fascist"? What if they're fascist? What if they post pictures on Instagram of themselves taking care of their children? What if they have a family to support? Then is it still cool to be in charge of things? And tell everyone else how to live, dress, work, behave, fuck, eat, communicate, make money, and love?

Imagining what a humbled America looks like is the same project as imagining a humbled form of masculinity. A figure who does not misuse his power, who accepts his place within an ecosystem rather than trying to dominate and control it, someone who gives way, someone who consumes only as much as they replace, someone who sees the rest of the world in a way other than as a supermarket of pleasures and treasures on offer and they're standing there with a pocketful of cash—it's difficult to imagine what that is even going to look like.

There is an obvious solution on the table. What if those sliding into a decline looked to those around them, those who never (or at least not within the time of the written record) occupied the top position, to learn how to do things differently. This is the problem of the impossibility of solidarity. People do not want to feel solidarity or identify with people of lower status than themselves. This is the agonizing disappointment with every project of inclusion. Straight men prefer not to align themselves with queer men. White feminists prefer not to align themselves with Black feminists. Cis women prefer not to align themselves with trans women. And Americans prefer not to align themselves with South Americans, Africans, Eastern Europeans, Asians, and so on. Doing so would require humility and admitting their position, which is an intolerable proposition.

As much as certain patriots and patriarchs have tried to convince us otherwise, that sense of dominance was always artificial. It was always based on coercion and violence. The patriarchy has generated self-serving myths of a god-given order to things (and when that didn't work it swapped out god for nature) with the patriarch always conveniently placed on the top. And then they used the fear of an impending chaos that would follow the destruction of the hierarchy.

This inability to humble oneself, to stand down, to face the reality of diminished powers seems to be a defining characteristic of contemporary masculinity. It generates defensiveness. But the humbling will come.

the patriarch falls

In the mid-nineties, as the peak of the Michael Douglas era was coming to a close, Michael Douglas movies offered two visions for the future of the patriarch. In the first, as shown in the film *Disclosure*, a man dissolves into a bilious froth of resentment and rage that the world no longer accommodates only him. His confusion about why nothing operates in the way that he expects curdles into resentment and disappointment, and he stubbornly refuses to adapt to changing conditions.

This version of masculinity is immediately apparent in the politicians who have been trying to roll back feminist advancements like abortion access and marriage reform, while deploying images of the traditional nuclear family in a "look at what they stole from you" form of manipulation. It's also in the masculine influencers who tell their followers that their failure to thrive is the fault of greedy women who will lie and cheat to get what they want.

In the second vision of masculinity's future, a man does the ridiculously difficult work of constructing a new identity after shedding the restrictive patriarchal exterior like a reptilian skin. He sees the past as something that is holding him back from real connection, true feelings, and an authentic sense of self. But he undertakes this journey as an individual, and he has the resources needed to hire the support staff necessary to bring him over to the other side. It's a false binary, but it does line up with how we think and talk about men today. Either they are bad men (incels, misogynists, bigots, contributors to rape culture) or they are good men (attentive fathers who contribute equally to domestic labor and always ask for consent when coming in physical contact with women). The bad men are men who have not "done the work." The good men are men who have "done the work."

What the work is, how it might be undertaken, what the results might look like is never fully explained. Therapy? Maybe one of those *Stoics for Dummies* books.

When women needed to "do the work" to liberate themselves from patriarchy, they had a whole industry willing to help them. There were philosophers and self-help columnists, consciousness-raising sessions and political advocacy groups, nonprofits to support women leaving abusive marriages and families or women entering into higher education or women getting ahead at work.

But because men have not wanted to conceptualize themselves as a gender, only as individuals, and because expanding their selves past these stiff patriarchal roles has not been seen as a legitimate goal, there is very little social or cultural support to help them address these issues as a group. Unless, of course, it's run by a charlatan who promises to make their followers into "real men" by teaching them how to pick up girls or make more money.

Not that there haven't been a few efforts. There was the mythopoetic "Iron John" movement in the 1990s, when men gathered in the woods to get in touch with their primal masculine selves by dancing around a fire and banging drums. There was the men's liberation movement of the 1970s that was tied to feminist ideas, but got twisted somewhere along the way and transformed itself into a conservative, anti-feminist group that wanted reinforced, hardened gender roles. The problem of solidarity re-emerges. When disempowered people gather, they find strength in shared experiences and power in organization. When empowered people gather, even if the project is voluntary disempowerment, they, too, seem to find power in organization.

This leaves the task to the individual, who might find it difficult to manage the discomfort of self-interrogation, go astray when seeking out guidance, and decide it simply isn't worth the bother to try to meet all these new and confusing social expectations. After all, what is the reward for these drastic changes?

There's no consensus about what a good new man even looks like, as an archetype. Does he co-parent in his marriage, or has he rejected marriage and the nuclear family as patriarchal institutions? Is he a great leader in his work, or should he have refused the position of power to allow a woman to take the high office? Is he a champion for the poor, or is that just mansplaining? There's a creeping suspicion about men who are deemed good men. What if they are simply bad men in disguise? What if under that façade of equality there's lurking a transphobe or a power imbalance in their relationship or a racist joke? A good man must continually re-establish his goodness daily.

As the institutions that helped to create and sustain patriarchy transformed themselves, the economic, legal, and social changes that removed the protections that had kept power in the hands of men were at this point mostly complete. And yet, there was no evidence of these changes in men's culture. There was no big *New York Times* exposé, no one created organizations and nonprofits to fill the gaps, there were no self-help manuals printed by *Esquire* or underground literature focused on illuminating the new world for boys and young men. They were left adrift and no one even seemed to notice.

Now masculinity was a personal problem. If you failed to become a good man, that was a matter of character, not a result of structural change. And while commentators started to bemoan the absence of good role models, or to throw any seemingly decent famous guy into the role as a model for young men to emulate, there was, for a long time, a fundamental misunderstanding of what was happening.

As professor of law Leigh Goodmark has noted throughout her work on the failures of the carceral response to domestic violence, there is not an image in American culture of a reformed abuser. There is an image of what a "wife abuser" or "woman beater" looks like, which is often overly reliant on classist and racist stereotypes. There is an image of what a "battered woman" looks like; she is often more passive, more pathologically damaged than real women who have experienced violence in their intimate relationships. And there are some ideas about intervention—the police are called, or the woman goes to a shelter. But other than prison, which often doesn't do anything to address the underlying issues and can indeed make a man more likely to offend once he returns to his home, and despite domestic violence continuing to be a very serious issue and one of the leading causes of death for married women, we have no idea how to turn a man who has abused his partner into someone who will not.

That is not to say that once a man hits his romantic partner, that's it, he is forever a domestic offender. But there is no immediately recognizable system in place to address the issue. There isn't a therapeutic regimen in widespread use for men who are abusive, there aren't resources for them to access—shelters, social workers, hotlines—in the same way that there are for women who have been abused. The reasons for this can only be speculative. Once a man has wandered over the line from respectability into criminality, he is frequently seen as disposable. Prisons are not rehabilitative, they are about punishment if not outright torture. Men who abuse were often abused or witnessed abuse in their childhoods, but there is no reliable, affordable system for therapeutic intervention with child victims. The failures of America's child protective services are well known and well documented. Often the specific social shame related to victimhood with boys and men prevents them and their caregivers from seeking help. And the social causes of domestic violence—and Goodmark has demonstrated that economic instability is often a triggering factor in abuse cases—are not top priorities for the political class.

When it comes, then, to the reformed man, the best anyone can seem to come up with is "I worked on myself," which turns a social problem into something embedded in the individual, who must go through some sort of mysterious and hidden alchemical process described in vague, therapeutic language about getting in touch with feelings or having to encounter one's dark side. People without the money and time to go take drugs with a shaman in the desert or go into years of one-on-one therapy have no recourse. There is no visible path to reform.

A lot of men who would have thrived under a more strictly patriarchal culture are flailing now, and that is because they are being left to their own devices to decide how to become a better man, or to discover what being a "better man" even means. *Disclosure* shows a man abandoned in this way in his workplace, as the old-fashioned patriarchal goals of business other than profit (pride in work, creating a quality product, advancing technological knowledge) are thrown over in favor of pure greed. His inability to acknowledge the changes and see the true culprits causes him to lash out and self-destruct.

But there is a second vision for the future of masculinity within the Michael Douglas canon. *The Game* is an antidote to this, pushing a man past his defensiveness and panic to a place where he can thoughtfully engage with the social and familial pressures that had convinced him that this limited version of a man was the best thing he could be. But in the end, this is a personal, individual journey he undertakes, and the audience is allowed to see only the deconstruction and not the final result. The question remains unanswered: What does a good man look like?

And while other groups adapted to the new reality, because they had spent decades building the support systems that allowed them to flourish, the man faltered. He stuttered, he got stuck. He fell.

There's a moment in watching *Disclosure* when the viewer might be thinking, "Um, excuse me? Sir? Sir, it is 1994." Maybe if it had come out in the early eighties a film like this would be acceptable. Maybe. But to come this late in the Michael Douglas Project, this late in human development even, starts to feel unforgivable. It's not just that there have been three waves of feminism by this point, multiple campaigns for racial equality and civil rights, and the beginning of the push for the expansion of marriage and protections for queer relationships. It's not only that art and film have begun to expand their boundaries to include and tell the stories of people other than straight white men and that figures like Kurt Cobain and Eddie Izzard have been showing up on the covers of magazines wearing dresses and redefining masculinity for the masses.

It's that this story of a man getting passed over for a promotion that instead goes to an undeserving woman relies on old and silly stereotypes about gender, business, and violence. It's a film not meant to entertain or enlighten but to rant loudly at you, up close, the spittle misting your face as you try to turn away.

The Anita Hill testimony about being sexually harassed by Clarence Thomas, who went on to become a Supreme Court justice, was a turning point in our culture, even if the immediate results were disappointing. Women felt newly emboldened and empowered to speak up about the abusive treatment they had suffered in workplaces. And people in workplaces were being forced to have difficult conversations about how things might have to change to create an environment where women workers felt not only included but secure. Even if only because of the looming threat of legal action or a scandal in the media.

But there was also a certain kind of man watching all these changes happen in front of him who, instead of responding with curiosity and flexibility, chose to dissolve into a bilious froth while screaming, "But what about me???" And that sense of entitlement and anger dates the film badly. For a movie about a technology company working on virtual reality and talking about the future of connection and communication, even upon its release the film felt unpleasant and passé.

But that's what grievance will do. It causes a person to retreat instead of advance. It ages a person prematurely, and a person trapped in their grievance will get left behind as society advances. But grievance is also a big business. And not just for men.

In 1995, a white woman named Jennifer Gratz was denied admission to the University of Michigan School of Literature, Society, and the Arts. In 1997, the same thing happened to a white man by the name of Patrick Hamacher. The university used a points system to determine acceptance, and each of these applicants had come up short. Certain facts about a student's education, upbringing, and activities, such as SAT scores or extracurricular activities, were designated a specific number of points. Had they crossed a certain threshold, they would have been admitted, and they each had failed that barrier. However, if they had been of a certain underrepresented minority or ethnic background, twenty points would have been added to their score and they would have surpassed the minimum and been allowed to study at the institution.

Together, Gratz and Hamacher decided to sue the university with the assistance of an organization called the Center for Individual Rights. It was a test case, meant to challenge the legality of such considerations in the effort to diversify the racial makeup of university student bodies. These standards had widely been put in place in the 1970s, as educational and corporate institutions tried to figure out how to adapt to changing expectations. If previous standards of admission and employment had been biased, due to unfair barriers certain demographics faced earlier in life, then there had to be a way to hedge against that.

This was part of what was widely called "affirmative action," and these new standards of merit weren't in place very long before various groups, mostly conservative organizations, tried to dismantle them. The *Gratz v. Bollinger* case eventually made it to the Supreme Court, where it was decided that such regulations were legal. But there were more challenges and lawsuits to come, and a continuing debate began about merit, fairness, and who deserves what and what metrics to use to measure that.

This process was meant to correct for the patriarchy and to assist in its dismantling. The education system, among other institutions, had been built by and for men. The elite education system, which includes universities and private schools, was built by and for a small subsection of men, the wealthy, mostly white, property-owning men.

One way of restructuring these patriarchal institutions for a postpatriarchal world was to design them for not just elite men but for the "deserving." The patriarchy would be replaced with the meritocracy. But the result of these reforms has been even more inequality, rather than less. Less social mobility, less opportunity for the disadvantaged, and a greater gap than ever before between the classes in opportunities, salary, and even markers like life expectancy and the amount of pain a person will experience in their lifetime. In Daniel Markovits's *The Meritocracy Trap,* he writes, "Today's meritocrats still claim to get ahead through talent and effort, using means open to anyone. In practice, however, meritocracy now excludes everyone outside of a narrow elite." Opportunities that were said to be made available to everyone, the most deserving recipient being designated through open competition, somehow keep going only to the rich. Much like how, previously, those same opportunities were blatantly reserved only for the men.

These decisions are still unfair, but they are unfair in a new way that is more difficult to identify. A person who has abilities and assets and skills that would make a useful contribution to a university or to a workplace but is not given the opportunity to make those contributions because they are deemed unworthy will struggle to understand their exclusion. Is it the fault of the system, which claims it is blind to color, gender, sexuality, and class and yet seems to favor one of those markers above all the others. And if it is the fault of the system, what are they to do about it? Or is it the fault of the person from a marginalized demographic, who is given an advantage that seems unfair. As Markovits puts it, "Meritocracy frames this exclusion as a failure to measure up, adding a moral insult to economic injury."

With fierce competition for opportunities that have a real material effect on a person's well-being and place in the social hierarchy, there will be a lot of people disappointed that their lives are not going to turn out the way they imagined. There will be nasty swipes about the "diversity hire" and the "quota kid." And there are also a lot of organizations, influencers, and entertainers who are more than happy to take that disappointment and harden it into resentment. The disappointed Michael Douglas in *Disclosure* is Tom, whose hard work is about to be rewarded with a promotion and a business merger that will greatly enrich him. People wander around the office making grand pronouncements about the "$100 million" to come. Instead, the position he expected to be his is taken by Meredith, a much younger and slicker figure who has, the movie suggests, climbed her way to the top through sexuality and beauty rather than merit. "She doesn't know the difference between software and a cashmere sweater," Tom complains, which isn't even a good joke, but his male co-workers all chuckle along.

Meredith then, in her new position of undeserved power, sexually harasses Tom and "nearly rapes" him. It's an upsetting scene not because of its depiction of sexual assault but because of all the heavy breathing and slurping sounds. "You wanna get fucked?" and so on, a very silly depiction of sexy times. He manages to escape from her clutches, to flee before the attempted rape becomes successful. Meredith then makes a false accusation of sexual assault against Tom to inoculate herself from his accusation against her, but because this time the victim is a man and the harasser is a woman, no one believes him.

Meredith shows up to a deposition to record her account of his sexual assault and lies prettily, feigning fragility and vulnerability to make sure all the men in the room pity her and feel compelled to take care of her. This is pretty typical MRA stuff, the idea that women are constantly falsifying accusations of abuse, assault, and rape in order to manipulate authorities and unjustly punish men to get what they really want (money, power, custody, revenge).

All of this is done in the name of pointing out that, Hey, women can be bad people, too. But Meredith is not a realistic depiction of a powerful and dangerous woman; everything she says and does in the film seems to come directly from the feverish fantasies of a certain kind of man. She swings from one misogynist stereotype to another with barely a moment to catch her breath in between.

Tom's boss announces Meredith's advancement with a speech that references his deceased daughter. Had she lived, he tells his employees, she probably never would have had the opportunity to run a company, due to sexism. That's why he's so proud to put another woman in a position for success. But, of course, none of this can be true. A world in which Tom, who is honest and good and doesn't hate women at all, doesn't get what he wants is a world that is fallen and corrupted. It is a world of conspiracy and greed. It is a world that must be investigated and made right again, so the people who deserve good things get them.

He's not against the advancement of women, as long as it happens in a way he approves of. And if it's not happening in the way he likes, then that must mean there is a vast conspiracy working against him and all that is good in the world. His job, then, as a white man, is to reveal the corruption and put the world right again. This would be a noble cause were he not so blinded by his grievance. If, in the middle of an argument with his wife, he didn't yell, "Why don't I just admit it? Admit that I'm that evil white guy everyone is always complaining about?"

Somewhere between affirmative action and the current day, it became obvious that taking a space that has been built specifically for one small group of individuals and transforming it into a space that is populated by pluralities requires an adjustment rather than simply inclusion. And as evidenced by the lawsuits and media coverage of childbearing women being driven out of the workforce and racism in corporate culture and the problems of navigating disability or health problems while employed, this adjustment is an ongoing process that requires imagination and input from all parties.

It is not just offices that have to change. In Caroline Criado Perez's book *Invisible Women: Exposing Data Bias in a World Built for Men,* she gets into the specifics about how much of the public world was built for the average male body. Medicines, urban design, the safety features of automobiles, and even the standard temperature of public buildings were all constructed around the accommodating and protecting of the average male body. Yet a car that is built to save a man's life might, in an accident, take a woman's life. A medicine that is tested on men might affect female biology differently. Having just one limited idea of what a body, a life, or a soul might need turns out to have harmful effects on everyone who deviates from that narrow norm.

It's not only women who suffer from this expectation, of course, but also men who diverge from the "average." Disabled men, homeless men, men with chromosomal abnormalities, men who are mentally ill, men who have sex with men, men with criminal records, and men with religious obligations are all men who in one context or another suffer from their inability to meet the standards of the designed world.

Building a world that is fair to all, then, means taking what has been unconscious as far as expectations and bias might go and making it conscious so it can be reconfigured. It's too much to ask one gender or multiple races or people of different faiths to constantly carry the burden of unforeseen consequences. To constantly be forced to accommodate one small demographic rather than having their own needs accommodated. Some of those demands for accommodation are going to be unreasonable, sometimes what one group thinks they need in order to be accommodated actively blocks another group's accommodation. There have to be methods of planning for the future that are not mired in constantly relitigating the past. Marginalized groups can have their own forms of grievance culture.

But the men of *Disclosure* resist the idea that the workplace might have to change to adapt to the presence of women. If women want to be in the public space, then it is the women who should change. The men should be allowed to make the same sexist jokes they did in all-male spaces—it's women who have to learn how to take a joke. The men should be allowed to create the same cut-throat competitive atmosphere where people are expected to work all night long and go without seeing their families—if women can't balance work and family they'll have to make a decision. The idea that maybe the men themselves would benefit from flextime, work from home options, or a less sexually charged environment never arises.

Disclosure doesn't deny the existence of sexual harassment. In the film, Tom's wife, Susan, is designated the "good woman" (maternal and accommodating, with no expectations that the world will change for her) in contrast to Meredith's "bad woman" (ambitious, manipulative, barren). Susan nastily informs Tom she's dealt with sexual harassment her entire career, but she does what women have "always done." She ignores it and moves on with her life. She doesn't make "a federal case out of it." Perhaps this is what the men who wrote and produced and directed the film think women should do. Adapt to the world as it already exists and move on. And indeed, the way Tom wins in the end is not through the legal action he threatens to take against the company, but through the usual masculine triumph of hard work and gumption.

Tom's first reaction when his assistant accuses him of creating a hostile work environment as he ogles her legs and casually slaps her ass is one of defensive anger. How dare she betray him in this way. How dare his intentions be misinterpreted. (And the work environment is worse than that, with multiple male colleagues making jokes referencing female workers' bodies and erections. One can guess that if Tom's assistant had complained about that, the retort would have been that she needs to learn how to take a joke.)

When Tom is asked if maybe the allegations that he sexually harassed Meredith instead of the other way around were true, he responds, incredulous, "Sexual harassment is about power. When did I have the power?" He doesn't seem to see that when he, for example, slaps his assistant's ass or laughs at a male colleague's joke about his erection in the presence of a woman he supervises, he has power over their ability to complain or leave or ask him not to do that. In order to avoid taking responsibility for the power he does wield in his life, he throws up his hands and claims total helplessness.

Unfortunately, much of this conversation has been taking place through the language of "privilege." Privilege is a rather clumsy and misunderstood way of trying to calculate the various levels of power in any group of people. The accusation of privilege is often wielded as a weapon rather than used as a tool, and it relies on gross stereotypes of identity markers. For instance, it's often assumed that a white person is always going to have more power than a Black person because of "white privilege," but while there are many situations in which that is frequently true—including interactions with police or bureaucracy—there are many contributing factors that quickly erode any racial privilege. Issues like mental and physical illness, income and housing security, education level, region of origin, employment history, relationship status, gender and sexuality, and immigration status all have a real effect on how people are able to function and how they are treated by others. Many of these mitigating factors also happen to be invisible or deceptive.

Being accused of having privilege in the form of an inherited advantage in the world often puts people on the defensive. America still has a powerful fantasy about the self-made individual, with a distaste for the aristocratic. And yet that is still how money, power, and influence works, even in America. Families accumulate wealth, businesses, and access, and these are distributed downward through the generations. But because the model of American success is the started-in-the-mailroom, walked-ten-miles-to-school, began-with-nothing-now-we're-here bootstraps narrative, any reference to nepotism or inheritance can damage the fantastically generated self-image.

It's an interesting role for our Michael Douglas figure because of what he has represented on-screen before taking this role. He has played, repeatedly, figures of great privilege. Lawyers, men of finance, detectives. And his character was written by Michael Crichton, a wildly successful writer whose books sold in the millions and were adapted into films by the likes of Steven Spielberg and Philip Kaufman. And yet now here these men are, complaining that the world is working against them, that they are at a disadvantage.

Many activists who have spoken or written in the hopes of drawing attention to the identity-based discrimination a particular demographic faces have become mired in one recurring conversation. This is a common complaint among feminist, anti-racist, and queer rights spokespeople, especially those who operate online.

The conversation goes like this: The activist attempts to state a problem of discrimination that has been backed up with research and easily accessible statistics. Take for example the statistic from Stop Street Harassment that approximately 80 percent of women report having experienced sexual harassment over the course of their lives. Then someone will interject something like this: "Well, what about men?" And it's true, which maybe the activist admits, that according to the same study something like 40 percent of men have also experienced sexual harassment, but that is only half the percentage of women. Women also report experiencing more material harm from that harassment, their pathways to advancement closed off, mental or physical health problems developing from the stress, and a loss in productivity and pay. Also, when men experience harassment, it is more often at the hands of male supervisors. Mean-

ing, men are by far more likely to be the abuser in a sexual harassment claim, no matter what the gender of the victim.

The activist is simply trying to state in a clear way the disproportionate problems that come with being a member of a specific racial,
sexual, gendered, or religious demographic. Bringing attention to a
problem and having it acknowledged as such is often the first step
in a long process of creating systems that counter that problem. But
instead of moving forward from awareness to action, the effort gets
mired in denials and defensiveness. And here we are talking about
men again, rather than what to do about this information. The
result is wasted time, on both sides.

Watching *Disclosure* is like experiencing a two-hour version
of this conversation. "Well, what about men?" say the men when
a woman says she's having a problem. What about my problem?
When are we going to talk about me again? If Tom had social
media, he would probably be typing #notallmen in response to a
feminist's Twitter post about the way women have been mistreated,
objectified, sexually harassed, and assaulted in the workplace.

The motivations of this conversation are clear, even if the person doing the instigating is unconscious of them. The protesting
men are trying to avoid the information that these problems are
structural rather than individual. If the world actually is set up to
disadvantage whole groups of people, it would require substantial
changes to rectify that. And if things do change, that might mean
that, after the changes, their position might decline. They might
have to question whether they deserve what they have acquired in
life. But there is also fear that maybe the sacrifices they made to get
by weren't actually necessary. Maybe they were like wolves who got
their paw caught in a trap and gnawed it off to escape right before
someone came to rescue them. And if they had simply waited, they
would still have their injured paw, instead of a bleeding, painful

stump. It's safer, then, to think of these interventions as unreasonable or an exaggeration, and to think of the people making these claims as weak and trying to create an unfair advantage. It's safer to the psychological integrity of the individual to reject the conversation entirely. This is the primary message of grievance culture: Do not accept your suffering. Every discomfort, every moment of confusion, every pounding headache caused by being confronted for misgendering someone or the use of an offensive word or phrase or touching someone without their consent, that is something you should not have to experience. Instead of using that discomfort and anxiety as a cue to rethink and adapt, grievance culture tells the offender they shouldn't have been made to feel that way in the first place. The victim is making the decision to take offense, they've decided to let it bother them. It's their actions that are unreasonable.

Grievance culture replaces discomfort with anger, to the point that the anger becomes a part of someone's personality. Instead of figuring out how to move forward, they hold their anger close. Anger is nurtured instead of interrogated. Grievance can cause a person to refuse to participate in the world until it meets their exact political, ideological, sexual, or social expectations.

And because patriarchal culture is harder and harder to participate in, because as we've discussed previously the benefits that used to be distributed through men are now reserved for the wealthy, grievance culture looks appealing to the struggling man. There's a huge blank space between these two cultures, one where adaptation and progress feel possible, but unlike with patriarchy and grievance there are no posted rules in this middle space. And the ability to flourish there often comes down to a matter of luck.

It's been sixty years since the beginning of affirmative action. And it's been fifty years of organizations trying to undo, undermine, and destroy those measures. Of dragging attorneys back to the courthouse again and again. Of drafting legislation that doesn't have a chance of passing. Of trolling for disappointed men and women and convincing them that instead of moving on with their lives and adapting to changing conditions, they should professionalize their hurt feelings. Make their disappointment the problem of everyone around them.

One wonders what they as individuals could have accomplished with those sixty years had they decided to give way rather than grow defensive and combative. One also wonders what could have happened if those who got trapped in grievance had directed their anger and outrage toward the institutions rather than one another.

In order to take root, grievance culture requires two things. The first is a competitive rather than a cooperative mindset. It's the shark mentality, eat or be eaten. It's the financialization of everything. It's Gordon Gekko, "lunch is for wimps," and so forth. Rise and grind. In that way of thinking, everyone is a competitor rather than a collaborator, and any assets that one group has will look like an unfair advantage. (It's why it's so important in *Disclosure* to portray Meredith as undeserving with the unfair advantage of her good looks and sexuality; in this way, it's easier to show Tom as just a good guy in a bad situation and Meredith as the usurper.)

The second requirement for grievance culture is a false sense of scarcity. These two ideas, competition and scarcity, feed off each other. That scarcity is generated by institutions. It's the corporation that gives CEOs $20 million bonuses while laying off thousands of workers. It's the university that limits admission based not on need but in order to increase the desperation to get in.

This dynamic creates animosity between groups, but it's particularly effective at getting hatred flowing downward. When the ground someone is standing on is unstable, it's going to piss them off to see someone else climbing up from below to join them. Men experience it with women, heterosexuals with queers, whites with

Blacks, cis with trans, and citizens with immigrants. And maybe that's enough to distract them from asking why the territory they've been given is so paltry and unstable in the first place. Grievance culture is different from racism, misogyny, or other forms of discrimination, although it often wears the same outfit.

Tom would insist he's not a bigot, as would just about every single Michael Douglas character. "I'm not a misogynist, but . . ." The "but" being, there are good women (the wife) and bad women (Meredith). There are women who "deserve" inclusion and those who are not competing fairly. In this way, Tom isn't against progress as long as it happens in the way he expects and accepts. As long as it doesn't disrupt his plans for how his life should look or how his business should operate.

Women keep telling Tom their stories. They, too, have been harassed and manipulated and abused and misused. They have found the promotions they rightfully earned given to undeserving peers. They, too, have been silenced and threatened. They offer Tom their condolences and companionship, while his male peers express exasperation and disbelief.

But Tom doesn't form a bond with these women. He doesn't think in terms of solidarity. He is instead horrified to find himself in the position of the woman, a common experience for Michael Douglas. Rather than thinking it's a problem that so many of the co-workers and women in his life have this shared experience and that it might mean there's something structurally wrong that needs to be addressed, he merely struggles, hard, to return to the position of unsullied masculinity under patriarchy. In the end, sexual harassment and mistreatment are not things that need to be understood as fundamental problems with hierarchical structures. Nor is there something wrong with the possibly unconscious and unexamined way men have been encouraged to see their women colleagues not as peers but as sexual objects, disapproving mommies, or children to be ordered around and pitied. Instead, it's a problem with this boss, this individual, and once they are ousted the whole ecosystem can go back to a state of balance.

While all of this is happening, Tom is being haunted by the ghost of unemployment, a sad and bitter middle-aged man who rides the ferry with him each day. He gave his life to this business, he tells Tom. But now the women are coming in and pushing good, hardworking men like him out. He doesn't say this directly, but he makes sad snipes about Tom's female assistant, and how she is probably gunning for his job. The women are climbing up from below, and they're going to take what naturally belongs to the men.

Grievance culture in America is overwhelmingly associated these days with Donald Trump. And both Trump and grievance are often associated with the white and rural poor. But it often looks a lot more like Michael Douglas. When you consider the demographic breakdown of who voted for Donald Trump and participated in the January 6 insurrection, it wasn't the poor. That demographic voted for Trump consistent with the numbers it had voted Republican for decades. One of the broadest bases of new support for Trump, clinching his election, came from the semi-professional. The disappointed. The middling. The people for whom things worked out okay but not to their full expectations. They were entrepreneurs who didn't have the regional dominance they had dreamed of. The middle managers and the third best salesperson this quarter. The students who didn't quite get into the university that was their first choice.

These leaders of grievance all say the same things: The world was great when it treasured and rewarded men. Now that it doesn't, at least not in the same way, there is something wrong about it. We must return it to its natural state.

Marginalized communities spent a lot of time and resources creating mentorships, scholarships, literature, and cultural materials to help facilitate their assimilation into the institutions of power. White men did not do the same because those institutions were always supposed to be for them. They were supposed to operate in their favor. Now that that is no longer exclusively true, men seem lost. They are more likely to drop out of high school and university, their achievement levels have dropped, and they are being outnumbered in professional accreditations.

White men still dominate the powerful positions within those institutions. At universities, white men are the dominant demographic of tenured professors, deans, and presidents. In corporations, white men outnumber every other demographic on executive boards, in CEO and vice president positions, and at the top levels of the hierarchy. White men are still mostly in charge of religious institutions, mass media outlets, and the justice system. And yet at the lower levels, younger men of the middle class and below are failing to gain a foothold.

THE GAME:
BRINGING PATRIARCHS BACK TO LIFE

Throughout this book, we've discussed the suffering of men under patriarchy and the necessity for men to create an identity outside of its limitations and restrictions. But how? Alas, there are many people online who are very eager to issue instructions.

Go to therapy. Oh, you can't afford it and your health insurance doesn't cover it? Or your job slashed your benefits, so you don't have health insurance at all? That just shows you're not prioritizing this and taking it seriously. Because even though we think men should be different than they are, we also think it's good for them to have traditional traits like being successful and rich. Okay, maybe be more like this celebrity who seems friendly in five-minute interviews he gives on late-night talk shows. Or this other celebrity who is always nice on his own well-produced Instagram posts. Or this celebrity, who said this one thing that one time about how it's important to express your feelings, he seems great. Oh, he what? He actually got arrested for punching his wife? That's surprising! Okay, not him, don't be like him, but the other ones are still okay. So far.

How about your reading material? No, not that book, that book itself is fine but the author said something weird about women once so now all of his books are bad. Here's a list, we can give you a list. Try Viktor Frankl's *Man's Search for Meaning* and then read *The 48 Laws of Power* . . . oh, who liked that one? Oh, he's bad, so the book must be bad. Maybe skip that one. You should definitely read some books by women, though, you need to take women seriously. I don't know which ones, there are a lot, I am not here to do your work for you!

You should definitely be healthy. Eat well and exercise, stop taking the Alex Jones supplements, maybe take these Goop supplements instead. The ingredient list is exactly the same, but it's important to support rich women more than rich men. Don't go to jiujitsu, there are rumors jiujitsu studios are red-pilling all their followers. And don't lift weights, an obsession with physical strength is just part of toxic masculinity, maybe try running instead. Or take a ballet class. I'm sorry, did you just say a ballet class would be a great place to meet women? Are you even taking this seriously?

Learn how to cook, it's important that a man know how to cook and will share in the domestic labor of the household. But it's really suspicious if a man likes meat, but also vegan men, there's just something kind of weird and feminine about a vegan man, so you should probably eat meat but, like, not too much.

What about your family? You should love your dad, but you should also think of him as a terrifying patriarch who ruined your life by instilling these corrupt values in you. You can hang out with him, but you should also hate him and the world he helped to create. And then you really need to look at his relationship with your mother, I mean, he was five years older than her when they met, that is just a shocking power imbalance. Your father basically raped your mother. It totally doesn't matter if they've been together for thirty years and are still in love, that is really messed up that he did that.

Speaking of relationships, how is your love life? You really need to stop being attracted to women who are shorter, younger, less educated, or a different race than you. That's a power imbalance, and that's a huge red flag. That's basically the same as rape. You can't date women who make less money than you, are from a lower economic class than you, work in a less lucrative field than you; you need to be exact equals. If you're attracted to richer, more powerful, older, or more successful women, you must really have some intense mommy issues and you should go to therapy for that. You should split the bill on dates because that's feminism but then you should always pay the bill on dates because historically women make less money so it's up to you to compensate for that.

Sex is also really tricky territory. You should masturbate, because we're really uncomfortable with the NoFap guys, we think they might be incels, but you shouldn't use pornography for that unless you are watching feminist pornography that centers the woman's pleasure. You can't pay for sex workers because that just means there's something wrong with your relationship to women and you just want to dominate them and order them around but you should definitely still support sex workers and give them money for GoFundMes because they are a really vulnerable group in our society. If you're having sex with a woman, you should never ever choke them, unless they want it and ask for it, because that means they're a strong independent woman and you should give them pleasure but you shouldn't like doing it.

You should be religious, kind of. Atheists are bad and they are all misogynists, but if you're really devoted to any of those patriarchal monotheistic religions like Christianity or Islam that means you think women should be enslaved by men. Spirituality is also bad, because that one yoga guy turned out to be a rapist. You shouldn't think it's weird or pathetic when a woman is into astrology but also you shouldn't be into astrology because that's cultural appropriation of women's spirituality practices. Maybe get into meditation, David Lynch was into meditation, and he's still on the list of good

men but we are actively looking into his history to see if there's anything bad there, which means you would have to give up meditation
to prove you care about the treatment of women.

Deep breath.

Trying to escape from toxic masculinity in today's society
becomes a deranged Choose Your Own Adventure where no matter what you decide or which page you turn to you end up falling
into the mouth of the volcano. There's no choice you can make,
no option to choose, no path to follow that doesn't immediately
become fraught.

In the 1997 film *The Game*, our Michael Douglas figure seems to
have been distilled into its purest form. All the facets he's performed
in the movies before are revealed to be part of the same crystalline
structure. The wealth of *Wall Street*, the personal failures of *Falling
Down*, the broken marriage of *War of the Roses*, the woman trouble
of *Basic Instinct*, the authority and power of *The American President*, the daddy issues from all of them. Here Michael Douglas is
MICHAEL DOUGLAS™.

The release of the film was timed perfectly to depict the way
the power structure of the world was changing—or had changed.
Here we have the end of the patriarchy, as shown by the fall of the
last patriarch, the Michael Douglas character Nicholas Van Orton.
Even in the small details, we see how the values and the mission of
patriarchy, both good and bad, have gone away. What the powerful
men of *The Game* are saying and the ways in which their conversation seems from another time marks the change in both the values
of the ruling class and their methods.

For example, the businessmen in *The Game* make reference to
attending the opera—one of the duties of patriarchy was the maintenance and belief in the vital importance of the high arts. It was
done grudgingly, maybe with a groan, but support of the arts was

still an obligation. The new wealthy and cultural stewards feel no such obligation, and arts programs have been closing down all across the country at an alarming rate since the fall of patriarchy. The rich are adorned in beautiful outfits, in well-tailored suits with subtle but expensive details like signet rings and watches. Michael Douglas mentions how much his Italian leather shoes cost him after one of them is chewed by a dog. The men who will replace Michael Douglas will come wearing hoodies and jeans, with a contempt for the responsibility of looking nice in public spaces. They will still feel the need to signal their wealth to the people around them, with clunky gadgets and ostentatious cars, but their dress will be pointedly slovenly and disrespectful.

These patriarchal obligations and responsibilities have become a shell, and the men underneath them need to emerge, soft and vulnerable like cicadas crawling out of the underworld and shedding their exoskeletons. Nicholas Van Orton has no sense of self outside of the identity that was provided to him by the patriarchy. It's very literal for him. His father built an empire, and after his father's death it was his obligation as the eldest son to take over the business and familial responsibilities. He has used his father as an example of how to be a man in the world, never questioning or rebelling against what he had learned.

And like his father, who committed suicide by jumping from the roof of their palatial San Francisco home, Nicholas has been made miserable by this way of life. (And "palatial" describes not just the size but the structure—the house would not be out of place in any other tormented story about the troubled father and son relationship, whether told by Henry James or by Victor Hugo. There is a separate structure for the domestic servants and a gate to keep out the peasants.)

Now Nicholas is the same age—forty-eight—as his father had been when he died, and there's great concern among his family and friends that he might be headed down the same path, that the burdens of patriarchal responsibility might break his psyche as well. But Nicholas has no way of stepping outside of the role he is playing. Things are "working" for him. He might be divorced and cranky and lonely but in the ways that matter to men—financial success, business reputation, social status—things are going well. This is the real midlife crisis, lurking under the fantasy version that Michael Douglas played in films like *Black Rain*. It's not a rejection of the obligations of domestic life, it's a real suffering from his inability to participate in them. It's feeling the intense absence of an emotional self, and a powerful incapacity for relationship. There is nothing in his life that brings him joy or pleasure or meaning, he is the empty suit, the Willy Loman who made it big but was still unhappy.

By contrast, his brother, Conrad, was very young when their father died, meaning Conrad did not grow up under his influence. For him the father was always a ghost, never an example. He didn't follow his father's strict rules, because they weren't real for him. So he drifted, from school to school, from drug to drug, from high to low. He asks his brother for money occasionally, or maybe to get him into a rehab facility. Unlike Nicholas, he is a failure in all the things that supposedly make a man. No job, no money other than inheritance, no empire, no social status. At an exclusive restaurant, Conrad tells Nicholas he had been there before. Nicholas assumes they had dined there together. But as Conrad clarifies, he sold drugs to the maître d'. Yet there is one way in which Conrad is superior to Nicholas. Everyone likes him. He's emotionally open, he's sweet and funny and has a sense of humor about his failings. No one likes Nicholas, and it's more important to him to be respected and feared. But everyone lights up around his little brother.

It's Conrad who introduces Nicholas to "the Game." It's billed as a little adventure, an expensive diversion for billionaires who have become bored with the usual entertainments for the very rich. The yachts, the expensive resorts and hotels, the VIP experience at the world's most exclusive restaurants and clubs. The Game is tailor-made to each individual's exact interests and needs, turning the city around them into an exciting mystery to solve. The line between the Game and reality quickly becomes blurry, and whether this is an elaborate con, a radical therapeutic treatment, or just one man spinning into schizoaffective disorder remains tantalizingly uncertain. But the Game has other ideas. By creating an alternate version of reality around Nicholas, utilizing his friends and family to create the illusion that his world is falling apart, they drive him relentlessly into a state of crisis. They are going to break Nicholas apart, in order to surgically reveal whatever might be authentic or special about him underneath all of his daddy issues. The Game is going to forcibly remove the patriarchal influence from his life, even if it kills him. It's going to turn him from a man into a human being.

And this is how they do it. It's like a road map to restoring the soul of lost men and guiding them out of patriarchy into authenticity.

STEP ONE: RECONTEXTUALIZE THE FATHER

Nicholas clearly believes the roles his father played in business as an investment banker and in the family as the patriarch were essential. They are so essential that it doesn't seem like he even considered any other possibilities for his own life other than to do what his father did. Continuity is key. He becomes the man of the house after his father's death, despite still being a child. He takes over his father's firm. He becomes his little brother's protector. And he doesn't question his inheritance, like, say, whether he still needs this big old house despite being a divorced man with no children. Or whether he still needs to employ his father's domestic staff. Or whether he has to have not only the same career but the exact same job as his father.

His path follows a very old-fashioned way of thinking about legacy and patriarchy. It's the thing of monarchs and emperors. The father manages the empire, the son replaces him as emperor. His only job is to protect what his father created, and his father before him, and to expand it in order to leave something even better for his own son. Nicholas as the eldest son took over his father's business, his father's role within the family, the family home and estate, and he even took over his wardrobe, wearing the same kinds of suits and the exact same watch. He even took his father's name.

The first thing the Game does for Nicholas is say to him: Hey, man, your dad was a clown. They place a figure in the driveway where as a young boy Nicholas saw his father's dead body, but instead of being a mannequin or a dummy it's a life-sized doll dressed as a clown. Your father wasn't noble, this gesture is telling him. He wasn't doing great things, he wasn't a towering figure, he was a fool who thought it was better to die than to change the way he was living. And this is your model for how to live your life?

We don't see Nicholas's father as a character; all we know of him is a few images from a nostalgic series of silent home movies. He is withdrawn and preoccupied, disconnected from his family. He is always walking away from the camera. Given the timeline, he would have been of the so-called Greatest Generation, the generation that went to war, saw and/or committed atrocities, and then got shipped back home and told to forget about it. The familial, societal, and cultural pressure on a man like that to earn money, start a family, become a success would have been immense. And yet when he cracks, that's a personal failing. A personality defect. Nicholas asks, anxiously, Am I like my father? He wants to be and yet he doesn't want to be. He can't help but be.

Since the sixties, there has been a way of thinking about and talking to our mothers and the women who raised us about how they felt about all that. If they wished they had done something different, made other choices. There is a whole intellectual sphere to recontextualize the unfair pressure put on women to satisfy certain societal roles and instead give women the space to think and feel and talk and make changes. That work was done almost entirely by women. But there is no corresponding way for men to talk to or about their fathers in the same manner.

When Nicholas's younger brother confronts him, saying that no one ever asked him to become their father, Nicholas shouts back, "Did I have a choice?" He truly believes he had no other option.

STEP TWO: SULLY THE EXTERIOR

Men's status is made legible through their exterior presentation. It's in the way we label men's level of success, blue collar versus white collar. (The invention of "pink collar" to designate women's support and care work doesn't really say much about women; it only really functions as an insult to men who take on the nursing or teaching or secretarial labor traditionally performed by women.)

Michael Douglas shows the world who he is and how he expects to be treated by the way he dresses. As Nicholas, it's old-fashioned but extremely well-made suits, the finest Italian-made shoes, the perfectly crafted briefcase, the signet ring and the wristwatch of old money and inherited status.

He demands deference and respect. And everyone at the private club, his office, his gym, and in his social life is happy to meet that demand. Until the Game intervenes. A waitress spills red wine on his suit and refuses to apologize. His pen leaks ink in his shirt pocket. A dog steals his shoe. His briefcase breaks. He gets grease on his jacket climbing out of an elevator shaft. Again and again he is stained, muddied, torn, and sullied. And the world stops treating him the way it used to, because the visual cues are missing.

Men's appearance under patriarchy is limited because it is a method of communicating with the world. It's a uniform way before it's a form of pleasure or play. It does so much unacknowledged work, holding an incredible amount of meaning. A certain knot in a tie tells everyone (at least everyone who also speaks that sartorial language) that the wearer had someone in their life to teach them to knot their tie like that. It announces who their fathers and mentors were, it can even signal where a person went to school. (A lack of a tie says just as much.) The shoes are there merely to tell everyone how much money the wearer has, whether they are wearing handcrafted leather loafers or limited-edition sneakers. Accessories announce the wearer's relationship to tradition—are these actual heirlooms passed through the generations, or is this obviously new money, or is someone running away from tradition by abandoning significant markers like cufflinks and wristwatches, or is someone trying to re-create a connection to the past that isn't authentic by wearing knockoffs or nostalgic reproductions of the patriarch's wardrobes? A person's outerwear tips everyone off to whether they spend any amount of time exposed to the elements and whether that exposure is necessary or recreational.

People remark upon the lack of variety and fun in men's clothing, but that's part of the point. The lack of experimentation and diversity in a man's wardrobe should be understood not only as a masculine trait but also as a limitation on what the world really wants from men. The world wants men to be only a couple of different things—either a man who works with his hands or a man who works at a computer or a man who works in institutions of power, and a person picks their clothes to tell the world which thing they are.

To strip a man of his wardrobe's language is to render him dumb. The world doesn't know what he's saying, so they don't know how to address him. And rarely will the world listen to the words coming out of his mouth, because how can the world interpret what he is saying without the context of the external surface? Nicholas's trashed clothing starts to disconnect him from his old life. He's no longer recognizable as himself. Which also means there is finally the possibility of becoming something new.

STEP THREE: KEEP HIM FROM WORK

The workplace is the man's domain. His place in the world of commerce and service defines who he is. "What do you do?" is the introductory question of the patriarchal world, so significant that in early patriarchy a person's job became their last name—Baker, Shoemaker, Brewer. He thinks of how he is doing by gauging how he is doing at work. Work is men's escape from the uncomfortable confines of the home and it is where he builds his social realm and his reputation. Severing that connection means forcing redefinition.

The Game mostly accomplishes this with petty inconveniences. An interview runs over, forcing Nicholas to cancel or delay other meetings. It keeps him up late at night, causing him to oversleep. It sends him on useless errands, picking up various items like his credit card and his briefcase from different locations. It puzzles him so his mind is elsewhere. It steals what he uses to conduct business to delay, interrupt, and bother him.

Job loss affects men in a different way from how it affects women, statistically speaking. With men, the loss is more existential. He's invaded by dread and anxiety that surpass the usual concerns about where money or health insurance or food is going to come from. It attacks the core of masculine identity, especially its standard form in the family man, as breadwinner and provider. A man's descent into violence or criminality is often precipitated by his loss of work. If he's not his job, who could he possibly be?

STEP FOUR: TAKE HIS MONEY AWAY

Money is a medium through which men interact with the world. But, like many men of means, Nicholas uses his money as a method of keeping the world at a distance. His house is located behind a gate. He dines at his private club to avoid the social mixing that might happen at a bar or restaurant. He waits for his flight in the first-class lounge instead of at the gate with other passengers. There's no one in his life, except for his brother, who is not on his payroll. His closest friend and confidant is his attorney.

The rich have always separated themselves from the rabble. They live on the top floors of buildings, they buy private islands, they have castles with moats and guards. Money acts as a shield. Money frees them from the morals, the expectations, and the company of the masses. That exclusivity is built into every daily activity, whether it's the VIP section of the club or the private jet or the executive bathroom or the private chef and private shopper and private driver. The rich fear the intrusion of anything novel, anything unexpected.

Without his money, Nicholas is forced to interact with people. He has to ask people for a ride. He has to go to the embassy like any other helpless tourist. He has to ride the bus. He has to call his ex-wife to borrow a car. He is no longer watching the world pass by through the window of his private car, he is in the mess and noise and populace. He's just another person again.

STEP FIVE: MANAGE THE SPIRAL

The consequences of this method have to be managed by the Game carefully. A man humbled gets himself a gun. (Nicholas pulls his gun out of a hollowed-out version of that Good Patriarch fairy tale *To Kill a Mockingbird,* a gesture that is itself worth several dissertations of symbolic unpacking.)

The kinds of pressure under which Nicholas finds himself—financial, business, reputational, romantic—are the "contributing factors" that inspire mass shooters, family annihilators, and anyone who engages in acts of spectacular violence. It's the ghost of D-Fens haunting *The Game.* Men who define themselves too greatly by the roles they play in the realm of business, family, social standing, or other external markers of success to compensate for the absence of an internal sense of self will, once those roles are threatened, try to compensate for their loss of self by annihilating other selves. Men who lose their job will often get a gun. Men who lose money will often get a gun. Men who lose face will often get a gun. Men who lose their wives will often get a gun. Michael Douglas loses all of these, and, of course, he gets a gun.

It's not helpful to get too far into the weeds as far as the "symbolic surrogate phallus" goes with all this gun talk, or even to pontificate about how an America in decline has decided to arm itself on an individual level as a mass event. But a man in crisis is prone to lashing out. It's a last ego-protective measure to make a mark on the world before going out, even if that mark is just blood splatter.

The Game provokes this response—crisis is just another word for opportunity, is it a breakdown or a breakthrough blah blah blah—and then must manage it in order to protect both Nicholas and the people around him. The first person Nicholas shoots is his brother, because a man who goes off to shoot strangers or enemies will often start by killing the people he loves most. That everything

that happened is a fantasy, from the loss of his money to the killing of his brother, and that it was all done in the name of making
Nicholas Van Orton a real human being again, enables Nicholas to
change. Finally.

But in the end, here is Nicholas, broken and vulnerable, forced
into a tender encounter with his community. And it took only
somewhere around a million dollars, a hundred or so paid employees of the Game, and an entire network of colleagues, family members, and friends to make this happen for him. As well as one very
alluring woman.

The only reason Nicholas allowed what the Game was doing to
him to happen was because of the mysterious and alluring blonde
leading him around like the white rabbit in *Alice in Wonderland*.
From *Bringing Up Baby* to *Something Wild* to *Forces of Nature*,
it's a recurring fantasy in film that a carefree and wild woman will
arrive and transform a straitlaced man into someone who can feel
and love. Or maybe it's not a fantasy after all, but rather the role
that many women take within a heterosexual relationship. It keeps
men from having to take responsibility for their inner development,
and it keeps women as less than autonomous beings. After all, these
women aren't wild and free for their own sake, they are just muses
and inspirations to the man who needs help loosening up.

It's a bit like the real-life billionaire Elon Musk telling his then-
girlfriend Grimes that he believed she wasn't real, that she was in
fact a simulation he created to be his perfect companion. If a man's
companion isn't real, her emotions, desires, identity, hopes, failures,
and disappointments are also not real, they are just there to add a
little variety to the central figure's life.

We know nothing about the blonde in *The Game*. She provides
different names, different backgrounds, and conflicting information about her role. She says she is midwestern, but she speaks with
the deliberateness of someone who has at some point unlearned an

accent. She is an actor, there to speak the necessary lines to keep the action moving forward, to lead or to push Michael Douglas into action. She needs no interiority if her entire job is to transform herself externally to keep her man interested and entertained. Michael Douglas becomes curious about who she really is only after he's been broken down and is in the beginning stages of being rebuilt. Only then can he see who she might truly be.

One reason this type of woman is a common fantasy and a recurring figure on-screen is that her role is one that many women have played through time. But especially now, as men drag their feet on incorporating into their worldview the changes that feminism and the assimilation of marginalized communities have wrought. These women are often there, pleading, teaching, nagging, begging, enticing. Spending their time trying to convince men to feel their feelings, engage with their children in a meaningful way, live a life outside of the narrow patriarchal expectations, be good partners. And Christine/Claire/Blonde, whatever this mysterious woman's name is, does this instead of living her own life. But at least she gets paid for her "emotional labor." A lot of women don't. And a lot of women are victims of men's difficulty in adjusting and giving up patriarchy's protections and comforts—murdered by husbands, victims of mass shooters, raped and abused, careers ruined by powerful men. Somehow the burdens for dealing with men's patriarchal traumas often fall on women.

The Game shows that making the adjustment from a patriarchal to a postpatriarchal society requires a bit more than finding the right role model and fixing some troubling and toxic behaviors. It's psychological, it's social, it's economic. And the world simply doesn't have the resources to Game-ify every single man currently living. Most men can't afford to hire a company to swarm their lives for a week or two, most of their family and friends have other things they'd prefer to be doing.

The film doesn't show the results. There is a broken, vulnerable man who has hit rock bottom and is now ready for real, sustaining change. But the story is left with a dot dot dot. He still has all that money, he still has that house, he still has employees and clients and a social calendar and family. Will he actually change, or will he relapse? Will he find the constant renegotiation and making conscious what was once easily, even if destructively, unconscious too difficult to manage?

This will be a recurring trope in Michael Douglas films that come after *The Game*. The dot dot dot. A man is in the process of transformation, but the screen fades to black right as he emerges from his cocoon. He gets into a taxi and off he goes, out into the world. What does a reformed man look like? Enter shrug here. If a man is "good" in a film, generous or kind or comfortable with feelings or capable of vulnerability or a pillar of his community, he is a singularity. He just is that way. Institutions and societal structures didn't shape him to become that, it's something in his character. He's fully formed, he's good.

The only male character who gets a whole redemptive or recovery arc in entertainment is the addict. The trajectory of that storyline is told so often that it has become a cliché. First the good times, then the dark times, then rock bottom, then the intervention or the plea for help, then the rehabilitation, then the struggle for reintegration and accountability.

But the so-called bad men of the world—the murderers, the rapists, the wife beaters, the patriarchs, the businessmen, the pimps, the tyrants—don't get redemptive arcs because contemporary culture does not seem to know what that would look like. Our imagination has its limitations.

. . .

For a long time in our entertainment we celebrated the renegade and the rebel, the uncontrollable genius and the rule breaker without considering what it's like to live around someone who won't take "no" for an answer. It turns out that living around someone who doesn't abide by laws, norms, and safety regulations isn't very pleasant. But also, what's lying behind the arrogance and antisocial behavior is very rarely misunderstood genius—dig under the surface of swagger and you're likely to find insecurity and incompetence.

So how does someone transform grandiosity into humility? Aggression into strength? In a culture that has given up on reform and instead prefers punishment and banishment, we're left with a multitude of "bad actors" with no new parts to play. Their stories dead-end into a dot dot dot.

welcome to
the postpatriarchy

By the late 1990s, the institutional supports of traditional patriarchy had, one by one, been dissolved. What replaced them was sneaky and amorphous, resisting clear definitions and labels. A lot of phrases get thrown around, most of them inadequate or confusing. Postpatriarchy, late capitalism, technocracy, oligarchy, a neoliberal hellscape . . .

It looks like a meritocracy, but that's not how it functions. It's a system that gives advantage to the already wealthy and has allowed the middle class to erode and protections for the lower classes to disappear. It's an era of increasing income inequality, lower life expectancy, and environmental collapse.

Thomas Piketty writes in *Capital and Ideology,* "Every human society must justify its inequalities: unless reasons for them are found, the whole political and social edifice stands in danger of collapse." Under patriarchy, the reasons men were placed at the top of the hierarchy and women were restricted in their ability to interact with the public realm had to do with women's inadequacies. They weren't as intelligent, they weren't logical, they had betrayed Adam and God in the Garden of Eden.

One of the reasons patriarchy failed, then, was because these reasons were shown to be false. Women could be educated, and they thrived in fields like science and technology where it was once assumed only men could function. Women could run nations, philosophize, program a computer, compose a symphony, and all the rest of it. It took a while, but once the justification for women's subjugation was proven to be false, it was inevitable the system would collapse.

But what came next was not the meritocracy or the free and equal society some suspected had to follow patriarchy. The hierarchy that structured society and the distribution of resources did not crumble; it was just rearranged. Piketty continues: "In today's societies, these justificatory narratives comprise themes of property, entrepreneurship, and meritocracy: modern inequality is said to be just because it is the result of a freely chosen process in which everyone enjoys equal access to the market and to property and automatically benefits from the wealth accumulated by the wealthiest individuals, who are also the most enterprising, deserving, and useful." The implication is also that if you are lacking these things, it can only be your own fault. How does one go about proving that those with the most wealth don't deserve it? No wonder people get stuck in grievance or trapped in hustle culture, trying to prove they deserve to be part of the elite.

Patriarchy is over. What we have now is worse.

In the years before, during, and after World War II, American patriarchy's golden age, psychologists were curious about what made people behave in the ways that they did. There are clearly social norms, but how did they arise? Are these behaviors logical or illogical? Are they conditioned responses—meaning, did people learn through social reward that certain behaviors were desirable and others undesirable—or are they instinct? If they are conditioned, can we condition humans to behave differently from the way they do now?

Simple reinforcement taught test subjects to repeat behaviors. The lab rat solves the maze, he gets some cheese. The pigeon presses on a lever, he gets a food pellet. But scientists could also induce illogical, irrational behaviors in their test subjects, simply by randomizing the distribution of reward and severing its timing from the behavior of the animal. Which is how B. F. Skinner and his assistants made some pigeons superstitious.

Skinner placed pigeons in the same boxes he used to teach test subjects to press a lever to get a food pellet reward. This time, however, the box was designed to send pellets on a random schedule, completely independent of what the trapped pigeon might be doing. They discovered that whatever the pigeon was doing when the pellet appeared, they would repeat that action in the hope of being rewarded with another pellet.

The birds were trying to control the behavior/reward setup. If it so happened that the bird was bobbing its head up and down when the food pellet appeared, the bird would continue to bob its head up and down, convinced this was the desired behavior that would bring food from the unseen source. If the bird happened to be flapping its wings when the food pellet appeared, the bird would continue to flap its wings.

Skinner wrote in his report, "To say that a reinforcement is contingent upon a response may mean nothing more than that it follows the response." The bird becomes programmed, if you will, only by the coincidence of action and reward. It only understands the timing of the connection, not the other factors like the desires of the laboratory staff or the functioning of the gadgets. It can't see beyond its own needs and desires to theorize what is happening.

This experiment has been used to explain primitive belief systems and magical thinking, from the ball player who refuses to change his underwear while the team is on a winning streak to the young woman who continues to visit and pay the psychic who correctly predicted she was about to meet a lover. When good things happen people try to control fate and make those good things happen again by creating superstitions.

This also explains the status of men in the postpatriarchy. Once, certain behaviors were granted certain rewards. The results were, for the most part, predictable. Young men who behaved in ways that made them "marriage material" to the culture in which they belonged mostly ended up married. Barring early death, war, or economic crash, if a man met the standards expected of him, his reward soon followed. That role and reward would differ based on a man's class, race, religion, place of origin, and so on, but the community around the individual man taught him what to expect from his life.

But now, a young man can be handsome, college educated, have a decent job, be personable and hygienic, and yet still a romantic failure. A man can go to a good college, have the right accreditation and certifications, and yet still fail to establish himself in the career he has chosen. A man can participate in his community and still be isolated and lonely.

The patriarchal connection between behavior and reward has been severed. This has made superstitious pigeons out of men. Flapping their wings, bobbing their heads, trying to get that food pellet, certain that there must be a reason for it, the answer must be here somewhere, the right combination of steps and gestures and vocalizations that will make the pellet come. Some of the pigeons will turn against the machine, say the reason that it's not working the way it should is because of feminists or gender confusion or cultural Marxism.

The men are told they will be rewarded with love, community, money, quality education, and meaningful work when they deserve it. But there are no visible markers, no metrics that will tell a man

WHAT IS WRONG WITH MEN

whether he's getting closer to his goal. Or if he's even moving in the right direction. The tools that he needs to become the man who deserves the things he wants—therapy or mentors or teachers—are elusive. And even if he goes into a shocking amount of debt to get the college degree he's told he should have to get a job that isn't in a factory that will either shut down four years later or injure him to the point that he needs opioids to function, he may still find people telling him it is his lack of other, less tangible things—gumption or grit or ambition—that are keeping him from finding employment in his field.

Michael Douglas the character stopped being a dominant force in movies following *The Game*. Postpatriarchy stories didn't really have roles for patriarchs. Michael Douglas became a marginal figure, either part of an ensemble, with supporting rather than leading roles, or the star of lower-budget, less successful films.

This fallen status of the Michael Douglas figure in the postpatriarchy tells us how big this shift really was. Much like masculinity itself, Michael Douglas looks lost in many of these films, past his prime, uncertain how he fits into the changing world. He's falling behind, he's drifting alone, he has no guideposts to put him back on track.

The social norms and institutions that used to tell him how to live a life are no longer invested in him. Despite past success, he's not wealthy enough to matter to the new order. Despite showing up on many Sexiest Men Alive lists, he's no longer heartthrob silver fox status. He has no heirs or protégés, eager to learn at his knee, he has lost cultural relevance and financial buying power. He is a man in decline. Meaning, he is a man.

TEACHING MICHAEL DOUGLAS TO LOVE:
AGE GAPS, POWER IMBALANCES,
AND OTHER HETEROSEXUAL INDIGNITIES

It's never a great idea to remake a Hitchcock film, but the *Dial M for Murder* update *A Perfect Murder* seemed particularly cursed. With Michael Douglas taking over the role of the older husband and the Grace Kelly–in–waiting Gwyneth Paltrow playing the unfaithful trophy wife, the filmmakers had forgotten, perhaps, to update the gender dynamics to meet the new era along with other details like wardrobe and characters' occupations.

Because what would have once gone unquestioned—the romantic pairing between one of Hollywood's most famous male actors and one of its hottest young starlets—suddenly became an issue. This age gap wasn't just a norm, it was tradition. Studios were clearly trying to launch Paltrow as a nineties waifish version of Grace Kelly or Audrey Hepburn, and hadn't Grace Kelly been matched on-screen to great acclaim and swoony admiration with Jimmy Stewart and Bing Crosby? Hadn't Audrey Hepburn been cast as the love interest of significantly older men like Cary Grant and a creaky Fred Astaire? No one had made a fuss even a few years before when Douglas was cast against the significantly younger Sharon Stone in

Basic Instinct. Producers, the director, and studio executives probably had no idea that the culture had shifted so far and so fast.

Because this core relationship and the twenty-eight-year age difference between the stars was all anyone wanted to talk about. The movie reviews kept asking why this old man was putting his liver-spotted hands on this fawn-like creature. Gwyneth Paltrow herself commented on it in an interview with *The Morning Call,* acknowledging that the idea of a real, offscreen relationship between herself and Douglas was "creepy."

Many conversations that had been grumbling around in the background began to emerge: Why are women over the age of forty relegated to mom roles or disappear from the screen altogether? Why is an older man still considered beautiful and desirable but an older woman is sexless and hag-like? Why is it normal for older men to be paired with younger women but when it's the other way around it's a perversion or disgusting?

A Perfect Murder still routinely shows up on lists of films in which there are relationships with problematic age gaps, even as every other fact about it has been forgotten. Douglas had come up in a culture in which a man, if successful, could do pretty much anything he wanted, and no one would comment let alone criticize. This was quickly changing. In fifteen years, Douglas would go from starring opposite Gwyneth Paltrow to having Diane Keaton as his on-screen love interest (still two years younger, but at least the gap was closing). The question was, how was an aging patriarch supposed to navigate an evolving romantic culture, and how do we teach Michael Douglas how to love? How does a man raised on patriarchal ideas find love in the new era?

There is a pattern to the romantic films that Michael Douglas appears in after *A Perfect Murder,* the object of which is to teach Michael

Douglas to adjust to the new world. In every new film, his character seems to carry the weight of all his past films, all the lying and
cheating and chasing of younger women. That might have been okay
behavior in the eighties, but now it's wrong, he's instructed, to treat
women carelessly. It's also wrong to assume he'll be loved only for his
successes and his money. It's wrong to use certain dehumanizing language around women, it's wrong to bail on relationships to prioritize
business. In most of these movies, Douglas eventually learns to love,
and he is rewarded for his progress with a partner who is age appropriate and also his intellectual match. So in film after film, from *Wonder Boys* to *Solitary Man* to *And So It Goes* and *It Runs in the Family*
and others, Michael Douglas treats women poorly. Michael Douglas
must be taught how to love. Michael Douglas learns an important
lesson. Michael Douglas falls for a socially acceptable match. The
movie ends with a Happily Ever After vibe. The next one begins.

It becomes a bit of a *Groundhog Day*–style cycle, where all progress is wiped away at the beginning of each new film and there is no
opportunity to enact in the world the lesson he has learned. He is
a lothario, he is reformed, he meets the right woman, and then he
must begin again. Perhaps it is a Sisyphean punishment for his past
transgressions? The man who must be schooled on the importance
of love like rolling a boulder up a mountain for all eternity? How do
we rescue Michael Douglas from his eternal torment?

A specific scene recurs. Michael Douglas tries to teach a younger
man—in *Solitary Man* the younger man is played by Jesse Eisenberg,
in *Ghosts of Girlfriends Past* he's played by Matthew McConaughey—
the lessons he has learned about how to attract and seduce women.
He tells these younger men, Women are for fun. They are to be
manipulated and conquered and then discarded for the next. The
younger and dumber you can get them, the better. It's important to
get experience with as many women as possible, because life is all
about having a good time and chicks are a really good time.

Then the younger man has to explain to Michael Douglas that actually he's wrong. Life is about love, about family, about connection. It's about relationships and being a good partner. It's not a numbers game, it's about the quality of life and the real goal is to find someone you can love over a lifetime. When Michael Douglas shows up in these films with a much younger woman, it's not sexy or cool, it's gross. It's pathetic. It's no longer about claiming women as trophies, it's about treating women as equals. Michael Douglas must unlearn the norms of the past and embrace new standards for love and romance, and that starts with learning to appreciate women who are closer to his own age, who are independent and intelligent, and who have often been mistreated by men a lot like Michael Douglas in the past. But then after a big kiss or a declaration of love the screen fades to black and the process restarts itself.

Maybe the reason the effort Michael Douglas makes to internalize the progress the world has made around him doesn't ever really take is that while the problems of the past are understood to be socially constructed, undoing them is left as a personal project. It's not like Michael Douglas came up with this idea that younger women are more beautiful all on his own. Desires might feel extremely intimate and individualized, but they are all shaped by the social context in which they develop. So if society created this problem, why is our hero left on his own to counteract it? Because his desires for the "wrong" kinds of women or his objectifying attitude toward women is seen as a character flaw, one he must overcome by confronting his issues and facing his demons.

This lines up with the postpatriarchal idea that a man must make himself deserving of love before he can find it. It's a fantasy as destructive and useless as the earlier fantasy that it was men's midlife crises—not women's dissatisfaction—driving divorce rates up in the eighties and nineties. It's an additional layer of confusion on an issue that is already difficult to navigate.

These what used to be called May-December romances are a controversial flashpoint not because there is anything inherently wrong with dating someone outside your age group. It's what it represents. If a man is dating or marrying younger women, that means he hasn't learned yet the new rules of heterosexuality. He becomes a target because his behavior evokes anxiety about the difficulty of changing norms, of the incomplete nature of the feminist project, and the creeping sense of dread that maybe all this so-called progress can be washed away in an instant.

The anxiety and exasperation of these relationships, whether they are about the latest Hollywood romantic pairing or a scandal about a professor dating a graduate student, are a proxy for a larger conversation about how to reimagine heterosexual relationships in a way that would do less harm. If women are truly going to be considered equal partners in a marriage or relationship, and not simply property handed over from father to husband, which is essentially what the patriarchal romantic structure was all about, then some things are going to have to change. The problem is that by focusing attention on the results of gendered power dynamics rather than the source, it's difficult to push past centuries of indoctrination and start to imagine new possibilities.

The age-gap relationship became and remains a target in these discussions because of its symbolic power. It is the distillation of what the culture still believes about both men and women. Men's worth lies entirely within their bank accounts. Women's worth lies entirely within their youth (read as fertility) and beauty. Breaking away from these limitations gives women the opportunity to be valued—by men but also by society and the workplace—for their artistic accomplishments, their intelligence, their physical strength, their wealth, their ambitions. Being valued means receiving some sort of reward for those achievements, like money or attention or love.

Seeing a traditional age-gap relationship, an older man with a beautiful woman, reminds women who perhaps aren't traditionally considered beautiful or at least don't want to spend all their time pursuing and maintaining their beauty, that this is an incomplete process, and many men are still trained and encouraged and socially rewarded for attaining a beautiful woman as a partner.

Less discussed but just as restrictive are the expectations placed on a man to make himself desirable to women. Men are still told they are valued for their ability to provide and accumulate, and if they would like to find the time and space to develop other sides of themselves—their kindness, perhaps, or their ability to care for others—or if they are simply unable to fulfill those expectations because the ruling system has decided to no longer accommodate your average man, they, too, run the risk of getting passed over on the sexual marketplace. So it's unclear why there has been less protest from men about the harmful norms displayed in these relationships and their implication that an older man is only lovable or desirable if he has tremendous wealth or success.

Actually, it's not unclear. Because women lose fertility as they age, and because the societal stereotype is that they also lose beauty, women are essentially walking around with a hole in their pocket, losing value as time passes. With men, the opposite is true. The belief is that men will accumulate value as time passes, as they gain status, skills, and money. The possibility for bounty is always just around the next corner. This keeps hope alive that they'll eventually get what they need to find a valuable mate at some point in the future.

From *Gentlemen Prefer Blondes* to 2019's *Hustlers,* the young hot gold digger is a feminist icon. She cannily understands the disempowered position she is in, and she uses the patriarch's tools against him. She schemes and devises and triumphs. Because it's understood that she is the victim of this relationship, anything she does to her oppressor (her lover) to manipulate or defraud him is not only justified but righteous.

The older man, however, is a buffoon, a creep, a mark. The Michael Douglas of *A Perfect Murder* must die because his choice to woo this significantly younger and more beautiful woman is so objectionable. By taking a young bride he has misused his power and he must pay for his transgression.

Even in the supposedly women-friendly reimagining of this relationship, somehow the woman is still treated as lesser than. Because her power, her youth and beauty, is still disregarded and diminished. She is not seen as the equal to her wealthy partner but instead as childlike or a victim. She needs to be protected and coddled. She can't be getting what she wants out of these relationships, unless she is running a con simply for the money, so there has to be something wrong with her. Daddy issues, maybe. A lack of self-worth. An insufficient political education. Which just goes to show how difficult it is, even for activists, to fight against this idea of the woman as lesser than—an idea planted in our imagination to justify the patriarchal forms of love.

It's not that the desire for rules by which we can more easily manage our romantic lives is somehow wrong. Relationships under patriarchy were maintained by institutions like the church, the law, and the family; community involvement; and social norms. These were deemed coercive—a pastor guilting a woman into staying in an abusive marriage by telling her that her soul would be endangered in a divorce, say—and inadequate for protecting both parties in the marriage.

It was foolish to think we could break with centuries of tradition governing how relationships are formed and supported and simply tell everybody, "Just do whatever feels right for you," and chaos wouldn't ensue. And romantic chaos has ensued. The percentage of young people who have no sexual or romantic experience at all is growing, divorce rates might be steady but that's only because marriage rates are way down, domestic violence rates are up, and the percentage of people reporting relationship satisfaction is down. People are unhappy, they're confused, and there is an enormous industry of consultants, apps, self-help books, therapists, online influencers, motivational speakers, spiritual retreats, pharmaceuticals, and pornography there to prey on and profit from, but not solve, their dissatisfaction.

Imagine the position of a romantic heterosexual young man today. Constantly blasted by images from advertising and pornography and entertainment of what an attractive woman looks like so that his desires, which feel intimately personal, are warped by outside influence. And while that image of the ideal woman has changed through the years to expand beyond its thin, young, white predecessor, there is still a sizable gap between the fantasy image and the real-life human beings walking around on the planet. He is told that a relationship these days can be anything he wants: polyamorous, monogamous, ethically non-monogamous. To find satisfaction, he only has to figure out what kind of relationship is authentic for him.

"Authenticity" has replaced the social role developed for patriarchy. It's the belief that the answer to how you should behave, look, love, fuck, and think lies within yourself rather than within a social norm. Philosopher Charles Taylor described this turn from the patriarchal role to authenticity in *A Secular Age* as "the understanding of life . . . that each of us has his/her own way of realizing our humanity, and that it is important to find and live out one's own [life], as against surrendering to conformity with a model imposed on us from outside, by society, or the previous generation, or religious or political authority."

This change, from the patriarchal role to authenticity, stretches past the boundaries of the romantic relationship and affects everything in a person's life, including a person's work. Carl R. Trueman describes the shift in *The Rise and Triumph of the Modern Self*. He writes, "The difference is stark: for my grandfather, job satisfaction was empirical, outwardly directed, and unrelated to his psychological state; for members of mine and subsequent generations, the issue of *feeling* is central."

The educational system turns from being a place in which a subject is shaped as a worker and taught the skills, ideas, and knowledge one will need to know to contribute substantially to their future workplace into a site where students discover their authentic abilities, dreams, and desires for their careers. Trueman continues, "Traditional institutions must be transformed to conform to the psychological self, not vice versa."

It's a utopian idea, but in the postpatriarchal era authenticity as achieved through satisfaction in work and marriage is only actionable by the very wealthy. They have the highest marriage rates and the lowest divorce rates, just as they make up the most significant demographic at Ivy League universities like Harvard and Yale.

This is why the language of money permeates the language of romance in a consumerist society. Just like a person is expected to find what is to their taste in their diets and execute those decisions in the marketplace of a grocery store, a person is expected to find out what they want in a romantic partner and execute those decisions in the "sexual marketplace." This is what sociologist Eva Illouz calls "the ideology of individual choice" in *The End of Love*. "By letting individuals negotiate themselves the conditions of their encounter with only very few regulations or prohibitions, this market-form creates a widespread and pervasive cognitive and emotional uncertainty," she writes.

Our hero might know what he desires and who he finds attractive (or more likely he is still deeply confused on this issue), and he then has to figure out how to go about bringing someone who matches his desires into his life. And here he receives conflicting and contradictory rules from all directions: peers, reality television programming, social media, pornography, Michael Douglas movies, teachers, family, and video games. There is a social justice conversation happening about the future of love and dating in academia and mass media, about how a man can be a feminist ally and more respectful of women, but maybe that trickles down to him and maybe not, depending on his class, his preference for pop culture consumption, and his access to universities, publications, and communities where those conversations are centered.

Mostly what he'll receive are negative instructions. Don't date women younger than yourself. Don't be creepy. Don't talk to a woman in this way or that way. When he sees a man meeting a woman in a movie, it all just happens so naturally. There's a meet-cute at the grocery store or the bar or at school, but these things never seem to happen to him in real life. The dating apps are designed to keep their patrons hooked in an endless scroll, with the tantalizing possibility that a slightly better version of the person in front of you is out there somewhere. The only positive advice he can find is to be himself, but clearly that self is wanting or else love would have found him by now. Desires are mass-produced but individuals are left alone to manage them.

It's easier to see now that the rewards are disconnected from the behaviors. When you're a little laboratory pigeon pressing the lever to get the food pellet, your little brain starts telling you this is how the whole world is set up. But when the food pellet stops coming, does every single pigeon figure out, oh hey, this is a construct and there are other sources of reward? Other forms of food? Other ways of being? Other spaces outside this box in a laboratory? Or are there a lot of birds in those boxes just slamming away at the lever harder and harder because at some moment that fucking food pellet is gonna come.

The superstitious pigeons think if they just exhibit more extreme versions of patriarchal behaviors with women they'll get fed from it. In the patriarchal romance, men prized women for their subservience, their youth, their emotional intelligence over other qualities because that met the community's standards for gendered divisions of labor and social expectations. But the values of patriarchy have been severed from their meaning. The prize of the younger woman today has nothing to do with her fertility, nor is her innocent heart prized for the way it informs her kind attention to others. So today masculinity influencers tell young men they should treat women like dumb babies and get them while they're still young and too scared to say no to you because that'll get you high fives from your bro peers who drink beer out of plastic cups. Persisting in this behavior, however, requires thinking that fleeting sexual stimulation and an emotional connection sustained through domination and the threat of violence is the equivalent of a lifelong partnership and participation in a like-minded community. For men, it's basically confusing the feeling of being dragged over a field of broken glass with ice-skating.

There are a lot of angry women in these movies. Wives, lovers, daughters, discarded exes who rage at the men for mistreating or underappreciating them. In *Solitary Man*, Douglas's daughter Susan is furious with him for the way he treated her mother, for his attitude toward women, for his inability to value her or participate in her family. She is all clenched jaw and tightened fist. But that's nothing compared to the halo of rage that energizes Douglas's wife, Rebecca, throughout *It Runs in the Family* as she is cheated on, neglected, and talked down to by the men in her life. Jenny is angry in *Ghosts of Girlfriends Past*, Sara is angry in *Wonder Boys*. With each of them their anger is not just personal, it's political. It is a tool with which they navigate an unfair world. It assists them, it is information for them.

But the men don't get angry. Maybe in the course of the narrative they become more self-aware, maybe they learn an important lesson, maybe they fall in love, but there's no scene in the movies of the men being just really pissed off at this shitty hand they have been dealt. There is a lot they could be mad about. They could be angry that they were raised to believe that the emotional sides of themselves were disposable or harmful, or that they were never taught how to care for the people they loved or appreciate women as full human beings with something vital to contribute to their lives or how to express that care in a way that didn't cause further harm. They could be pissed that they were asked to sacrifice such large parts of their lives and that the rewards for those sacrifices never really materialized. Or they could have a righteous fury that the world has limited the lives of the women they love, and that they themselves have unknowingly (or knowingly) hurt their mothers, wives, daughters by refusing to reject their patriarchal inheritance. But it doesn't happen.

This is a continuing problem in heterosexuality. Women have all these different ways of making meaning out of their romantic issues. Not all of them are productive, obviously, but women's media, books, community, and family assist women in figuring out how to improve their chances for romantic satisfaction or find alternative forms of emotional support if a life partner doesn't appear. There is technology to help women form families and bear children outside of heterosexual partnership, there is a tradition of living in alternative forms of housing, women are encouraged and instructed on how to form emotional bonds outside of romantic ones. When women suffer romantic disappointments, there are alternatives waiting for them.

"Could I Be My Own Soul Mate?" asked *The New York Times* in 2019, exploring whether someone could be cool enough, confident enough, fulfilled enough not to go looking for a partner to complete them but could instead be happily independent, and used women as the primary examples. Women had been experimenting with single parenthood for a while now, finding themselves increasingly in the position of reluctant head of the household not because of a broken marriage but because they couldn't find a partner to begin with. And they blamed men for not stepping up, for being commitment-phobic, for preferring subservient women, for not having basic housekeeping skills like cooking or having box springs under their mattresses.

An increasing number of women decided to try to break free from heterosexuality, as best they could. They developed wedding ceremonies to declare a lifelong commitment to their own self. They developed platonic marriages with female friends. They proudly declared themselves spinsters. They chose themselves.

Men, however, do not have these advantages. They mostly have negative influences, whether that's an incel forum that tells sexually frustrated men that no one will ever love or desire them or it's an intellectually dubious book of evolutionary psychology that tells them men are biologically destined to rape and spread their seed and use women for sex. They have fathers and mentors who possibly don't understand times have changed. They lack the cultural influences that could help men develop themselves emotionally.

It takes infrastructure to make relationships work. But there's another way the logic of the market has taken over the emotional sphere: There are no safety nets. There are no forms of assistance when people are down on their luck, and those who are failing become the subject of scrutiny and jokes. Due to the new rules of the postpatriarchy, disguised as a meritocracy, it's easy to believe people deserve what they have.

. . .

Under patriarchy, romantic love wasn't just about warm feelings and shared experiences and photos taken in front of the Christmas tree in matching pajamas. It's about money. It's about property law and taxes and legal protection and wealth management. It's about the creation of future generations of the workforce and the ideological indoctrination of children and the genetic optimization of offspring.

The traditional rituals of mating and starting a family are as much about inheritance law and the careful distribution of material resources as they are about creating emotional bonds. This is still true. But as marriage as an institution was increasingly destabilized, this traditional meaning of the heterosexual pairing was omitted from the conversation.

As a result, the language we use for love is so idiotic and flimsy, all this silly airiness about destiny and connection and "I just knew they were the one." If the patriarchy actually cared about men, instead of just the wealthy, when the rates of divorce started to increase, when people waited longer and longer to marry, when larger percentages of people started to live alone, there would have been other ways of distributing these rights and material advantages through arrangements other than marriage. The patriarchy would have cared as much about single men as married men and made sure they had equal access to health insurance, immigration assistance, tax breaks, and all the other benefits that are granted to the married. Young men would not have been left alone to manage structural disadvantages all on their own, unorganized and with no pathway toward solidarity.

This might be why all the films of this era end on their dot dot dot. Trying to break down lifelong indoctrination with maybe a couple self-help books and a round or two of getting yelled at online by women for being toxic in order to create a wholly enlightened new self is a bit like taking someone who has never left New York City to the woods and releasing them with an ax and a shovel and expecting them to figure out how to live off the land. I mean, point some cameras at them and document their failings—it's sure to be a good show—but more likely than not they'll be dead by Tuesday.

How do we really think getting Michael Douglas together with Diane Keaton is ultimately going to work out? He'll probably truly be in love, maybe really believe he can make it work this time, then six months later an ex still in her twenties texts him or maybe his new bride gets a cancer diagnosis (statistically that's a high-risk time for women to be abandoned by their spouse, because in a patriarchal relationship it's the woman who is supposed to be the caretaker, not the other way around) and all those switches flip back to their factory settings.

And what is witty, quirky Diane Keaton getting out of this? Surely there are better ways for her to spend her time than trying to convince a guy who previously thought of her as a dried-up hag that she has worth as a loving partner.

The current setup only creates resentment and confusion. Young men are raised to believe themselves and their partners are romantically disposable, only good for taking whatever they can get. Young women are raised to believe their value is tied to their youth and thus eroding every second, and they always have to be on the lookout for predatory behavior. The prevailing belief is that no one can possibly be satisfied in love, and in each case it is the other group's fault. It's women's fault for wanting too much. It's men's fault for refusing to evolve. The animosity is real and spreading. It's hard to convince anyone that the thing that is afflicting them is also afflicting their counterpart, and only through that realization can there be progress. Only by reclaiming love from its current market venue can it flourish again.

DADDY ISSUES:
FATHER HUNGER AND THE SEARCH
FOR AN HEIR

It's remarkable how few children Michael Douglas has in his films. He is childless in *Romancing the Stone* and *The Jewel of the Nile*, *Basic Instinct*, *The Game*, and *Wonder Boys*. He is the weird uncle in *Ghosts of Girlfriends Past*, providing an eccentric and erratic influence on his nephew.

A man having sons is the basic foundation of patriarchy, which is about promoting and protecting male inheritance. Having sons is still the standard reason for the nuclear family. Researchers at the University of California noticed that men are more likely to stay in marriages with sons than those with daughters. The results of these studies have been borne out consistently—families with sons are more likely to have a father present in the household or in the role of an active parent.

Traditionally a man without sons was considered a failure. Henry VIII killed a lot of wives simply to avoid the knowledge that his sperm seemed incapable of creating heirs. Under the new rules of masculinity—or perhaps we should say under the lack of rules for the new masculinity—a man's life is lived primarily for his own self. There's no need to sacrifice oneself for future generations, it's about living the best life you possibly can for now.

But it's also true that Michael Douglas doesn't seem to be having a great time, freed from the responsibilities of patriarchal duties. The values of patriarchy—stewardship, sacrifice, conformity—are at odds with this culture of hedonism and authenticity. But the hedonism is revealed to be empty, draining rather than sustaining. He is, if anything, in something of an identity crisis about his lack of sons and heirs. He hunts for substitutes, he is always seeking out young men to look after and teach his wisdom to. It's all wrapped up in a fear of death, the fear of disappearing from the earth without having left a mark. A son who will carry on his father's work soothes the aging patriarch with fantasies of legacy and influence and importance. Having a son is the next best thing to paying Harvard to name the new wing of a library after you. But without this assurance, there's a restless anxiety in these films, a searching wonder at whether what he's accomplished will be enough.

If Michael Douglas does have children, he has daughters, who do not function as potential heirs for some reason. They are not viewed as vessels for male wisdom, they are not raised to follow in his footsteps. In *Fatal Attraction, Falling Down, The American President, Wonder Boys,* and *Traffic* he is a kind of omen for the bad romantic futures to come for these girls. No doubt he is setting them up for a lifetime of "daddy issues." Women's "daddy issues" are blamed for everything from women's emotional unavailability to their clinginess, their ambitions on Wall Street to their involvement in sex work. And somehow these issues are always regarded as their fault, despite the patriarchal origin point.

These films seem to pick up on something in the culture, a worrying disconnect between father and son, something that was disrupting patrilineal inheritance. Like maybe what the fathers were handing their heirs was not the great gift they were pretending it was. They weren't setting them up for success, they were dropping their children into what feels like the last hour of a wild party. All the fun has already been had, all the bottles are already empty, and there's a guy named Steve passed out in the bathroom. Maybe the newer generation didn't want to work to preserve their legacy, maybe their fathers were a bunch of sex pests, greedy capitalists, and warmongers. Maybe their inheritance was a burden, as, if anything, what the younger generations were handed was a dying earth, a crashing economy, and a disappearing future.

The previous generations of men had not been responsible stewards for the future generations, or so the accusation against the baby boomers goes. Maybe that had been something of a lie all along, this idea that men had been sacrificing and preserving and saving for the future. Looking back, all that faithful stewardship starts to look like squander and pillage. Whether it's the choking exhaust from monstrous cars crawling down the freeway at peak traffic hours or the strip-mining of every last diamond, shred of lithium, and chunk of coal for frenzied consumption, there appears to have been no real plan for preservation of the future.

What does our Michael Douglas character have to leave his children, other than his anxiety, his failings, and something like an object lesson in how not to be a good person? There is the legacy of his films, of course, but when the next generation is all gathered to hear the collective last will and testament of this generation of men, how will they value what they are bequeathed?

Michael Douglas might not have sons, but in many of these films he's looking for an heir. He's looking for some younger man to instruct and pass along what he has learned and accumulated. In *Wall Street,* he takes the young Charlie Sheen on as a protégé for his financial business. He teaches him all the things a successful father would: how to dress, how to deal with women, how to get ahead in business. In *Solitary Man* he tries to help a lovesick young man bag a woman, using him as a vessel for all of his tricks and lessons on how to successfully manipulate potential sexual partners. He plays a professor in *Wonder Boys,* dealing with a student whose family doesn't seem to understand him and whose strange behavior makes Michael Douglas think he needs a father figure to put him right. In *Ant-Man,* he's struggling to find someone to take his scientific research seriously and keep it going.

But in most of these stories, the knowledge Michael Douglas has to offer is corrupted and rejected. In *Wall Street* his selected heir turns on him and hands him over to the authorities. In *Solitary Man,* his surrogate son tells him to his face that his ideas are worthless. In *Wonder Boys,* his influence can't penetrate his student because he's already a fully developed man.

In each case, there's a sense that this younger generation doesn't want to live in a world of Michael Douglas's construction. In the case of *Wall Street,* his unethical dealings and corrupt worldview are rejected because the younger man rejects those values. Where every rule is just there to be broken and the ends justify the means, as long as the ends involve swimming in cash.

This notion, that living like Michael Douglas would make the world inhospitable, is behind every rejection he suffers by his surrogate sons. There's a hope for something better, even if it means managing the uncertainty that comes through this clash of the generations. The young men in all these stories seem all right. They may be scared or floundering a bit, but they are smart enough to reject a mentorship that is useless to them.

But there's a constant anxiety about young men without mentors or father figures, someone to point the way for them. This lack of leadership is the reason given for young men falling into fascism, misogyny, or under the sway of cult leaders and masculinity influencers. If only they had a paternal figure in their lives to show them alternatives. Which would seem to ignore the myriad men in public life, in the worlds of entertainment and media, in politics, sports, education, and business, as shining examples of how to live a life.

This is similar to the destructive rhetoric about "broken families" within various marginalized communities, most vocally directed during this era at struggling African American families. The "dead-beat dad" soon took the blame for all the difficulties of those communities, from violence to school dropout rates to drug use to crime. If the father had been responsible and present, so the political rhetoric goes, then all these families would be better off.

This is a fundamental misunderstanding of what a father figure actually does. Men aren't suffering because they don't have an image of what successful, non-fascist, non-misogynistic men look like. Those are all around. But the basic function of patriarchy—to prepare boys and young men for a social role, complete with rigid boundaries and incentives for desired behaviors—has broken down. It's material support that's needed, not an inspirational pep talk.

The steps to getting from the dream to the result, however, have all been destabilized. Now achievement is linked completely to capital. Access to education is linked to capital. Access to romantic love is linked to capital. Access to meaningful work is linked to capital. Access to mental and physical healthcare services is linked to capital. Accessing access to capital is linked to capital. The chances of being able to become a good man are greatly improved not through any internal workings or ability to mimic the behaviors of the fore-fathers but through cash reserves.

If there's one prevailing characteristic of the American father in film over the last eighty or so years, it's disapproval. Don't do that, don't wear that, don't go out with her, don't follow your dreams, don't drive that car, don't you talk back to me, young man, don't shirk your responsibilities, don't read that book, don't hang out with those low-life friends of yours, don't wear your hair like that, don't drink that, don't experience joy, don't think you're better than me, don't go there, don't look at that, don't you talk to your mother that way, don't put that in your mouth, don't feel those feelings, not while you're living under my roof.

It's very Freudian, this notion that a society is in part defined by what is forbidden. And since society and its institutions were primarily built for and around an idea of men, masculinity in itself under patriarchy was defined by what is forbidden. The father ruled via the no, but this no was an act of care. He knew from experience that the world wanted only a very limited form of expression from men, and he attempted to pass along that information to his son to help prepare him for the world. Some of the things men had to sacrifice are obvious: same-sex desire, soft feelings of empathy and vulnerability, fanciful dress or self-expression, and so on. A lot of these sacrifices were the parts of oneself that could be understood as being feminine, of course. And it was helpful for men to denigrate or belittle what was deemed as being "for girls" as a way of getting boys to repress it within themselves. For instance, replace crying—something girls do—with anger or violence—something boys do.

And while the punishment against transgression along with the no wielded by the father has been a defining characteristic of patriarchy since the beginning, it's relatively new that there was a basic understanding that this was oppressive. Authenticity, as the patriarchy started to fall apart, was defined by rebellion against the father. But much like the no that the father attempted to pass down to the son to prepare him for life, and much like the valorizing of the Lilith figure as discussed in the chapter about *Basic Instinct,* rebellion against the father isn't really a satisfying answer to the question of how one should live a life. It's hard to build from a space rooted in the negative. It's hard to tell where to go when you start from "Okay, well, not that."

This is especially true when the form of masculinity currently being rebelled against—in these films at least, the Michael Douglas baby boomer figure—was in itself constructed as an act of rebellion. Baby boomer masculinity rebelled primarily against the notion of sacrifice. These men were against the war because they rebelled against the idea that it was their role to sacrifice their lives for their nation. They were against sexual prudishness because they rebelled against the idea that masculinity required that they sacrifice eroticism for the sake of monogamy and family stability.

Rebelling against rebellion simply leads all the way back to tradition. This is why there is a resurgence of military culture (even if only as modeled in boot camp–style workouts and "thank you for your service," rather than actual enlistment) and things like the NoFap movement online and the masculinity influencers like Andrew Tate, Jordan Peterson, and Kevin Samuels. They are picking up on nostalgic versions of masculinity in order to fight against the hedonism and meaninglessness of contemporary consumer life. The problem is that these sacrifices are no longer rewarded. At one time, joining the military was a method of social mobility. One could expect to leave the service and enter a university or find a middle-class job. But for decades now, the budgets for veterans programs like the GI Bill and healthcare for veterans have been slashed, which has led to problems like untreated PTSD. There's also a stigma in the culture at large against military service after several unpopular and illegitimate wars and military interventions, which can make isolated veterans vulnerable to being radicalized and joining white nationalist groups and militias. The military is no longer the doorway to social mobility. Which leaves the individual attracted to something like the military out of a desire to serve their country with the decision of whether to enlist anyway and hope for the best, believe in an outdated fantasy, or be drawn into pseudomilitaristic cultures on the political left or the right.

This is the same with conservative sexual culture. Sexual conservativism is no longer rewarded with guaranteed spousal monogamy or acceptance into a religious community, so the only way to judge whether it is good or not is how it makes one feel. How to measure the pleasures of self-restraint versus the pleasures of indulgence? Normally people will restrain themselves in order to achieve something, but if there is no direct correlation between restraint and reward, the sacrifice becomes a meaningless gesture.

Under postpatriarchy any outer constraints are considered to be an obstacle to authenticity. We are a culture obsessed with the idea of authenticity without, again, any structures in place to help average boys and young men discover what might be authentic about themselves. The search for the father is a nostalgia for the no, the support that limitations provide. The younger characters seek Michael Douglas out for guidance because they are tired of trying to figure it all out for themselves. But Michael Douglas has no no to offer. He is a representative of the so-called liberated masculinity that finally broke away from hundreds of years of repression. Any guidance he can offer is corrupted by the prevailing belief of modern masculinity that the only responsibility one has is to oneself. There is no public role for a Michael Douglas figure. He is here in this lifetime to enjoy himself, and the younger generation eventually realizes how empty that impulse really is, or how out of reach it might be for someone without the money to buy one's way to pleasure.

In *Solitary Man,* the Michael Douglas character is a figure of masculine waste. Without the limitations that a traditional social role provides, he's spilling out in every direction. He wastes his money.

WHAT IS WRONG WITH MEN

He wastes his time. He wastes himself sexually. He once occupied a very formal role as husband, provider, and father, but after a health scare he decides to abandon those roles and enjoy his liberation.

Released from the obligation of being a husband, he as a man in his fifties hits on and sleeps with college girls. Released from the obligation of being a provider for his family, he goes to work at a friend's diner. Released from the obligation of being a father, he does whatever he wants with no thought toward the future. His health problem means he could die at any moment, so he spends his time trolling for college girls and attending parties and enjoying pointless leisure.

He languishes. He betrays his surrogate son, he cheats on his girlfriend, he gets into a fight. And he seems surprised that people think he's pathetic. The teenage girl he sleeps with has no interest in continuing the relationship, the people he encounters think he's a loser. When he's not connected to the community via his social roles, his display of money and his general attractiveness—neither of which are that substantial—are not enough to broadcast to the people around him that he is of value and is worthy of respect.

The limitations of patriarchy didn't just give men rewards, it gave them a context in which their value could be understood. Michael Douglas is surprised that having abandoned his patriarchal context he is not immediately granted the treatment he is used to. He doesn't exactly say, "Don't you know who I am?" but that is the general tone of a lot of Michael Douglas characters after *The Game*. Richard Sennett wrote in *The Fall of Public Man*:

> In a milieu of strangers, the people who witness one's actions, declarations, and professions usually have no knowledge of one's history, and no experience of similar actions, declarations, and professions in one's past; thus it becomes difficult for this audience to judge, by an external standard of experience with a

particular person, whether he is to be believed or not in a given situation. The knowledge on which belief can be based is confined to the frame of the immediate situation. The arousal of belief therefore depends on how one behaves—talks, gestures, moves, dresses, listens—within the situation itself.

Again, context is replaced with money. If evaluation is going to happen without any other information—which under patriarchy was provided by family and work and community—people mostly rely on metrics, financial metrics being the most powerful. The striving classes wear representations of their wealth on their body when out in public: limited-edition sneakers, expensive watches, bags and clothing by elite designers that are branded with their logos. Stripped of these external cues, removed from the traditional context, a person risks disappearing or being treated like a member of the lower classes. Placement on the hierarchy must be established and re-established with every interaction.

The thing that sets this version of Michael Douglas free is his impending death. He's given a medical diagnosis that means he could die at pretty much any moment. He could live for another twenty years or another twenty seconds. With no future, the primary mechanism of patriarchal masculinity—conservation, or the big no—makes no sense. He has no heir (girls don't count), so the sacrifice that is built into the roles he's been playing in his life becomes nonsensical. If there is no future, there is nothing to wait for.

He is liberated from the roles of father, provider, husband, but there is nothing with which to replace those. Outside of those relationships with his family and with his community, there is only selfish pleasure. His apocalyptic thinking is easy to see in contemporary culture. NO FUTURE might as well be the name of every oil rig, every piece of fracking equipment, every bank building, every shoddily built housing project. Of course, not every CEO was diagnosed with the same heart problem all at once, but the No Future mentality is caused by the pervasive sense of doom—the source of the coming catastrophe being environmental, geopolitical, and/or economic—that hovers above the culture. Some of that is legitimate, like the sense that we started doing something about weening ourselves from our reliance on fossil fuels too late. But some of our apocalyptic thinking is like what afflicts Michael Douglas, an inability to find meaning in a new way of living. The traditional ways in which men found meaning are disappearing.

The dying of colonialism has destroyed the sense that "Western civilization" is a force only for good. Even if your average American man had nothing to do with the international community, he could, simply through citizenship, feel like he was participating in something great. That America was the greatest nation on earth, the pinnacle of Western civilization's values and accomplishments, that the rest of the world was vastly improved by America's existence.

But now, living in America does not give the average citizen the same sense of pride and belonging. There are too many dissenting voices and counternarratives from people from places that were violated and destroyed by American power. There are too many ambivalent feelings about America's history, now that there's a conversation within the mainstream about its darkest moments, from slavery to genocide to unjust wars.

Historical narratives are being debated as if they were contemporary issues. Questions about American history, about whether the Founding Fathers were glorious or immoral, whether all the wars fought were legitimate, and the real reasons for the Civil War have become contentious. Politicians have been frantically trying to rewrite history books to erase dissenting voices about the history of slavery and genocide and re-establish the master narrative.

The shifting role of the father and his unquestioned authority within the family has many questioning what the point of the father is anyway. When the father was essentially the king of the household, then he, simply by marrying and impregnating his wife, could think of himself as important. He had created life, he had people who depended on him, people he could control. And even if he was violent or neglectful, society believed his role as a father was more important than interfering with how he was choosing to play that role.

But now, how does a young man find meaning by being a father? Now that being a father no longer guarantees respect, or even participation within the family as single parent households rise in number, now that men are expected to contribute an equal part of the domestic labor, now that the courts can and will intervene in poor parenting on the part of the father, then why bother going through the whole mess and expense of childrearing? This has manifested itself in low rates and long delays in both marriage and having children.

This sense of hopelessness has fostered what Natalie Wynn, the philosopher who runs the YouTube series ContraPoints, calls "revolutionary ideation." Wynn has been documenting the fringes of political belief over the last decade, and the way political violence—on both the left and the right—has become attractive to disillusioned young men in particular. They feel oppressed by the economic system of capitalism and see no hope in reform, so they dream of revolution as the solution to the problem of meaning.

"It's a kind of fantasy escapism," Wynn explains in her essay "Voting." "It's an alternative to politics." But keeping the political imaginary engaged in fantasies about what life will be like "after the revolution" disengages it from the ever-pressing present and the looming future. Because the whole imaginative capacity is focused on a world that will not exist, it becomes another form of waste.

The end of patriarchy has created a crisis of meaning. As old forms crumble, and new ones "struggle to be born," as the philosopher Antonio Gramsci would say, what's left is a selfish, narcissistic impulse. If a person actually does live every day like it's going to be their last, they create the kind of environment in which we now live. Use up every fossil fuel, make every dollar possible from every potential asset, and rush for the apocalypse.

This is why younger men have this father hunger. They are looking for someone to tell them how to find their lives meaningful. What they find is a conservative trend among masculinity influencers, who tell them things were better under patriarchy. They are nostalgic for meaning, recognition, and community, and these fantasies of a better life in some distant time, whether it's the 1950s or the Roman Empire, become just another thing erasing their potential futures.

This anxiety about the end of the world has created an entertainment industry all about titillating the death wish. Thanatos has been professionalized. Big-budget films about environmental collapse, about a battle of civilizations with AI or advanced alien species or brilliant supervillains have dominated the box office over the last twenty years. The world keeps threatening to end, and yet here comes the dot dot dot.

It's often said that the older generations and people in power are in denial about how bad things are. If they are not moving with some urgency to address climate change, it must mean they are science deniers. If they are not embracing the possibilities of socialism, they must be in denial of the signs that capitalism is failing as a global system. If they are not adapting to the changing times by empowering women and people of color, they must be in denial that patriarchy is falling apart.

It might be more accurate to say they are less likely to be in denial and more likely to be flirting with the apocalypse. Otto Friedrich illuminated this embrace of Armageddon in *The End of the World: A History*. He writes:

> The end of the world is, in a way, a pun. The end can mean not only the conclusion but also the purpose of the world. Just as it has been said that a man's life can be understood only at the moment of his death, so the end of the world, the destruction of the world, seems to imply that there is some higher purpose in the world's existence. Thus, the end of the world makes manifest the end of the world.

The end of patriarchy is illuminating in the same way.

SPECULATIVE MASCULINITY:
THE RISE OF THE MASCULINITY INFLUENCER

As we saw in the previous part "The Economic Actor," the financial world during the Michael Douglas era was beginning to look a lot like gambling. Just straight earnings were no longer enough to keep a family financially solvent, let alone prosperous, which pushed a lot of amateur investors into the market. Banks were incentivized to take bigger and bigger risks, and if anything catastrophic happened there was a safety net provided by the taxpayers. Short-term windfalls were prioritized over long-term investments. You place your bets, there's a small chance you'll cash out big, but the house—in this metaphor, the house is the international banking system—will always win, because the political infrastructure will always choose the banks over the individual players.

Under traditional finance, a bank's relationship with their client was understood as a kind of symbiosis. When the client flourishes, the bank flourishes. Now, because of deregulation and the removal of consumer protections, the relationship between the bank and the client is more like predator and prey. Banks need overdrafts so they can meet their expectations each quarter for fees (collectively, American banks make $15 billion a year simply charging their clients for going into the red on their accounts), the short-term loan industry makes the vast majority of its money from late fees and interest on missed payments, and when banks are accused of perpetrating fraud against their own clients, they are rarely effectively punished.

Everything Susan Strange documented in the 1980s about the way that banks were no longer incentivized to help their clients thrive financially but were in fact encouraged to gamble with their money and profit off their losses, became crystal clear with the global crash in 2008. Banks had placed a wild bet, they lost, and it was they, not their clients, who were bailed out by the government. No meaningful reforms to the financial system emerged after the crash, setting the system up for another potential fall in the future.

There was a large group of people who saw the government prioritize the banking institutions over the individual and they divided into two camps. On one side, there was the Occupy Wall Street movement and its corresponding resurgence of the idea of a socialist future for America. This has led to grassroots campaigns for progressive political candidates, community-based activism for things like mutual aid funds and debt cancellation, and organizing for things like tenant rights and access to healthcare. These have had mixed results, with small successes usually confined to local elections and municipal victories, but groups are making active investments in their neighborhoods and communities in an attempt to fight off apathy and displacement.

Another group responded to the realization that the financial system is rigged against them because it is set up to enrich a small number of people at the expense of everyone else, making sure those few people are enriched rather than the people who are exploited. They decided the problem with the system being rigged was that they weren't the ones who were able to profit from it.

This was one of the primary motivations for the invention of digital peer-to-peer cryptocurrency and the development of Bitcoin in the years following the global financial crash. Documentarian Dan Olson explains in *Line Goes Up*, "The principal offering wasn't revolution, but at best a changing of the guard. The gripe is not with the outcome of 2008, but the fact that you had to be well connected in order to get in on the grift in 2006." Cryptocurrency was a speculative asset that would enrich a different demographic, cutting out Wall Street and instead enriching the inner circle of innovators and investors, mostly in the tech community.

But the wild fluctuations of cryptocurrencies—which are mostly run like a pyramid scheme—created losses among the small-time investors and big wins for the venture capitalists and wealthy investors who could game the system. In other words, they created a system that would enrich a small number of people at the expense of the many. The crypto crash of 2022, which destroyed over $2 trillion of wealth worldwide, was a small-scale version of the 2008 crash—a whole financial sector cratering due to speculation and fraud, with the losses suffered mostly by individuals while the majority of the offenders evaded prosecution and oversight.

A lot of people lost a lot of money in the crash of the housing market, and other people lost a lot of money in the crypto crash of 2022. Trillions of dollars disappeared. But, of course, it wasn't just the disappearance of a number on a screen. People lost their houses. Cars. Savings accounts. The ability to retire. Their marriages fell apart. Ater the 2008 financial crash, in Europe and America there was a spike in the number of suicides, with most of them committed by men. After the 2022 crash, forums that had been devoted to encouraging investment in cryptocurrencies were now posting the numbers for suicide hotlines and emergency counseling.

Twice as many men as women invested in crypto. And while gender essentialists might want to make grand pronouncements about why that is (testosterone makes men more impulsive and drawn to risky behaviors or whatever), the truth is that masculinity is still tightly intertwined with money. A number on a bank account is a visible marker of how manly you are. And when having a dependable, respectable job with benefits is getting harder to come by, when savings accounts will not grow to keep up with inflation rates, when pensions can disappear thanks to the decisions of a bank that is not even based in your country let alone your community, when the real estate market is skyrocketing and individual buyers are having to compete with LLCs that are paying in cash and offering 25 percent over asking price, and forums are full of anecdotes about overnight millionaires and instant wealth, then putting the entirety of a savings account into a crypto market that has the slim possibility of quadrupling its worth overnight starts to look all the more attractive.

What's going on with the financial sector is essentially what has happened to masculinity as a whole. The traditional ways of functioning as a man are not likely to pay off. But there's like a 5 percent chance that a man investing all his time and energy into one exaggerated and risky opportunity will pay off big.

There's a moment in the *Wall Street* sequel *Wall Street: Money Never Sleeps* when Michael Douglas as Gordon Gekko, newly released from his prison sentence for insider trading, expresses disbelief at what manhood has become. His little insider trading habit looks like a child's game next to the devastation wrought by the next generation of traders. His infidelity and salacious behavior are almost respectable next to the porn addiction and rank misogyny of the younger men around him. The men who followed didn't just use Gordon Gekko's ideas as a useful tip, they went all in.

Call it speculative masculinity, a vision of manhood that looks an awful lot like a desperate man in a casino, placing wild bets on impulses he confuses for rationality, hoping for a jackpot win.

Robert Jay Lifton, the professor of psychology who has for years investigated the control cults and other so-called brainwashing organizations have over their followers, remarked that these groups become immensely attractive during times of turmoil. Lifton considered, in 1993, in *The Protean Self: Human Resilience in an Age of Fragmentation,* that the postpatriarchal era we have been discussing has disrupted the expected stability of existence. He writes, "We feel ourselves buffeted about by unmanageable historical forces and social uncertainties. Leaders appear suddenly, recede equally rapidly, and are difficult for us to believe in when they are around. We change ideas and partners frequently, and do the same with jobs and places of residence. Enduring moral convictions, clear principles of action and behavior: we believe these must exist, but where? Whether dealing with world problems or child rearing, our behavior tends to be ad hoc, more or less decided upon as we go along. We are beset by a contradiction: schooled in the virtues of constancy and stability—whether as individuals, groups, or nations—our world and our lives seem inconstant and utterly unpredictable."

During these fragmented times, a cult or guru who offers easy answers—there's a UFO coming that will take you off this planet and into a better life, or if you follow this system women will fall at your feet—will have more sway. They can step into the void created by "fatherlessness, homelessness, and the absence of clear mentorship." The father, according to Lifton, "is identified with social and moral authority," and those without the resources to take advantage of the freedom to create one's own sense of social and moral authority are vulnerable to making a substitution with a false father.

Lifton has noted that the following that politicians like Donald Trump and other extremists collect tends to be more cultish than the crowds showing up for your traditional politician. Their support for the politicians of their choice tends to be more devotional and irrational than typical political affiliations, and they resist rational arguments against their leaders' positions. And these supporters are often overwhelmingly men.

Enough men have taken up such extreme positions in culture, politics, sexuality, and finance that it's become difficult to retreat. There's no steady ground to retreat to. There's a term in crypto lingo, "diamond hands." It's an exhortation to stay in the risk, even as all signs are pointing to disaster. Even if the investment is crashing, even if the investor is seeing everything they own disappear, it is a sign of true integrity to stick it out. The "diamond hands" mentality says it would be cowardice to sell now and try to recover whatever might be possible in a dire situation.

But selling to contain the damages also requires the investor to admit they've been led astray. With so many men who feel lost glomming on to influencers and con men who profit from their confusion, these investments take on a cultlike, fantastical quality. It's difficult for a person to admit they've been duped. It's difficult for a person to admit that things are not going to improve, that years have been wasted maintaining this extreme position. Getting out of a cultlike mindset, as Lifton has documented, whether religious or political, can require years of psychological and intellectual work that is often referred to as "deprogramming." But the longest process is often the one that leads up to the break with the collective, which requires the follower to admit they were vulnerable to persuasion in the first place.

This is how men get trapped, grinding it out. The understanding that this is a waste of time, that their failure is not only certain but also very useful to a small number of people is easy to avoid. There are a million podcasts to listen to, YouTube channels to subscribe to, e-books to download, friends who will reinforce a person's worst fantasies. Never stop hustling. Just keep holding, the payoff has to be right around the corner. The endless stream of content that will reinforce irrational worldviews and extreme positions keeps a person trapped in their own delusions.

There are many entry points to this cycle. Crypto is one, hustle culture is another. Physique is a big one. Weight lifting, bodybuilding, martial arts, extreme diets where the ultimate goal is to reach some impossible or painful marker of muscle mass or body fat—all become tied into feelings of insecurity around masculinity. When the results don't show up, there's always something new to try, some supplement, some illegal or unregulated mix of hormones and injectables, some new guru, some new diet, some new product to buy, some new trendy workout gear or gym. If raw food doesn't work, let's go paleo, let's go keto, let's go all beef, let's go vegan.

Even if a man does reach his goals, he is never really done. There is always one more marker, further off in the distance, that he can strive for. Five more pounds of muscle. One more millimeter of fat to lose. One more belt ranking to advance to. One more zero on that number in your account. One more gun for the collection. One more side gig, one more passive revenue stream, one more subscriber for his YouTube channel about how to hustle harder.

One way to silence self-doubt is to proselytize. Which is why men who get sucked into speculative masculinity end up perpetuating it by advising others to adopt its extremes. They are easy to find on social media, professing their loyalty to scams and con artists, picking fights with anyone who dares to disagree.

There is an idea that has governed our understanding of both economics and each individual man acting in a larger financial system: the *Homo economicus*. It's the theory that each man is capable of rational thought. Each man knows what he wants and what is good for him, and, given the opportunity, he will pursue his interests in a rational manner. The market, which also acts rationally, will respond and adjust itself to the man's rational decisions, correcting itself through natural processes. This interaction between man and market will allow for the best possible outcomes, as desires are met, discernment is rewarded, and relationships are built through mutually agreeable interactions of supply and demand.

This progressive notion of the market—that world peace will be spread through the interconnectedness of international trade, that resources will stay in a fluid state of movement rather than being hoarded, that it is in the rational self-interest of the wealthy to keep the market fair and accessible to all—hasn't really materialized.

This arrangement only really works if sacrifice is rewarded. If, by knowing the future is mostly predictable, one can act rationally with long-term goals. Economically speaking, that means that a pension or retirement account will still exist in the future, that Social Security and Medicare will still be operational, that an individual can reasonably assume that what they pay for expenses now will remain within a certain boundary.

Instead, volatility rules. The sociologist Aris Komporozos-Athanasiou notes in his book *Speculative Communities: Living with Uncertainty in a Financialized World,* "All aspects of life now revolve around collective experiences of uncertainty in the form of labor precariousness, rent dependency, indebtedness, emotional insecurity, and political instability." This has led, Komporozos-Athanasiou theorizes, to the death of *Homo economicus* and the creation of *Homo speculans:* the economic actor who makes decisions not through conservation but through wild bets.

Instead of seeing this behavior as irrational, it's better to understand it as rational given the irrational environment in which an individual operates. Let's say our theorized man is an American voter. He has seen, for decades now, a disconnect between what the populace wants, what the politician promises, and what the government delivers. This is, on some level, how politics has always worked, through compromise and balance. Crowds are not always wise, they sometimes want things that are immoral or foolish or bloodthirsty. And sometimes they don't want things that are better in the long run but painful in the short term, like higher taxes or military action that is motivated by justice rather than enrichment. But never before in American politics has there been such a wide gap in what voters state are their priorities and what they are given by the government. Abortion rights are extremely popular with American voters. They were taken away in large parts of the nation by state legislatures. A large majority of American voters want the government to provide health coverage to its citizens. Efforts to create such a system have been blocked by politicians of both parties for decades. Americans want higher corporate taxes, environmental protections, a return of the manufacturing sector, free public universities. Many politicians have made grand promises on all these issues, then dropped their pursuit upon entering office.

There is also a growing gap between the benefits of freedom and the ability to access those benefits with capital. Pankaj Mishra notes in *Age of Anger: A History of the Present*, following the thinker George Santayana, that "most human beings" are "temperamentally unfit to run the race for wealth," and suffer "from impotent resentment." Bearing the weight of being a "loser" can drive an individual into increasingly desperate acts or into extremist ideologies that give distorted explanations for why they are lacking the things they want.

It's not that the values of patriarchy—stewardship, loyalty, sacrifice—have disappeared, but that men are economically and politically compromised when it comes to connecting those values to action. In a nihilistic age, the declaration of values—a politician declaring themselves a traditional Christian—is more important than acting on those values, as with the politician's decision to pay off a mistress to coerce her into terminating a pregnancy. In a system without social coherence, economic stability, and political feasibility, speculation is incentivized over investment.

If the sacrifice of time, money, and hope that a voter devotes to the political process comes to nothing consistently, why are people who divest themselves from the national political process in one way or another often referred to as acting "against their self-interest"? Whether they are matching volatility with volatility by voting for erratic politicians with extreme belief systems or they are not voting at all, given the environment in which they live these actions can be understood as rational.

Time and energy and money are perhaps better spent, then, on the hyperlocal and the immediate. Union organization is up across the country because it promises immediate and visible reward. It gives its members the power to negotiate better pay, working conditions, and scheduling. But it's also clear how this newly invigorated support for labor organization is created by the failures of national government. It is a result of the government's inability to pass legislation for an increased minimum wage (another issue that the majority of Americans strongly support but the government will not act on), stronger labor protections, and access to the benefits that mostly come through employment (like health insurance and childcare) for everyone.

Local public offices that once were almost an afterthought have become heated and contentious battles during elections. The reason there is so much investment in things like the school board—another place where changes can be seen immediately and visibly—is due to the national government's failure to provide quality, consistent education to all children regardless of class, location, or race. But if even something like a local school board is volatile, with wild turnover and widespread death threats for those who hold that office, then uncertainty truly has permeated every facet of life.

The long-term political investment required to change things structurally is hard to imagine. There is a logical argument for the creation of a third political party, in order to avoid legislative gridlock and to give those who are politically unrepresented in the current American two-party system a voice. And while smaller political parties do exist on the local level, where results are more likely to be immediate and visible, it is hard to imagine a stable and effective third national party as things stand. These are the sort of things that take large investments of time, money, energy, and imagination, and the payoff is delayed probably past an individual's lifetime. Maybe a change like this would have an effect on the life of one's child by the time they reach adulthood. Maybe. But why invest when the uncertainty is so great? The country could fall into fascism, environmental collapse, pandemic, it might break into several smaller nations, a civil war could break out. Or it could just turn out the way your vote for one of the other political parties turned out: like it never mattered in the first place.

Hence the incentives to speculate. Komporozos-Athanasiou points out that people have been living under these conditions of uncertainty and volatility for longer than what has been previously discussed, with many pinpointing the origin of international instability around the beginnings of the American War on Terror. Strange published her book *Casino Capitalism* in the 1980s, but she was pointing toward changes that had already been under way for decades. You can see part of the outcome of these changes in the 2008 global crash. While there was outrage about the results, the individuals in the financial sector who made the decisions that caused the crash were not condemned. They were "respected for their upfront, if unapologetic, pursuits of capital accumulation," in Komporozos-Athanasiou's words. They had used the system available to them in a way that profited them. Their actions made sense given the logic of the system in which they existed.

In a speculative system, Komporozos-Athanasiou writes, "Relations and transactions alike are underpinned by a compulsion for instant gratification in an economy that rewards speed, reveres immersion in the present, and endorses volatility." And the widening gap between the haves and the have-nots, the increased suffering and shorter lifespans of the growing population of the "have-nots," are the logical results of casino capitalism and speculative masculinity.

There comes a time in every writing project, when one must surrender and use the obvious and cheap, but extremely useful, metaphor that is dangling in front of their face. What we are talking about here is impotence. The inability of the average man to exercise free will and change his life. If slow and steady, reasonable behavior is not met with predictable and reasonable ends, force becomes useful. The philosopher Franco "Bifo" Berardi writes in *Futurability: The Age of Impotence and the Horizon of Possibility,* "Violence is replacing political mediation because political reason is determined to be devoid of potency." The consumer is impotent to change the fact that the price of food has risen due not to necessity but to greedy corporate whim. He can, though, attack the clerk at the grocery store who tells him the total of his order. The voter is impotent to change the mind of a politician who has once again betrayed him, but he can arm himself and occupy a government building. The father is impotent to force his child to meet his expectations for gender expression, but he can go down to the public library and bar or harass a drag queen. Violence is another big bet one can make on the world.

Berardi is careful to define impotence as distinct from powerlessness. The powerless have at many times in history, through organization and democratic methods, been able to exert their will on the world. Whether through the peaceful revolutions in Czechoslovakia or Portugal, or through the establishment of new institutions through electoral politics, people were able to stand up against power and make changes. But working in this way requires collaboration and solidarity. Impotence is the affliction of the resentful and the isolated.

Speculative masculinity has created an environment in which the primary goal for the modern man is triumphing over everyone else, winning at the expense of all. It codes every other person as an obstacle or a competitor, everything you want as a scarce resource, and the method of attaining your goal as the annihilation of your enemy. Everyone is betting against everyone else.

As Lifton has shown in his extensive work on radical politics and cultish programming, the way to pull someone away from their extreme positions and back into reality is not by attacking the position they've taken but by creating a space into which they can retreat. It doesn't work to try to disprove what their guru or leader is saying, the indoctrination resists interrogation. Instead, the most successful approach is to work on reversing their isolation. Let them know their community misses them. Inject alternative ideas and ways of thinking into conversation. Help the person create new and strengthen old bonds with people, animals, ideas, fantasies, experiences. When someone is out on the ledge, it's not very helpful to start throwing rocks.

It's much like the project Michael Douglas undergoes in *The Game*. The best way to keep someone from walking off into oblivion is to tether them to the world. But it doesn't make sense to continue these projects on an individual basis. We require collective projects of reimagining what a life beyond patriarchy could look like, a life that is not based on venal competition and the sacrifice of the many to better the financial position of the few, a life that requires moving into the future rather than venturing back into nostalgic re-creations of the past.

The skills of solidarity are very different from the skills of competition. Most political organizations today call themselves "inclusive." Inclusivity is very different from solidarity. Calling yourself inclusive still suggests a gatekeeping mechanism, since inclusion has within it the shadow of exclusion. There are still standards that must be met, some form of control. It's a way of limiting the number of people you have to care about.

Inclusion lays down rules for association. Before a community that comes together based on some shared sense of identity or purpose, whether that be white nationalists or a yoga cult or a political organization, includes someone else, they require knowing where they stand on vaccinations, trans healthcare, water rights, which podcasts they listen to, what they think about Michael Douglas movies, how they voted in the last five elections or if they voted at all, what their position is on the estate tax, land usage, the 1982 Farm Bill, the Russian invasion of Ukraine, what astrological sign they are, whether they think astrology is a hoax, what they thought of the last Taylor Swift album, what their take is on Elon Musk, on *The New York Times,* on veganism, on laws that restrict pit bull ownership, on laws that restrict chicken ownership within city limits, on laws in general, which *Law and Order* series is their favorite, where they stand on Scorsese versus the Marvel Cinematic Universe, if they think treatment or criminal prosecution is the best way to deal with the opioid crisis, if they know anyone who has overdosed, if they know someone who has experienced sexual violence, if they know someone in Ukraine, if they know someone who voted for Trump, if they know Todd, where they buy shoes, where they buy food, if they are a cat person or a dog person, if they were a horse girl, if that shirt they are wearing was bought at a chain store that sources clothing made with sweatshop labor, if they recycle their plastic, if they own property, if they're a landlord, if they're an INFJ or an ESTP, if they are a nepo baby, if their father was working class, if their parents are still married, if their parents are still alive, if their great-grandfather owned slaves, if their DNA is more than 5 percent East Asian, whether or not they have unacknowledged privilege due to the fact that their mother cooked them dinner when they were a child, if they believe the eucharist literally turns into the Body of Christ during communion or if they think it is merely a symbol, which kindergarten they went to, do they even lift, bro?, whether they think *Moonlight* or *La La Land* should have won the Academy Award for best film, their opinion on the protests to take down Confederate monuments, their opinion on the protests to defund the police, their opinion on the police—are they good or bad?, whether or not they have student debt, if they went to college, okay but did they go to the right college, how do they feel about the right of this white woman to write a cookbook about dumplings, whether doing yoga as a white woman is cultural appropriation, whether doing Brazilian jiujitsu as a white man is cultural appropriation, whether cultural appropriation in a flat world is even a thing, how they feel about the scandal with Ivanka Trump, the scandal with Armie Hammer, whether they think fireworks during the day are a psyop, whether the CIA killed JFK, whether the CIA killed Marilyn Monroe, if aliens built the pyramids, if mankind lived at the same time as the dinosaurs, if dinosaur bones were put in the ground by god to confuse humans, if Jesus was a real person, if Jesus ascended bodily into heaven, if it is blasphemy to depict the prophet Mohammad, if Muslim and Jewish women should be forced to show their arms and their hair, if Muslim and Jewish women are oppressed because they can't show their hair, if it's impossible to have democracy if Muslim women don't show their hair, if California should secede, if California should be split up into four separate states, if California should fall into the ocean, if Florida should fall into the ocean, if terminally ill people should be able to make the decision to die, if very depressed people should be able to make the decision to die, if everyone should die, if people should have a lot of children to save our nation, if no one should have children, if children are too loud, if children are precious angels who should be allowed to run free, if they eat gluten, meat, shellfish, carbs, vegetables, if autism is caused by vaccines, if autism is caused by a global conspiracy, if ADHDers should be a protected class, if ADHDers should be put on a national registry, if they boycott Disney, if they boycott Shein, if they boycott TikTok, how much they have in their checking account, their savings account, their retirement account, if they think America's primary national enemy is Russia or China or the global elites otherwise known as the Illuminati, if they laughed at that joke that was made at the expense of women, if they do their own research, if they said the word "Jew" in a weird way that one time, if their definition of woman is exactly the same as mine, if they bought a Harry Potter book after it was revealed that J. K. Rowling was a TERF, if they don't drink single-origin fair-trade coffee, how they feel about this picture of a dead Afghani, a dead woman, a dead Yemeni, a dead Mexican, what is the first word that comes into their head when someone says "Mexico," now "HBO Max," now "women's sports," now "Islamophobia," now "Salman Rushdie," now *"Charlie Hebdo,"* now "the Mormon Church," now "puberty blockers," now "Havana Syndrome," now "9/11 was an inside job," now "socialism."

Solidarity is the antidote to all of that. It is the understanding that if there is a shared need, that creates a bond, and then the other disagreements can be forgotten. Whatever someone does with their money, their hair, their cattle, their body, their brain is extraneous and separate from this bond, which is precious.

Everything about speculative masculinity fights against solidarity. But there's no true liberation without it.

CONCLUSION:

IMAGINING A POST-MICHAEL DOUGLAS WORLD

In June 2023, the leftist political podcast *Know Your Enemy* released an episode called "What's Wrong with Men?" A discourse had been circulating that year that the political left had a "man problem." The problem was that the political right, including extremist fringes like the alt-right and white nationalist groups, recruited new members by reaching out to young men in crisis about seemingly innocuous matters like romantic disappointment and "rules to live by" that included things like caring about your physical appearance and cleaning up your room. From there it was a slippery slope down to "Jews will not replace us" and "feminism was a mistake."

These were essentially political black holes—once men felt the gravitational pull it was too difficult to escape. Manosphere groups clustered around men like the accused sex trafficker Andrew Tate, the anti-trans psychologist Jordan Peterson, and the ideologically incoherent politician Donald Trump. They promised a return to manliness through the dehumanization of others, whether that be immigrants, women, or the trans community.

To counter this movement, many insisted, the political left needed to give these young men an alternative kind of mentorship, one that created the possibility of participation in leftist groups and politics, radicalizing them into ideas like socialism and identity politics.

But this was not a political left akin to the socialists of early twentieth-century America, populated by and advocating for the working classes. This was a political left that was dominated by people from the middle and upper middle class, who had attended university and postgraduate degree programs, and who were well versed in political theory. The American left had been drifting away from the working class since the 1970s, when the Democratic Party decided to shift its recruitment efforts toward the educated class, believing they were more receptive to ideas about civil rights, feminism, and gay rights. As such, the left was used to considering most of the problems of the world as being the fault of conservative white men, who were often depicted as bigoted, homophobic, and misogynistic.

Which must be why this attempt to reach out to the lost men who had been radicalized by the right was so damn awkward. In the *Know Your Enemy* podcast episode, the hosts let out nervous giggles almost every time they used the words "manliness" and "masculinity" in a way they would never do before saying "femininity." The political left has spent decades theorizing and conceptualizing womanhood, Blackness, homosexuality, and transness. But the idea of understanding something like whiteness or masculinity from an insider position—rather than as part of a critique from an outsider—remains taboo. Due to dubious and politically disgusting groups centered on masculinity and whiteness, all that is left for the good man or the good white person is to transcend or deconstruct their identity, rather than try to understand it.

Men who profited from a system that benefited those with material resources gained entry into exclusive and highly desired fields like the arts, journalism, politics, or publishing, and were happily married, and seemed to struggle to conceptualize the possibility that other men might have it worse. Having internalized ideas about male privilege and patriarchal power, they couldn't seem to understand that their ability to circumnavigate the difficulties other men faced might be directly tied in with their gender. And because they had certain difficulties—student loans, for example—they assumed the problems they overcame in their climb to success did not vary in quality from the problems faced by men without their specific advantages.

Which is why, for all the opinions and hand-wringing and moralizing about the problem of men, the conversation dead-ends in very predictable places. Either a nostalgic appeal to the male roles of the past, or the exhortation to transcend gender and try to be a good person instead of a good man.

The changes of the Michael Douglas era divided our world into winners and losers. The losers saw their assets exploited, their traditions broken, their resources squandered, and their voices silenced.

The winners, on the other hand, have created a suffocating monoculture that encompasses mass and social media, politics, entertainment, and business. It is often said that we live in a time of political polarization. That the right and the left in this nation are so divided that they have found themselves at a standstill, unable to govern effectively and provide resources to their citizenry. This is not accurate. The political class is absolutely in agreement that the losers of society are there to fight their wars, break their bodies in work, and enrich the corporate class. It is almost unanimous in our governing bodies that people do not have the right to quality and affordable healthcare, clean water, excellent education, and a sustainable path into the future.

The issues on which they appear to be divided are mostly cultural issues, their differences amplified to distract from where they overlap. And in that overlap is the willingness to let conditions continue to degrade, to let the housing crisis push ever greater numbers into insecurity and the open air, to let the sick languish, and the schools of our children go without teachers, supplies, and effective lessons.

The intellectuals of our time are mostly spokespeople for the elite. "Elite" is a tricky word these days, used to conjure Versaillesian fantasies of wealth and decadence, an easy political scapegoat for the failures of the current moment. But it is true and worrying that our writers, philosophers, and teachers come from the same small, educated class as the political rulers and the entertainers, not just unfamiliar with but hostile to the lived experience of much of the nation.

People at the top of the hierarchy often fail to see the reality of people living closer to the bottom. This is why civil rights movements went through decades of splintering. Feminists broke with leftist movements because the men who ruled them failed to see the validity of women's concerns and requests. This is why trans groups had to break from the larger queer rights movement, why the colonized had to separate themselves out from their colonizers, and so on.

The task at hand, then, is one of reintegration, starting with the very local. Resentment keeps a person impotent, scarcity keeps them selfish and paranoid, and grievance keeps them isolated.

Bad habits must be unlearned. The tools of patriarchy—exclusion and dominance—will only create new divisions. And the tools of the postpatriarchy—greed and competition—will destroy a collective's goodwill. Even the preferred entertainment of the postpatriarchy era—the competition reality show—reinforces that the only way to "get ahead" is to betray alliances, go for broke, dehumanize everyone around, and hoard the spoils of competition.

Moving out of postpatriarchy into something less hierarchical means finding different ways of relating to one another and rein-vesting in the commons. One of the messages of postpatriarchy is that everyone is alone, wholly responsible for their own socially cre-ated problems. Counteracting the system means counteracting that belief, and re-creating the shared meaning and resources that make a life worth living. This means learning and teaching new skills, learning to give way to others, to take only what you need, to share resources, and learning adaptation and resourcefulness.

What the winners have denied the losers they will have to learn to provide for themselves. That means reinventing public assets like education, health clinics, public spaces, and forms of leisure that suit the collective rather than those who want to monetize them. If the winners want consumers, the consumers will need to learn to become creators, artists, innovators, collaborators, and diplomats instead. Only in redefining their selves as something beyond the limits the culture wants to impose can men find true liberation.

Part of this will require turning our attention away from the endless stream of the winners' faces, houses, cute little paintings, and books that clog up social and mass media. If what you see on these screens does not appeal to you or reflect your own existence, it is right and good to create alternative forms of expression. It's acceptable to find the mainstream boring and to replace it with more interesting influences. It's a time for learning from the past, for creating connections with other nations, for deciding a new set of priorities. It's not enough to rage against those who have more—ultimately, getting angry and resentful only harms us and not them. Rejection can be a political act. Rejection of their ideas, their words, their policies.

There will always be those who disrupt these processes with infiltration and manipulation or violence. The guy who joins the protest not because he believes in the cause but because he nihilisti-cally wants to burn something down. There are those with charisma who will try to hijack and derail proceedings for their own ends. Practicing discernment is essential.

Perfection and purity are lost causes. Utopias don't exist. But communities do.

On a personal note, as I worked on this book I would occasionally make the mistake of telling people about the project. I got the same comment from several people. "You must really hate Michael Douglas to write a whole book about him." I am not writing this book out of hate. I can't imagine spending years thinking about someone or something I hated. I'm writing about Michael Douglas because I love Michael Douglas.

When I was a kid, growing up in a very small, conservative town in Kansas, one of my only outlets to the outside world was through the television. We had HBO. This was very decadent for the time, a "premium channel" on a cable package that came with about fifteen channels. We didn't even have MTV, it wasn't available. But we had HBO.

I watched these films as if they held secrets I would need to know about being an adult in a place other than a small, conservative town in Kansas. I learned about gender. A real man was Michael Douglas, Mel Gibson, Richard Gere. A real woman was Julia Roberts, Kathleen Turner, Michelle Pfeiffer. I learned about money, how a person would need a tremendous amount of it to have a good life. I learned about what was expected of me for success, the conformity, the ambition, the killer instincts.

As soon as I left my small town I learned that none of this was really very helpful when it came to living a life. That what made my life meaningful, the work I do and the people I know and the love I give and receive and the art I encounter and the kindnesses I bestow and which are bestowed on me, was mostly invisible in my childhood entertainments. It required less money than one would expect, more flexibility and empathy than anticipated, and a sense of curiosity that was not only not fostered but actively discouraged in the town I grew up in and the stories I consumed.

And still I see people with their noses pressed against their screens, believing the fantasies that this is what is required of them, this is what a good life is, this is what creates happiness. And it's all still about money, ambition, property. It fosters envy instead of curiosity. It stunts development and lets whole sectors of the human psyche go to rot.

When I say I love Michael Douglas, this is what I mean: I don't want to live in Michael Douglas's world. I've done too much of that as it is! And not even he seems all that happy there. What I want, instead, out of love, is to invite him into mine.

SELECTED BIBLIOGRAPHY

INTRODUCTION

Bly, Nellie. *Ten Days in a Madhouse*. New York: Norman L. Munro, Publisher, 1887.

Connell, R. W. *Masculinities*. Cambridge, U.K.: Polity Press, 1995.

Eliot, Marc. *Michael Douglas: A Biography*. New York: Crown Archetype, 2012.

Freud, Sigmund, and Joseph Breuer. *Studies on Hysteria*. New York: Basic Books, 1955.

Micale, Mark S. "Charcot and the Idea of Hysteria in the Male: Gender, Mental Science, and Medical Diagnosis in Late Nineteenth-Century France." *Medical History* 34, 1990.

PART ONE: MICHAEL DOUGLAS AND WOMEN

Fatal Attraction: Caught in the Crossfire of the Mommy Wars

Bronfen, Elisabeth. *Home in Hollywood: The Imaginary Geography of Cinema*. New York: Columbia University Press, 2004.

Cooper, Melinda. *Family Values: Between Neoliberalism and the New Social Conservatism*. Brooklyn, N.Y.: Zone Books, 2017.

Faludi, Susan. *Backlash: The Undeclared War Against American Women*. New York: Broadway Books, 1991.

Leonard, Suzanne. *Wife, Inc.: The Business of Marriage in the Twenty-First Century*. New York: New York University Press, 2018.

Milanich, Nara. *Paternity: The Elusive Quest for the Father.* Cambridge, Mass.: Harvard University Press, 2019.

Schlafly, Phyllis. *Who Killed the American Family.* Washington, D.C.: WND Books, 2014.

Self, Robert O. *All in the Family: The Realignment of American Democracy Since the 1960s.* New York: Farrar, Straus and Giroux, 2012.

War of the Roses: Court-Mandated Fatherhood

Bly, Robert. *Iron John: A Book About Men.* Reading, Mass.: Addison-Wesley, 1990.

Coontz, Stephanie. *Marriage: A History: From Obedience to Intimacy or How Love Conquered Marriage.* New York: Viking, 2005.

Gibraldo, Alessandra. *Unexpected Subjects: Intimate Partner Violence, Testimony, and the Law.* Chicago: HAU Books, 2021.

Nobel, Loretta Schwartz. *Forsaking All Others: The Real Betty Broderick Story.* New York: Villard Books, 1993.

Schmidt, Susanne. *Midlife Crisis: The Feminist Origins of a Chauvinist Cliché.* Chicago: University of Chicago Press, 2020.

Sheehy, Gail. *Passages: Predictable Crises of Adult Life.* New York: Dutton, 1976.

Basic Instinct: What If We Just Got Rid of All the Men?

Cremin, Ciara. *Man-Made Woman: The Dialectics of Cross-Dressing.* London: Pluto Press, 2017.

Faxneld, Per. *Satanic Feminism: Lucifer as the Liberator of Woman in Nineteenth-Century Culture.* Oxford, U.K.: Oxford University Press, 2017.

Halberstam, Jack. *Female Masculinity.* Durham, N.C.: Duke University Press, 1998.

Jordan, June. *Civil Wars: Observations from the Front Lines of America.* Boston: Beacon Press, 1981.

PART TWO: THE ECONOMIC ACTOR

Wall Street: A New Economy, and a New Masculinity, Emerges

Day, Kathleen. *S&L Hell: The People and the Politics Behind the $1 Trillion Savings and Loan Scandal.* New York: W. W. Norton, 1993.

Dowd, Kevin, and Martin Hutchinson. *Alchemists of Loss: How Modern Finance and Government Intervention Crashed the Financial System.* New York: John Wiley and Sons, 2010.

McCartin, Joseph. *Collision Course: Ronald Reagan, the Air Traffic Controllers, and the Strike That Changed America.* Oxford, U.K.: Oxford University Press, 2011.

Nembhard, Jessica Gordon. *Collective Courage: A History of African American Cooperative Economic Thought and Practice.* University Park, Pa.: Penn State Press, 2014.

Robinson, Peter. *Flying Blind: The 737 MAX Tragedy and the Fall of Boeing.* New York: Doubleday, 2021.

Strange, Susan. *Casino Capitalism.* London: Blackwell Publishers, 1986.

Falling Down: The Aspirational Mass Shooter

Berardi, Franco "Bifo." *Heroes: Mass Murder and Suicide.* Brooklyn, N.Y.: Verso, 2015.

Enzensberger, Hans Magnus. *Civil Wars: From LA to Bosnia.* New York: New Press, 1994.

Hall, Stuart, Charles Critcher, Tony Jefferson, John Clark, and Brian Roberts. *Policing the Crisis: Mugging, the State, and Law and Order.* London: Macmillan, 1978.

Isenberg, Nancy. *White Trash: The 400-Year Untold History of Class in America.* New York: Viking, 2016.

Ramsey, Donovan X. *When Crack Was King: A People's History of a Misunderstood Era.* New York: One World, 2023.

Wilson, William Julius. *There Goes the Neighborhood: Racial, Ethnic, and Class Tensions in Four Chicago Neighborhoods and Their Meaning for America.* New York: Knopf, 2006.

Wolfe, Tom. *The Bonfire of the Vanities.* New York: Farrar, Straus and Giroux, 1987.

PART THREE: A WHITE MAN IN A BROWN WORLD

Black Rain: America Hits Its Midlife Crisis

Amano, Ikuho. *Financial Euphoria, Consumer Culture, and Literature of 1980s Japan.* Abingdon, Oxon: Routledge, 2023.

Rangel, Carlos. *The Latin Americans: Their Love-Hate Relationship with the United States.* Piscataway, N.J.: Transaction Publishers, 1987.

Samet, Elizabeth D. *Looking for the Good War: American Amnesia and the Violent Pursuit of Happiness.* New York: Farrar, Straus and Giroux, 2021.

Todd, Emmanuel. *After the Empire: The Breakdown of the American Order*. New York: Columbia University Press, 2006.

The American President: Finding Meaning in the Drone Bomb

Edwards, Brian T. *After the American Century: The Ends of U.S. Culture in the Middle East*. New York: Columbia University Press, 2016.

Esty, Jed. *The Future of Decline: Anglo-American Culture at Its Limits*. Redwood City, Calif.: Stanford University Press, 2022.

Robbins, Bruce. *Perpetual War: Cosmopolitanism from the Viewpoint of Violence*. Durham, N.C.: Duke University Press, 2012.

Said, Edward. *The Politics of Dispossession: The Struggle for Palestinian Self-Determination*. London: Chatto & Windus, 1994.

Walter, Jess. *Ruby Ridge: The Truth and Tragedy of the Randy Weaver Family*. New York: Harper Perennial, 2002.

PART FOUR: THE PATRIARCH FALLS

Disclosure: Please Report to Human Resources

Cruz, Manuel. *On the Difficulty of Living Together: Memory, Politics, and History*. New York: Columbia University Press, 2016.

Kennedy, Randall. *For Discrimination: Race, Affirmative Action, and the Law*. New York: Knopf, 2013.

Kern, Leslie. *Feminist City: Claiming Space in a Man-Made World*. Brooklyn, N.Y.: Verso, 2020.

Mishra, Pankaj. *Age of Anger: A History of the Present*. New York: Farrar, Straus and Giroux, 2017.

Perez, Caroline Criado. *Invisible Women: Exposing Data Bias in a World Designed for Men*. London: Chatto & Windus, 2019.

The Game: Bringing Patriarchs Back to Life

Gray, John. *False Dawn: The Delusions of Global Capitalism*. London: Granta, 1998.

Phillips, Adam. *On Giving Up*. New York: Farrar, Straus and Giroux, 2024.

Sennett, Richard. *The Corrosion of Character: The Personal Consequences of Work in the New Capitalism*. New York: W. W. Norton, 1998.

PART FIVE: WELCOME TO THE POSTPATRIARCHY

Teaching Michael Douglas to Love: Age Gaps, Power Imbalances, and Other Heterosexual Indignities

Goffman, Erving. *The Presentation of Self in Everyday Life*. New York: Doubleday, 1959.

Illouz, Eva. *The End of Love: A Sociology of Negative Relations*. Oxford, U.K.: Oxford University Press, 2019.

Taylor, Charles. *A Secular Age*. Cambridge, Mass.: Harvard University Press, 2007.

Daddy Issues: Father Hunger and the Search for an Heir

Connor, Steven. *Giving Way: Thoughts on Unappreciated Dispositions*. Redwood City, Calif.: Stanford University Press, 2019.

Elias, Norbert. *The Loneliness of the Dying*. New York: Blackwell Publishers, 1985.

Hall, Stuart. *The Fateful Triangle: Race, Ethnicity, Nation*. Cambridge, Mass.: Harvard University Press, 2017.

McRobbie, Angela. *Feminism and the Politics of Resilience: Essays on Gender, Media and the End of Welfare*. Oxford, U.K.: John Wiley and Sons, 2020.

Sennett, Richard. *The Fall of Public Man*. New York: Knopf, 1977.

Speculative Masculinity: The Rise of the Masculinity Influencer

Franklin, Samuel W. *The Cult of Creativity: A Surprisingly Recent History*. Chicago: University of Chicago Press, 2023.

Komporozos-Athanasiou, Aris. *Speculative Communities: Living with Uncertainty in a Financialized World*. Chicago: University of Chicago Press, 2022.

Lifton, Robert Jay. *The Protean Self: Human Resilience in an Age of Fragmentation*. New York: Basic Books, 1993.

Piketty, Thomas. *Capital and Ideology*. Translated by Arthur Goldhammer. Cambridge, Mass.: Harvard University Press, 2020.

Spence, Lester. *Knocking the Hustle: Against the Neoliberal Turn in Black Politics*. Santa Barbara, Calif.: Punctum Books, 2015.

ABOUT THE AUTHOR

JESSA CRISPIN is the author of several books, including *Why I Am Not a Feminist: A Feminist Manifesto*, *The Dead Ladies Project*, and *My Three Dads*. She is the editor and founder of *The Culture We Deserve* as well as host with Nico Rodriguez of TCWD weekly podcast. In 2002, she launched Bookslut.com, one of the first and most treasured literary websites of the era; it ran for fifteen years. She is originally from Lincoln, Kansas, and currently lives in Philadelphia.

A NOTE ON THE TYPE

This book was set in Adobe Garamond. Designed for the Adobe Corporation by Robert Slimbach, the fonts are based on types first cut by Claude Garamond (ca. 1480–1561). Garamond was a pupil of Geoffroy Tory and is believed to have followed the Venetian models, although he introduced a number of important differences, and it is to him that we owe the letter we now know as "old style." He gave to his letters a certain elegance and feeling of movement that won their creator an immediate reputation and the patronage of Francis I of France.

Typeset by Scribe,
Philadelphia, Pennsylvania

Designed by Casey Hampton